TJ 163.3 .I555 1997
OCLC: 36138296
WHY ENERGY CONSERVATION
FAILS

W9-AAK-417

DATE DUE

DEC - 2 2003	
DEC 1 8 2003	
GAYLORD	PRINTED IN U.S.A.

THE RICHARD STOCKTON COLLEGE
OF NEW JERSEY LIBRARY
POMONA, NEW JERSEY 08240

WHY ENERGY CONSERVATION FAILS

WHY ENERGY CONSERVATION FAILS

Herbert Inhaber

Q

QUORUM BOOKS
Westport, Connecticut • London

THE RICHARD STOCKTON COLLEGE
OF NEW JERSEY LIBRARY
POMONA, NEW JERSEY 08240

Library of Congress Cataloging-in-Publication Data

Inhaber, Herbert, 1941–
    Why energy conservation fails / Herbert Inhaber.
      p.   cm.
    Includes bibliographical references (p.   –   ) and index.
    ISBN 1–56720–120–2 (alk. paper)
    1. Energy conservation. I. Title.
TJ163.3.I555   1997
333.79'17—dc21   96–6576

British Library Cataloguing in Publication Data is available.

Copyright ©1997 by Herbert Inhaber

All rights reserved. No portion of this book may be
reproduced, by any process or technique, without the
express written consent of the publisher.

Library of Congress Catalog Card Number: 96–6576
ISBN: 1–56720–120–2

First published in 1997

Quorum Books, 88 Post Road West, Westport, CT 06881
An imprint of Greenwood Publishing Group, Inc.

Printed in the United States of America

The paper used in this book complies with the
Permanent Paper Standard issued by the National
Information Standards Organization (Z39.48–1984).

10 9 8 7 6 5 4 3 2 1

This book is dedicated to three loving people. The first two are my late parents, my mother Mollye and my father Sam. They both bred in me a spirit of questioning those things that everyone else accepted on faith. This lesson has gotten me into trouble from time to time but, on balance, has served me well.

The third person is my wife, Donna. She stood behind me when the demands of research and writing were great, and I will forever be in her debt.

Contents

Figures and Tables

FIGURES

TABLES

Introduction

Over the past two decades, Americans have been subjected to an unprecedented barrage of government edicts telling them to save energy, water, natural resources, and many other substances. Gone is the self-imposed frugality of the Puritans and Calvin Coolidge, who said, "Use it up or do without." What we save individually is not enough now. Society as a whole has to conserve, and Washington would show us how.

All this would be harmless, and perhaps even beneficial, if conservation on a national scale truly existed. It is the thesis of this book that it does not.

This surprising conclusion seems at variance with all common sense. If we trade in a large car for a small one, surely we use less gasoline, all other factors being equal. This cannot be disputed. But what is forgotten in this example is what happens to the gasoline that is "saved." We may imagine that it remains in the ground somewhere, waiting its turn to be pumped up in future generations. This does not happen.

If Mr. A saves gasoline (or any other form of energy, for that matter), there is more gasoline on the market that has not been used. When there is more of a commodity on the market than before, its price will go down. Obviously, the few gallons that Mr. A saves will not depress the price significantly, but if there are millions of Mr. As who conserve, either voluntarily or through government rules, the price will fall.

• • •

Again, using simple economic reasoning, when the price of a commodity falls, more of it will be used than if its price had remained constant. Many more fresh strawberries are eaten when they are in season and priced low than in the winter, when they are flown in at high cost from Mexico or South America.

So one group saves energy, making its price fall, and another group uses more as a result. What is the net effect? Overall, it is a wash, or even an increase in energy use. The proof is in a host of statistics. For example, gasoline use in this country has risen, not fallen, after the imposition of strict mileage standards for cars in the late 1970s. According to those who advocated those laws, gasoline use should have dropped.

Even if Americans could actually reduce gasoline consumption by superhuman efforts like mandating everyone ride around in Geo Metros or even walk, the same effect of no overall conservation would occur on an international level. If the United States reduced total—not per car—gasoline use, the international price would drop below what it would have been without this action. Thus, consumers in China or India would use more than they would have if all factors had remained constant. The overall effect would be similar to sending convoys of oil tankers to other nations and not charging them for the fuel. Even the most ardent advocate of foreign aid in Congress would never propose that foolish scheme. But that is what we are doing with many conservation measures.

• • •

This, then, is the simple thesis of this book. I back this up with numbers, but the emphasis here is not on dry charts and equations. Rather, I try to explain how we got into this situation, and how we might extricate ourselves from it. I believe in the part of the Hippocratic oath that states, "First, do no harm." The well-meaning advocates of government-controlled conservation have done harm, and I illustrate this with a series of examples.

Language itself has been thrown under the wheels of the juggernaut called "conservation." For example, conservation proponents use strange terminology, such as *negenergy* and *negagallons*, to prove their points. I demonstrate that these terms have no meaning.

Waste is something that everyone is against, but we find it difficult if not impossible to define. This is not merely an accident of language. True energy waste, except in the most extreme examples, does not exist any more than conservation. Some energy use has lower utility, in the jargon of the economists, but it is rare that the utility is zero.

Chapter 6 deals with how conservation has been treated in the newspaper comics. Given that conservation has been raised, in the minds of many people, to the level of Mom, apple pie, and Chevrolet, it is rare to hear criticism of it. However, some cartoonists, including Gary Trudeau, the creator of *Doonesbury*, have made some trenchant observations. I include them here.

• • •

A note on terminology: When I use the term *conservation*, I am, unless otherwise specified, talking about *energy* and not other forms of conservation. I use the one word as shorthand for the two-word phrase to save endless repetition. The word *conservation* can sometimes mean the conservation of land, animals, and plants (as in the Endangered Species Act), or other entities. While these latter subjects are fascinating, they are not the focus of this book.

There is a reason why the conservation of animals and the like are not considered here. As I will point out, many of the confusions we have about energy conservation are based on a disregard or lack of knowledge of elementary economics. These economic laws generally do not apply to endangered species, as far as I can tell. For example, who can place an economic value on a threatened spider, the entire species of which may total only a few hundred somewhere in the heart of Brazil with no humans within fifty miles? We do not have to be economists to realize that a question of this type is vastly different from how much money we should or could spend on insulation or smaller cars. So, for brevity, I mean *energy conservation* when I write *conservation*.

There is a peculiar economic effect in conservation. I can save energy by buying a small car, bicycling to work, wearing a sweater around the house in the winter, and a host of other measures. I may imagine that if I multiplied my savings by the millions of people who might also adopt these measures, billions and billions, in the well-known phrase of Carl Sagan, of gallons of oil will be saved. My arithmetic might be correct, but I will be dreaming with my eyes wide open.

• • •

It is all too easy to throw stones, as any political campaign reveals. It is more difficult to construct a house out of the rocks that have been hurled. Some of what follows is indeed critical of how we have gone about the business of conservation. In the last chapter, I try to paint a picture of what, if anything, can be done about the potential problem of running out of energy. The answers will not be satisfying to everyone, but they build on the specific points I make in the preceding chapters.

1

Fundamentals of Why Energy Conservation Fails

Does conservation as it is described and applauded every day on TV, in our newspapers, and in other media truly exist? Or is it just a figment of our imagination, one that provides fascinating stories about cars that go 1,000 miles on a drop of gasoline, but does not truly happen?

What we perceive as conservation does not take place. We get little effects here and there, much as waves ripple the surface of a lake, but what many of us hope and long for—a reduction in our total energy use—always seems, like the hoped-for recovery in the depths of the Great Depression, just around the corner.

There are four types of conservation in common parlance. Yet the mirage is more than a matter of semantics and definitions. The differences among the four illustrate why, in spite of government programs in this nation and around the world, few have been effective in creating true conservation.

The first type of conservation is imposed by price. When the price goes up, all other factors being equal, less energy is used. The second is due to government laws and regulations. Examples of these are gas-guzzler taxes on large cars, fuel-economy standards for all autos, home building codes requiring specified amounts of insulation, and the like. While the first type undoubtedly works, it is not clear that the second type really produces a reduction in total energy use as opposed to that of a single homeowner. Those who favor government intervention in a wide area of the economy will tend to believe that it is effective; those who are opposed to this intervention will generally think that it is not.

The third type is what could be called *personal* conservation. That is, one person, or a group in society, decides to use less energy (or a specific type of energy, such as petroleum), for moral or other reasons. The question is, since the consumption of this person or group goes down, does overall use in society drop? Finally, there is *total* conservation, that is, a fall in energy use by a whole town, state, province, nation, or the world.

The four types of conservation, all related to each other, account for much of the confusion over the question, "Does conservation exist?"

The second type of conservation is clearly related to the third. If enough people in a nation decide that using what they call "too much" of a certain type of energy is immoral or unethical, they may try to set their feelings into law. The law or regulation that results is based on the presumption of the small group that their neighbors are not being cooperative enough in the supposed moral crisis. Examples of small organizations securing legislation of this type are legion. One example is the fuel-economy standards for autos imposed in the 1970s. They were pushed by some environmental activists who felt the nation and the world were running out of oil.

• • •

Do the second and third types of conservation produce less energy consumption in society? There is little question that a specific person may use less energy than in the past, under force of law or his or her own ethics. But does society as a whole use less?

If someone uses less energy as a result of the second or third types of conservation, there will be more energy available for you (or somebody else). All other factors being equal, you will use a bit more than you otherwise would have. The result is that total energy use remains about the same.

That reasoning does not apply to the first conservation type, which will be called *economic*. In that case, since the price has gone up for everyone, there is an incentive for all to use less energy. Only the richest will be unaffected by the increase in price.

Most people would claim that this type of conservation is not conservation at all; it is just the working of economics. Whether it is really conservation is a matter of semantics. Nonetheless, for many people, conservation comes about only when the government imposes it or a group of people acts, out of sense of self-sacrifice, to impose it on themselves.

In that sense, people who buy small cars because they want to save gasoline would be regarded as conserving. People who buy small cars because they do not like the paint colors in big cars or the look of larger vehicles would not be regarded as conserving. Yet the overall effect on petroleum supply would be the same.

• • •

What type of energy could or should be conserved? Consider oil, an international commodity. It is easily traded and exchanged. The price in one part of the world is rarely substantially different from that in another, taking transportation costs into account. (We will exclude, for purposes of this discussion, government price controls of one type or another.) As a result, how prices change with supply and demand plays a key role in how much energy is used.

Few people are concerned about coal conservation, as opposed to petroleum conservation. There is a rational basis for this attitude. World coal reserves are enormous, and would take hundreds of years to dissipate at the present rate of consumption. Oil reserves are measured in decades, not centuries. Yet when energy conservation is discussed, it is almost invariably in terms of oil, not energy as a whole.

Electricity prices vary sharply from one part of the United States to another. (Prices are sometimes uniform within certain foreign countries because of government policies, not because of economics.) The price per kilowatt-hour on Long Island in New York could be four or five times that of some hydroelectricity-served parts of Washington State. The price of electricity on Long Island has nothing to do with that in Washington State, because the two power systems do not have anything to do with each other economically.

If those in Washington State want to "waste" electricity, there is little effect on Long Island. But this rule does not apply to petroleum. If Americans decide to save or be wasteful with this commodity, this affects the world price.

Most of what we call conservation is the second or third type. Yet the only true conservation is the fourth type, or *global* conservation. When the fourth type takes place, not only does one person use less energy; her block, her neighborhood, her town, her state, the nation and the whole world does. Everything after the phrase, "one person use less energy" in the last sentence is more difficult—vastly more—to achieve. Yet true conservation will effect everyone, not merely the few who have decided to do without.

• • •

Energy efficiency should be easier to define. After all, if a Geo takes two gallons to cover 100 miles, and a Cadillac takes six, it is obvious that the first car is more efficient than the second.

It is not so simple. Dr. Len Brookes of England, a former head economist for the U.S. Atomic Energy Authority, notes that there are at least three definitions of energy efficiency.

Besides the quasi-economic efficiency which can be described by miles per gallon, there are two other physically based efficiencies. The first law of thermodynamics states that energy cannot be created or destroyed. Using the law of physics, the second type of efficiency relates the output of a system to the heat input. Electricity ranks low on first-law efficiency compared to other fuels, since it takes about three units of heat—coal, oil, nuclear, or gas—to produce one of electricity.

The second law of thermodynamics states that a system and its surroundings tends to an increased disorderliness, or entropy. Without going into the equations, it can be shown using the second law that electricity is more efficient than burning coal, oil, or gas. Thus there is an apparent conflict between the definitions of efficiency based on the first and second laws.

Which of the three types of energy efficiency should we use as a gauge? Most of us, not being physicists, lean toward the economic definition. It is true that a mile or a gallon are not economic measures, but when we fill an automobile tank we are most concerned about how much money will leave our wallets never to return. We do not care if the distances driven are miles or kilometers, or the volumes gallons or liters. If an electric-powered Geo costs 10¢ to drive a mile, and a conventional Cadillac only 6¢, almost all of us will award the blue ribbon to the larger but cheaper (on a cost-per-mile basis) vehicle. We will not pay that much attention to the laws of thermodynamics, the definitions of which most of us have forgotten, if we ever knew them.

• • •

What do economists say about conservation? A check of a few dozen economic dictionaries and textbooks shows little or nothing on the subject. Was there a conspiracy of silence? Rather, the idea of conservation was so vague, so confused, that economists—ordinarily reasonably clear thinkers—could say almost nothing of a substantive nature about it.

In the interests of brevity, I have not listed all the texts. They include *Palgrave's Dictionary of Political Economy*, for many years the main economics dictionary, that had not a word on the subject. The following are only two that did. The problem was that they did not define it in a way that most people do.

• Christine Ammer and Dean S. Ammer, in their *Dictionary of Business and Economics*, had a general description as the care and preservation of natural resources. No specific economic discussion was given, but there was a listing of government agencies related to conservation in some unspecified way: Department of Interior, Environmental Protection Agency, Department of Energy, and so on.

• Harold S. Sloan and Arnold J. Zurcher, in *Dictionary of Economics*, fifth edition, only have three lines: "care and preservation . . . of natural resources."

If the economists rarely mention a term with as many economic consequences as conservation, it makes one wonder if it truly exists in a definable sense.

Magazines like *Popular Science* have pages with ads for scientific equipment and books. Some are illustrated and large. But at the back of the magazine appear much smaller ads, crammed with words. They advertise books, but not the ordinary ones on light, sound, and mechanics. They often deal with someone's attempt to overthrow Einstein's theory of relativity. *Why Einstein Was Wrong!* would be a typical title.

Physicists dismiss these books as the work of cranks. On the rare occasions when the credentials of the authors are described, only unknown schools are listed.

Are those who question conservation as it is presently understood in the same rank of cranks? In a word, no. Stanley Jevons, perhaps the first to point out the fallacy of reasoning on conservation, is an icon to economists. There were no Nobel Prizes in economics when he lived. If there had been, he certainly would have received one.[1]

Others who have written on the subject are also not oddballs. Their papers, published in reputable journals (the authors of the books decrying Einstein never appeared in the major journals in the field, such as *Physical Review*) are noted in the rest of this book. Just to take a few names at random, Paul Joskow is a professor in the economics department at Massachusetts Institute of Technology in Cambridge, Massachusetts. Kent Anderson works for National Economic Research Associates, a major economics consulting firm. Leonard Brookes was, as previously noted, formerly Chief Economist at the British Atomic Energy Authority. Stephen Brown works at the Federal Reserve Bank of Dallas. Hendrik Houthakker is a Nobel Prize winner in economics. Jerry Taylor is a leading figure at the Cato Institute, a Washington think tank.

If these people were put into a room, they might disagree on some aspects of conservation and energy. But those outside the room would have to agree on one thing: They were not cranks.

• • •

One of Bartlett's most-used quotations is "Beauty is in the eye of the beholder." In a modern-day context, it can be paraphrased as "What does she (or he) see in him (or her)?" In the summer of 1993, Julia Roberts, one of the movie beauties of the day, married Lyle Lovett, a singer with an odd face and an even odder hair style. It was only the latest example. We observe a strange-looking individual, with the characteristics that *GQ* and *Vogue* try to eliminate from males and females, respectively. To their partner, a Greek god or goddess walks. You cannot measure beauty with a ruler. It is in the heart of the one smitten.

There is probably a good genetic reason for all this. If we all waited for Greek gods or goddesses before we gave away our hearts, the human race would have died out long ago. Somehow our mind tells us to settle for less than perfection.

What does all this have to do with energy waste or conservation? Just as with beauty, it is all in the mind of the beholder. If Joan buys a medium-sized car, Joe down the road, who uses a bicycle whenever possible, may think she should have purchased a Geo or Kia. "Just a waster, that's all she is," may run through his mind.

Max, living at the other end of the street, drives a giant Buick Roadmaster. He does not worry at all about Joan's wasting energy. "A little chintzy, isn't she?" he may think about her, if he ever thinks about her at all, "She probably could afford a real car if she wanted to."

Nobody makes public policy on beauty. We do not have the government formulating rules about how attractive people could or should be. Yet many of us are only too willing to have the government set standards on what is or is not wasteful in energy and other resources. If we draw the analogy with beauty, we realize how futile it all is.

Dave Rossin, an energy consultant in the San Francisco Bay area, is fond of asking, "Just what is a shortfall? I hear about a shortfall in this or that, but they never say exactly what it is. Can you enlighten me?" This question had a connection with conservation. Rossin's query suggests that what we understand by conservation is often so vague as to be undefined.

Leaving aside dictionary definitions, what does a shortfall mean? It is a situation in which an expectation is in a person's mind and is not met. For example, the Russians may foresee a crop of 100 million tons of potatoes this year. If they harvest only 90 million, then there is a shortfall of 10 million tons. What could be simpler?

It is easy only if we do not probe beneath the surface of the definition. If we say that 100 million tons are expected, somebody somewhere has estimated the land available, the number of harvesters and farmers, and their productivity, thrown in other factors like the cost of labor and land, and come up with a number. Somebody else, or another estimating agency, could have derived a projected figure of 110 million tons. In that case, there would be a shortfall of 20 million tons. Or they could have estimated 90 million tons, in which case there would not have been any shortfall at all.

Who do we believe? If we want to emphasize the problems besetting Russian potato farms, we will pick the higher value that we think the Russians should harvest. That way there is a giant shortfall. If we were Russian potato-crop managers without much confidence in the whole system of estimates, we might act like used-car salesmen. We would "low-ball" the numbers to 90 million tons. That way the shortfall would disappear.

All of this would be just a tempest in a bowl of potato soup if we did not take the word shortfall seriously. Most of us do. When the we hear about yet another shortfall—tax collections, number of engineers graduated, or the Russian potato harvest—we usually nod our heads in agreement. Yet the size of the shortfall—or whether it even exists—depends strongly on the person or agency making the estimate of expected taxes collected, engineers graduated, or potatoes harvested.

The people or agencies coming up with the numbers often have political, not scientific, reasons for choosing the numbers they do. An organization whose purpose is developing science, like the National Science Foundation (NSF), will not generally underestimate the shortfall in graduate scientists and engineers. In fact, in the early 1990s many observers criticized the NSF for estimating enormous projected shortfalls of scientists and engineers. According to the critics, the NSF was feathering its own nest by saying that far more money should be devoted to scientific training to cope with a bogus shortfall.

Conservation enthusiasts often complain about missed opportunities. "If only we had installed fluorescent bulbs instead of incandescent," or "If only we drove Hondas instead of Lincolns, we could save so many tons of oil, or not have to build that nuclear reactor," we are told. This is merely another way of stating a shortfall, at least in their estimation. We have fallen short of the goal, in their eyes, of reducing energy consumption by the "right" amount.

If the shortfalls for potatoes or engineers are on shaky ground, so are the conservation shortfalls projected by those who have decided we should use less energy. For various moral and ethical reasons, they have concluded that we as a society are wasteful. Once that has been decided in their minds, all sorts of conservation shortfalls are conjured up. These tortured shortfalls do not mean much more than the clumsy ones developed for the Russian potato harvest.

We can see through the vegetable shortfalls rather easily, since they do not involve ethical questions. We have a little more difficulty in dealing with shortfalls for energy conservation. As Dave Rossin implies with his questions, we have to remember that any shortfall of any commodity or service is a construct of the person or agency playing with the numbers. It does not take too much brains or skill to project a shortfall of practically anything, even shortfalls themselves.

• • •

Consider the phrase, "Can't do any harm. Might do some good." It pops out when a decision that did not have obvious bad consequences had to be made, like whether someone should visit an aunt for the afternoon. Not much damage, other than a boring few hours, might result.

Society uses that phrase when it comes to conservation. Some of us are skeptical over whether it will really work. But we say to ourselves, "Just in case there's something to it, maybe we need a few programs along these lines. Maybe not as many as the fanatics would propose, but at least a few. Consider it a type of insurance policy." The reasoning sounds persuasive. After all, we buy insurance for a myriad of dangers, ranging from death at an early age, to medical costs, to malpractice insurance for physicians. What is wrong with a little insurance against the dangers of running out of energy on some distant day?

Yet we do not buy insurance for everything. Iowans do not take out policies against tidal waves. Florida farmers do not buy policies against drought. Alaskans do not have heat-stroke insurance.

Did George Washington have a veteran's benefit policy signed by the Continental Congress? The concept of trying to insure ourselves against all possible misfortunes is a relatively new phenomenon.

Advocates of conservation policies might say in response, "We're not talking about billions or tens of billions here. Just a few million wisely spread, along with a handful of regulations, will do the trick."

It is true that a few million spent on trying to improve insulation or develop a more efficient engine will not bankrupt the American $5 trillion economy. Rather, it is the various regulations proposed by conservation advocates that will end up costing the economy serious money.

Economists have known this for a long time. The actual amount spent on an activity by the government or private enterprise may not be that much. But the regulations imposed by the government to further that activity, and paid for by consumers or yet other government entities, may be enormous. For example, in the unrelated field of education, the Federal government spends little money directly on handicapped students. But it can require school boards across the country to spend large amounts to take care of these students—a highly commendable goal.

So the insurance policy for conservation is not the nickel or so a month we might imagine. It is a far larger amount that is required as a result of all the conservation regulations that are being enforced every day. That money could be going to find new sources of energy and build new power plants. Instead, it is being spent trying to conserve what is regarded as our ever-dwindling store of energy, just as a squirrel might starve himself to conserve the tiny amount of nuts remaining in his tree trunk.

The seemingly innocuous regulations will indeed do some harm, as energy researchers are diverted away from more sensible goals to pursue the chimera of conservation. The aphorism, "Can't do much harm, might do some good," definitely does not apply to conservation.

• • •

We have all thrown pebbles in a fast-flowing stream at one time in our lives. Some of us may have kept on after the first two or three were thrown, attempting to build some kind of dam behind which the water would accumulate. Unless we were extremely persistent, nothing much happened. We heaved stone after stone, watching them disappear into the drink. Then there was silence.

The wilder ones among us may have tried to move boulders into the stream, and cemented them with smaller stones. With a bit of luck in placement, we may have been able to create a small dam, with some water being diverted from its natural course.

But if we came back a few weeks or months later, chances are our handiwork was swept away, and there was no trace of our past work. Nature had restored things pretty much to the way they were before we interfered with her.

Energy use can be thought of like the Mississippi River, flowing with almost unbridled force through our lives and our planet. When the snow melt in the mountains is great, the river flows faster. When drought stalks the land, it is slower. But the big river is still there, and we can never walk between its banks.

Some people, in the form of conservationists, propose to alter its flow by heaving pebbles into it. They toss and toss, but the stones sink to the bottom without trace. The more vigorous among them rent bulldozers and shove giant boulders into the river. The boulders pile up and cheers ring from the riverbank. Then, the next morning, the river has done its work again. There is no trace of the previous day's handiwork.

If we are going to have the conservation that some people feel in their gut is necessary, we will have to do more than figuratively throw pebbles in the stream. We will have to adopt the large-scale measures needed to build a big hydro dam. The river itself will have to be diverted and harnessed in a Herculean way.

The river in real life does not protest when we build a big dam. Thousands of fish die, of course, and migrating ones have their ancient paths completely ruined. But fish do not vote in elections.

Yet the river of energy is really us, and all of us can vote. If the conservationists try to do more than heave a few pebbles, and try to get to the stage of stopping up the river completely, they will encounter massive protests or even revolution. Their bulldozers will be blown up, and they themselves may suffer the same fate. Right now, we are at the pebble stage. The next stage, if it ever comes, is likely to be a lot less pleasant.

By early 1997, Ukraine had severe electricity problems. The Chernobyl accident and its aftermath had removed some of the biggest power plants from its electric grid. There was still a surplus of coal-fired capacity; but observers said that this had come about because the nation was economically prostrate—a result of the collapse of Soviet-style centralized planning. As soon as economic activity picked up, the Ukrainians said, they would need much more electricity. Then they would want to restart some of the reactors at Chernobyl.

The Western nations thought this was a bad idea. They had some leverage, since the Ukrainians wanted to borrow Western money to restart the reactors. Western nations appointed a commission, through the European Bank of Reconstruction and Development (EBRD), to investigate the situation. They concluded that neither restarting some Chernobyl reactors nor completing some other reactors whose construction had been abandoned with the end of the Soviet Union was the best approach.

Instead, the commission proposed a series of energy conservation measures that they believed would postpone or even put off completely the day that the incomplete reactors would start up. Each of these conservation measures would apply to a specific field of activity only, such as rehabilitating the nation's district heating system. But the majority of the panel believed that the Ukraine as a whole would reduce its electricity needs. Conservation, in spite of its uncertainties, would save the day.

This conclusion was met by a strong dissent by one of the panel members, Sweden's Prof. Lennart Hjalmarsson of Gothenburg University. In an appendix to the EBRD report, he said, "I have not managed to find one single evaluation of energy conservation programs published in a scientific journal that shows the program has managed to reduce growth in electricity demand at a national or regional level and the program has been cost-effective."[2]

I agree.

NOTES

1. Some of his many books are *The Theory of Political Economy* (London: Macmillan, 1871); *The State in Relation to Labour*, 4th ed. (New York: A. M. Kelley, 1968); *The British Coal Trade* (New York: A. M. Kelley, 1969); *The Theory of Political Economy*, 4th ed., ed. R. D. Collison Black (Harmondsworth, U.K.: Penguin, 1970).

2. *Nuclear News* 40, no. 3 (March 1997): 71.

2

Strange Terminology

The idea of energy conservation at all costs has spawned its own strange lingo or jargon. Confusing to the uninitiated, it is equally confusing after it has been explained.

National Public Radio once reported on a demonstration in Czechoslovakia against a nuclear plant. It was followed by an interview with Jessica Tuchman Matthews, an official of the World Resources Institute in Washington. The interviewer noted that nuclear power was associated with the previous discredited Communist regime in Czechoslovakia. As a result, some wanted to eliminate it, if only for that reason.

Much of Czechoslovakia's electricity came from brown coal. There were few if any antipollution devices used on the stacks of these coal-burning plants, giving Czechoslovakia the dubious distinction of being among the most polluted countries in the world. On a personal note, I drove through much of the Czech lands in 1971. I had never seen such a devastated landscape. It looked like something on the moon, not on earth.

The interviewer asked Matthews, in effect, if Czechoslovakia doesn't use nuclear and coal, for the reasons we discussed [association with the previous regime and suffocating air pollution, respectively], to explain what could they use to produce electricity.

In response, Matthews used, for one of the first times on a national broadcast, the term *negenergy*. She said that negenergy is the amount of energy produced by conservation. Enough conservation will produce enough energy. A barrel of oil saved is a barrel of oil generated.

The Czechs apparently generate very little electricity burning oil. The emphasis on oil indicated Matthews's U.S.-dominated thinking, where saving oil is the god of conservation.

No matter how much the Czechs save, negenergy or any other mantra-like concept will not produce one kilowatt-hour or light one bulb. When the Czechs plug in their appliances, the energy must come from somewhere. If they save 10, 20, or even 99 percent of present consumption, it will not turn on even a night light.

• • •

The Czech example may sound theoretical, but consider the negenergy programs proposed for some electrical utilities. Conservation enthusiasts want the utilities to pay a bonus to those of their customers who conserve energy more than a given level—usually unspecified. But the customers who install insulation and otherwise save energy already expect to save money from their actions. Why pay them a bonus on top of this?

Professor Paul Joskow went on from negenergy to negagallons. He writes, "Oil companies do not have 'negagallon' programs, and they do not view consumer opportunities to drive more fuel efficient cars as 'supply sources' allowing them to produce less oil."[1]

Oil companies could see, after the first oil shock of 1973, that consumers were going to be driving smaller cars in the future. If negagallons truly existed, the oil companies would then have said, "When people drive lighter cars, it's going to produce billions of negagallons. You can phone our exploration people and tell them to throw away their drills and oil rigs. We won't need them any more." There may have been a few oil companies that said this, but they are no longer in business. All the rest did precisely the opposite. Regardless of whether they thought negagallons really existed, they doubled, tripled, and quadrupled their exploration budgets. New oil fields were found all over the world as the roughnecks worked around the clock. The oil for the needs of society was found in the ground, not in mythic negagallons.

Suppose negagallons truly existed. When a large car was traded in for a smaller one, gasoline would be saved. But the purchaser would not be satisfied with this savings. He or she would be phoning Exxon, Chevron, and Atlantic Richfield, demanding to know when their bonus for generating negagallons would arrive.

Most people would regard this as excessive greed, even if it were the wealthy oil companies shelling out. Not content with legitimate savings, car owners would be dunning them for extra cash to do what they would have done anyway.

Prof. Joskow extends the analogy to grocery stores, noting that "My neighborhood supermarket doesn't have a 'negafood' program that pays me to eat less and doesn't see my going on a diet as a 'supply source'." A consumer might switch from filet mignon to chuck steak to save money, but they would not be satisfied with the extra dollars in their pocket. They would tell the grocery that they want a bonus for the wonderful sacrifice they have made. After all, they produced a lot of negafood by their actions.

These unhappy consumers would probably be thrown out of the supermarkets and the oil company towers. It would be for an eminently sensible reason: Regardless of protestations, negafood and negagallons do not exist any more than negenergy does.

• • •

Consider another analogy, that of the phone. All of us use it. Almost all of us wish that our phone bill was a little—or a lot—smaller. What does this have to do with conservation?

Prof. Joskow says this:

The local telephone company does not have a "negacall" program that pays me to talk less on the phone and does not view less talking as a "supply resource" making it possible to install fewer telephone switches. [My] talking less on the phone may . . . be [a] very worthwhile public policy goal [but] how best to achieve [it] does not follow naturally from the kind of centralized planning and decision making framework we are asked to apply to electric utilities. Instead, if I suggested that this framework be applied in these other contexts most people would laugh.[2]

Phone companies and electric utilities are what the economists call "natural monopolies," so they are similar in many respects. Building more phone exchanges to accommodate the ever-growing number of calls uses up some of the world's resources, just as supplying electricity does. Yet if you managed, through self-control, to cut down your phone bill from $50 a month to $45, would you expect an extra bonus from the phone company? As Joskow points out, it is to laugh.

NOTES

1. Paul L. Joskow, "FERC Should Not Include Demand-Side Bidding in Its Rules," *Electricity Journal* (Aug./Sept. 1988): 36–38.

2. Quoted in ibid.

3

Psychology of Energy Conservation

Tied closely to the notion of conservation is that of waste. If we are wasteful, then we are not conserving. If we do conserve, then we are, by definition, not wasteful. Case closed. But there is no exact standard for what is waste, and never will be. So whether or not we consider ourselves wasteful depends on our psychological attitudes, not on a chart or equation.

• • •

What is energy waste? Is it like pornography, which many people cannot define but say they will know when they see it? Or is it a more hazy phenomenon, whose definition depends on where we stand? Consider a classic example of alleged waste—electric toothbrushes. As debates over building nuclear plants in the 1970s and 1980s raged, many said, "It's crazy to build these huge and dangerous reactors to power a few electric toothbrushes. We can get along just fine without the plants and the toothbrushes."

The implication, rarely explicitly stated, was that using electric toothbrushes was a waste of energy. It had to be a waste, since everyone could clean their teeth using a regular toothbrush with little effort. After all, how lazy can people get?

Was it really a waste? First, let us dispose of the argument that huge power plants had to be built to power tiny appliances. One of these plants operating for a second could probably generate enough energy to power all the electric toothbrushes in the country for years to come. The power that went into these toothbrushes was an infinitesimal fraction of total output. The rest went into activities that most people would not claim was a waste—lighting homes, operating motors in factories, and a multitude of other uses.

So the statement that eliminating peewee devices will eliminate the need for power plants, whether nuclear or coal-fired, just will not wash. You do not have to be an engineer to figure that one out.

Nonetheless, some people would probably say, "Electric toothbrushes *are* a waste. People are incredibly slothful, if you let them be. Those toothbrushes should be banned." Lazy perhaps, but a waste? The ads for the toothbrushes claim that at least some dentists' organizations endorse their use. The dentists are quoted as saying that the power brushes do a better job of removing plaque. So if their word means anything, at least some uses of electric toothbrushes are not wasteful.

Suppose someone can avoid just one visit to a dentist to remove plaque by using an electric toothbrush compared to a manual one. The savings he or she would make by eliminating that trip would be far greater than the total cost of electricity to power that toothbrush—for decades. There would be savings in this case, not waste.

Now consider the plight of parents, who often find it difficult, if not impossible, to get their children to brush regularly. If children do not brush frequently, they usually spend a lot of time in the dentist's chair, running up bills for their parents. Children who use electric toothbrushes tend to brush more often, because the sound and vibration fascinate them. Again, parents can often save money by investing in electric toothbrushes. They can avoid some expensive trips to the dentist.

Not everyone needs electric toothbrushes. The point here is that what looks like energy waste on the surface can save money for some people. Waste is not as simple as it first looks.

• • •

Consider another example, waste of gasoline in autos. Someone may see a Rolls Royce or other gargantuan car go by and mutter, "What a waste of energy! He could get to wherever he's going by using a much smaller car."

Of course he could. Whether it is waste depends on where we stand.

To other Rolls Royce owners, that driver is not wasting energy. He is just using a reasonable means of transportation, given his income and wealth.

The Rolls uses much more gasoline than your car. Conversely, your car probably uses much more gasoline than a Chevrolet Geo or the defunct Yugo. These miniboxes produce about fifty to fifty-five miles per gallon (mpg). Other similar small cars are freely available on the American market, but certainly do not dominate overall sales. The vast majority of cars sold, probably including your own, get much less gas mileage.

So when a Geo or a Yugo owner (if there are any of the latter left) sees your larger car go by, he may mutter, "What a waste! All that gasoline being used when mine would save many gallons."

The story does not end there. Millions of people in this country use public transportation, such as buses and subways, to get where they are going. The energy used per mile of public transport is much less than for private vehicles. When someone waiting at a bus stop sees a Geo or a Yugo go by, he may say, "What a waste! True, they get fifty miles per gallon, but total gasoline use would be much lower if everyone took the bus."

The story still is not over. Most of the people in the world get to work, in factory or field, the same way that our ancestors did—by walking. As they trudge along the road, a bus passes them. We will assume that a Rolls Royce or Geo has never been seen on those parts. The man marching along says, "What a waste! All that gasoline being used up, when God gave us all two legs. What is the world coming to?"

What we call energy waste depends on where we sit—or ride. What seems like a foolish or wasteful activity to one person may be essential to another.

All this said, does true waste, on which everyone can concur, exist? One specific example occurred in the Gulf War of early 1991. The Iraqi troops, to provide cover for their movements, set hundreds of Kuwaiti oil wells on fire To complicate the movement of U.S. and allied ships in the Persian Gulf, they let other oil wells spill petroleum into that body of water. The waste of that oil served no conceivable purpose, except that of war. In that sense, it was a complete and utter waste.

All war is a waste, in that its purpose is to destroy what humans have painfully built up. Energy waste in war may be the only type of waste on which we all can agree.

• • •

When we waste, or think we waste, we feel guilty. As a society, we seem to have a fixed amount of guilt on public policy issues. Instead of the physics concepts of conservation of mass and energy, we have "conservation of guilt." Think of a hose with a constant flow, sprayed first on one target and then another. That hose is now pointed at energy waste. In the minds of millions, we are bad in some sense because we are frittering away our energy heritage.

The hose has sprayed over different targets in the past. In the mid-1960s, guilt over how the nation had treated its black citizens in the past produced laws designed to correct abuses. A host of agencies sprung up to enforce those laws. Many white people ventured into all-black communities, performing such tasks as teaching in majority-black schools. They never would have dreamed of doing so a decade earlier.

By the 1980s, the hose had gone on to other issues. While a case could be made that some people in black communities were not much better off than in the past, the national sense of guilt on this subject was largely assuaged.

After Pearl Harbor, the government removed Japanese-Americans from their homes to isolated camps. For many years, there was little sense of guilt over this action: "They were enemies, weren't they?" Over the subsequent decades, guilt gradually built up. Finally, in the 1980s Congress passed a bill compensating the victims of the removal. While some of those displaced and their descendants continued to insist that the United States was still at fault, it is likely that national guilt over this action has been forever removed.

Another bout of national guilt, perhaps not viewed that way at the time, was that felt over left-wing affiliations in the 1930s and 1940s. Those affiliations by millions of Americans seemed reasonable to many when they were made. They were an embarrassment by the 1950s, when the nature of Soviet communism was finally evident. Senator Joseph McCarthy of Wisconsin and others seized on the sense of national guilt in that period.

By the 1960s, virtually all guilt over this had dissipated. J. Robert Oppenheimer, whose security clearance had been lifted in the 1950s, received a medal from President Johnson in the 1960s. By the 1970s, attention paid to the subject had virtually dried up, with the exception of a few fringe groups.

Millions of us suffer from guilt over energy waste. We imagine our generation foolishly guzzling all the world's petroleum through giant straws, leaving only a few drops for our descendants. As the examples given here show quite clearly, this guilt over our supposed waste is grossly misplaced. It is easy enough to waste time, but finding cases of true energy waste is much more difficult.

4

Mathematics of Energy Conservation

This book does not spend much time on numbers, because many eyes glaze over when confronted by lengthy tables. But there are mathematical and data aspects of conservation that deserve some discussion.

There is always a lack of data when it comes to energy conservation. Buy a house that the owner claims is stuffed to the rafters with insulation, and you never know exactly what your fuel bill will be. Buy a car, and the Environmental Protection Agency gasoline mileage numbers on the back window may not prove to be true.

If there is one thing that both proponents and skeptics of conservation agree on, it is that a system for which data are scarce will tend to be used less than systems for which data are abundant. Many examples could be cited in support of this. In the 1980s, in the interests of energy conservation, General Motors (GM) pushed the use of diesel engines in their Oldsmobiles. But most consumers knew little about diesels, other than their use in trucks. As a result, regardless of the merits of diesels, they failed in the marketplace.

As a footnote to history, the GM diesels turned out to suffer from various mechanical problems whose cost of repair far exceeded any potential gasoline savings. Their disappearance from the market was probably inevitable, regardless of consumer knowledge of diesels.

Consider the Vegamatic, often advertised in the ultimate hard sell on late-night television. Most people have seen it only on the screen, so real understanding of whether it does all the wondrous things that are claimed is not great. Whether the Vegamatic is truly as grand as the barking announcer says, our lack of knowledge of how it really works prevents tens of millions from ordering it.

• • •

We can never know all we want to about any form of energy or its conservation. When an oil field is discovered, its owners usually state that it contains so many millions of barrels. But when it is finally drained, the amount collected often differs substantially from that estimate. Although the petroleum engineers gave it their best shot, they did not comprehend everything about that field.

The same situation applies in saving energy. When a home buyer considers a house, he or she rarely has access to the energy bills of the previous owner. Even if they are supplied, the prospective buyer does not know if the previous owner left the windows open in winter or walked around wearing three sweaters.

According to conservation advocates, the problem of lack of data is easily solved. Since the average consumer cannot know all that is necessary about the cost of efficiency or conservation measures, government rules and regulations should supply them. Thus he does not have to spend so much time gathering energy data. So we have the Corporate Average Fuel Economy (CAFE) standards for cars, rules about insulation for houses whose mortgages are insured by the government, and so on.

Even here there are many problems. When someone goes to buy a new hot water heater, for example, they see a label for the estimated annual energy cost. But the buyer may be extremely frugal, or take a shower every hour. There is no way of translating the official government number into the particular lifestyle of the buyer.

In reality, the ineffectiveness of conservation data is not completely hopeless. In fact, we are bombarded every day with information on the subject. We get far more now than a decade or even five years ago. Home builders label some of their new projects as energy efficient. We may not know exactly how much we will save if we buy one of those houses, but we can assume that our fuel bills should be lower. For years, new cars have had the EPA gas mileage stickers. Refrigerators and other appliances tell us approximately how much electricity they will use. The argument could be made that we do not suffer from too little conservation data, but rather too much.

Even if these labels and stickers were not there, we could always use that old standby, common sense. Even the most ill-informed car buyer knows that a Cadillac will use more gasoline than a Geo, and that a Chevrolet or Buick would be somewhere in between. Everyone knows a big hot water heater will almost always need more energy than a small one, regardless of how much insulation the two have.

We may not have all the information we need, but we have a fair amount. Yet some conservation advocates assume that they have all the data and answers. "Stay away from large cars: They use too much gasoline," they may caution, even though large cars may be safer than small ones. "Ride the subway instead," they may advise, although many are fearful of mass transit. This attitude smacks too much of elitism for many tastes.

• • •

Figure 4.1
Price versus Time in a Rational World

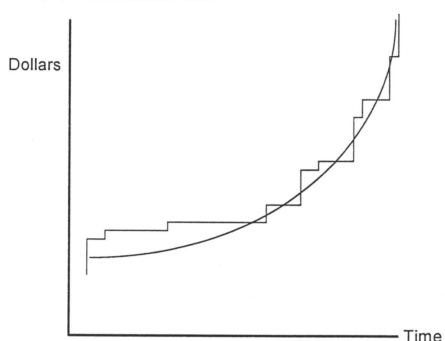

In a rational world, the energy price would remain constant until a small shock disturbed the system. Then the price would rise to the next level. The price would only rise, not fall, because energy is a depleting resource. The slope of the price rise might be determined by the work of Hotelling or other economists.

The mathematics of energy conservation can be applied to how energy prices might rise in the future. If the conservationists are right, we are running out of energy at an ever-increasing pace. When we run out of something, prices should rise steadily. Price versus time might look like the smooth increase in Figure 4.1. In reality, because of sudden shocks, the price chart will probably look like the series of irregular steps approximating the smooth curve.

For much of the 1950s and 1960s, the oil market behaved in the step mode. This was because of the oligopoly of the major oil companies, known at the time as the "Seven Sisters." Oil prices remained about constant in real terms, or even fell. (This is demonstrated in Chapter 5.) In Figure 4.1, this is close to the bottom left-hand corner.

After the oil shock of 1973, prices behaved in a much more erratic manner. The OPEC nations, which took control of international oil pricing, turned out to be much less of an oligopoly than the Seven Sisters. They tried to set prices, but rivalries brought frequent sudden lurches in oil prices. The behavior of oil prices in the past half-century is definitely not the smooth price rise expected on the basis of conservationist predictions.

What does all this prove? There are random variations in the prices of commodities, superimposed on broad variations. This explains why oil prices have not moved steadily toward infinity as the supply has been gradually used up. If we were really running out of oil at a steady rate, we would not have all these variations.

5

Petroleum and Gasoline

For many conservationists, the ultimate argument is over how much petroleum and natural gas is available underground. Some believe that nuclear energy has fatal flaws, and that coal, while abundant, will always be too dirty. The renewable energy forms, like wind and solar, are highly desirable in their estimation, but may not be available in sufficient quantity before the oil wells run dry. Hence the urgency to improve mileage standards and generally use much less of the desirable fossil fuels.

• • •

Just how much oil and gas is there? It has been estimated that the planet contains over 6,000 trillion metric tons of organic carbon that is cycled through two major cycles. Only about 18 percent of that contributes to petroleum production.[1] The primary cycle has a half-life of days to decades. This could be the decaying organic matter we see in fields and forests.

The large secondary cycle has a half-life of several million years.[2] Much of this organic carbon is too dilute or inaccessible for current technology to recover. However, the estimates represent centuries to millennia of fossil fuels, even with continued consumption at current or increased rates.[3]

The concern about running out of oil arises from misunderstanding the significance of a petroleum industry measure called the reserves/production ratio (R/P). This monitors the relationship between production and exploration. The R/P is based on the concept of *proved* reserves of fossil fuels. Proved reserves are those quantities of fossil fuels that geological and engineering information indicate with reasonable certainty can be recovered in the future from known reservoirs under existing economic and operating conditions.

The R/P ratio is the proved reserves divided by the production in the last year. The result is the time that those remaining proved reserves would last if production were to continue at the current level.[4] Economics and technological aspects affect the R/P ratio. As the price of oil increases (or new technology becomes available), marginal fields become proved reserves. As more fields become economic, we are unlikely to run out of oil.

Investment in exploration is also linked to the R/P ratio, and the world crude oil R/P ratio typically moves between twenty and forty years. However, tax breaks and bonuses to discover oil can extend that range upward.

Concerned people often refer to the Hubbert curves, which predicted fossil fuel discovery rates would peak and decline rapidly. The geologist M. King Hubbert calculated in 1982 that the ultimate resource base of the lower forty-eight states of the United States was 163 billion barrels of oil, plus or minus 2 billion. He estimated the ultimate production of natural gas to be 24.6 trillion cubic meters, plus or minus 0.8 trillion, with some additional qualifiers.

As the sum of past production and proved resources in 1982 was 147 billion barrels of oil and 22.5 trillion cubic meters of gas, Hubbert was implying that volumes yet to be developed could only be 14 to 18 billion barrels of oil and 1.3 to 2.9 trillion cubic meters of gas. Technology has confounded those predictions, so we hear little about the Hubbert curves these days.[5]

In 1995, the U.S. Geological Survey (USGS) increased their assessment of U.S. inferred reserves of crude oil (not just the lower forty-eight states) by 60 billion barrels, and doubled the estimate of gas reserves to 9.1 trillion cubic meters. When combined with the estimate of undiscovered oil and gas, the totals reach 110 billion barrels of oil and 30 trillion cubic meters of gas.[6]

The world R/P ratio has increased from 27 years (1979) to 43.1 years (1993) (see Table 5.1). If the crude oil price exceeds $30 per barrel, then alternative fuels, such as tar sands and oil shales, will probably become competitive. At $50 to $60 per barrel, coal-derived liquid fuels are economic, as are many biomass-derived fuels and other energy sources.[7] (Later in this chapter there is a discussion of why the U.S. Synfuels program, aimed at using coal to produce petroleum products, failed in the early 1980s.) The term *running out* may fade from our vocabulary.

• • •

Conservation rarely discusses price or value of resources. There are at least three ways in which we can consider prices and value of petroleum and its products that illustrate some of the fallacies of conservation.

First, we will consider the value of a barrel of oil, perhaps the prototypical example of energy resources. Second, we will see that how much gasoline we can buy with a fixed proportion of our income suggests if we will or will not conserve. Third, since how far we can travel on that proportion of our income is more important than the pump price of gasoline, we will consider the implication of that quantity in terms of conservation.

Conservation implies that we know—or can know—the true value of a barrel of oil or other fuel. This should be going up, as supplies inevitably dwindle and disappear. Is this true?

Table 5.1
World and U.S. Reserves of Fossil Fuels

	Proved Reserves (units as specified)	Reserves-to-production ratio (years)
	Crude oil (billion metric tons)	
Middle East	90	95
U.S.	4	10
Total World	140	43
	Coal (billion metric tons)	
U.S.	240	270
Total world	1,040	240
	Natural gas (trillion cubic meters)	
U.S.	5	9
U.S. Geological Survey data (1995)	9	17
Total world	142	65

Sources: BP Statistical Review of World Energy (June 1994), proved reserves at end 1993, p. 2; *1995 National Assessment of U.S. Oil and Gas Resources* (Denver: U.S. Geological Survey Information Services, 1995).
Note: Values have been rounded off; one barrel of Arabian Light crude oil = 0.159 cubic meters or 0.136 metric tons.

One way of determining the value of a barrel of oil is to compare it to average income. The simplest measure of American income is what the statisticians call *personal disposable income*, after federal, state, and local taxes. In what follows we will use dollar amounts in nominal dollars (in the year under consideration). Since we are also using the cost of a barrel of oil in nominal dollars, the calculations will not be biased by inflation.

The value of a barrel of oil can be defined as its cost divided by personal disposable income. For brevity, in the following we will use "income" as synonymous with "personal disposable income." The inverse of the value is the number of barrels that one year's income would buy.

For example, in 1937, the first year considered in Table 5.2, one barrel cost $1.10. Income that year was $549. Thus, the number of barrels of oil that could be bought was

$$549/1.10 = 499$$

The value of each barrel is the inverse of this (1/499 = 0.00200), as shown in Column 3. Since the value is always a tiny number, an index taking the years 1976 to 1978 as equal to 1.0 is used. These years were chosen because they marked the last period of relative calm before the massive fluctuations of the 1980s. The index changed only about 10 percent during 1976 to 1978.

Table 5.2
The Value of a Barrel of Oil

Year	Dollars per barrel (nominal)	Personal disposable income (in nominal dollars)	Value (column 1/column 2)	Index of value
1937	1.10	549	0.00200	1.47
1938	1.06	501	0.00212	1.56
1939	1.06	534	0.00199	1.46
1940	1.03	570	0.00181	1.33
1941	1.03	690	0.00149	1.09
1942	1.12	863	0.00130	0.95
1943	1.16	972	0.00119	0.87
1944	1.16	1,051	0.00110	0.81
1945	1.16	1,065	0.00109	0.80
1946	1.58	1,122	0.00141	1.03
1947	2.30	1,168	0.00197	1.45
1948	2.51	1,278	0.00196	1.45
1949	2.48	1,254	0.00198	1.45
1950	2.50	1,355	0.00185	1.36
1951	2.50	1,457	0.00172	1.26
1952	2.50	1,506	0.00166	1.22
1953	2.80	1,571	0.00178	1.31
1954	2.80	1,574	0.00177	1.29
1955	2.80	1,654	0.00169	1.24
1956	2.84	1,731	0.00164	1.20
1957	3.12	1,792	0.00174	1.28
1958	3.00	1,821	0.00165	1.21
1959	2.90	1,898	0.00153	1.12
1960	2.87	1,934	0.00148	1.09
1961	2.87	1,976	0.00145	1.06
1962	2.87	2,058	0.00139	1.02
1963	2.87	2,128	0.00135	0.99
1964	2.83	2,278	0.00124	0.91
1965	2.83	2,505	0.00113	0.83
1966	2.87	2,597	0.00111	0.81

In a year with an index of 1.00, 733 (1.0/0.00136) barrels of oil could be bought with one year's income. In a year with an index of 0.75, 978 (733/0.75) barrels could be bought.

In the late 1930s, when Table 5.2 begins, the price of oil was about constant, due to its control by the Seven Sisters. Income dropped by about 10 percent in the recession of 1937 to 1938. The value of oil rose slightly from 1937 to 1938 as a result. It then dropped slightly until U.S. participation in World War II in 1941.

With the onset of war, there was tremendous pressure for an oil price increase. However, stringent price controls kept it from rising above $1.16 from

Table 5.2 (*continued*)

Year	Dollars per barrel (nominal)	Personal disposable income (in nominal dollars)	Value (column 1/column 2)	Index of value
1967	2.92	2,740	0.00107	0.78
1968	2.95	2,930	0.00101	0.74
1969	3.00	3,111	0.00096	0.70
1970	3.30	3,489	0.00095	0.70
1971	3.36	3,740	0.00090	0.66
1972	3.36	4,000	0.00084	0.62
1973	3.89	4,481	0.00087	0.64
1974	6.87	4,855	0.00142	1.04
1975	7.67	5,291	0.00145	1.06
1976	8.19	5,744	0.00143	1.05
1977	8.57	6,262	0.00137	1.00
1978	9.00	6,968	0.00129	0.95
1979	12.64	7,682	0.00165	1.21
1980	21.59	8,421	0.00256	1.88
1981	31.77	9,243	0.00344	2.52
1982	28.52	9,724	0.00293	2.15
1983	26.19	10,340	0.00253	1.86
1984	25.88	11,257	0.00230	1.69
1985	24.09	11,681	0.00203	1.49
1986	12.51	12,496	0.00100	0.73
1987	15.40	13,157	0.00117	0.86
1988	12.58	14,111	0.00089	0.65
1989	15.88	14,948	0.00104	0.77
1990	20.03	15,898	0.00126	0.93
1991	16.54	16,741	0.00101	0.74
1992	15.99	17,616	0.00091	0.67
1993	14.24	18,225	0.00078	0.57
1994	13.19	19,003	0.00069	0.50
1995	14.58			

Sources: Column 1, prices from 1937 to 1973 are from *World Oil* (Feb. 15, 1975), 74. They are the average of (1) Oklahoma-Kansas 36–36.9 degrees gravity and (2) West Texas sour, 30–3 degrees API. From 1973 to present, prices are domestic first purchase price, from U.S. Department of Energy, Energy Information Administration, *Monthly Energy Review*, various issues; column 2, U.S. Bureau of the Census, *Statistical Abstract of the United States* (Washington, D.C.: The Bureau, annual); *Survey of Current Business* (Washington, D.C.: U.S. Department of Commerce, monthly).

a pre-war price of $1.03. The index of its value dropped substantially during the war because of a surge in income by war workers. It dropped from 1.09 in 1941 to 0.80 at the end of the war in 1945, a decrease of about one-quarter.

Peace brought an end to price controls. The price rose to $2.30 by 1947, a doubling. As a result, the index of value went back up to 1.45, close to what it had been in 1937, a decade previously.

The Seven Sisters controlled the price for about the next quarter-century, until the first oil shock of 1973. This control was subject to some outside forces, primarily the U.S. government. In 1950, with the onset of the Korean War, prices were frozen at $2.50. With the armistice of 1953, the price rose quickly to $2.80. The index of value declined by only 10 percent from 1947 to 1957, and the price rose at about the same rate as income.

The price remained almost constant from 1953 to 1956. It rose to $3.12 in 1957, after the Israeli–Egyptian war and Suez crisis. While we tend to think of the oil shock of 1973 as the first one, the Suez crisis provided a portent, as petroleum shipping was blocked to many countries. The price gradually dropped back to $2.87, close to the pre-crisis price, by 1960.

The year 1957 marked the beginning of the longest decline in value in modern history. The index gradually dropped from 1.28 in 1957 to 0.62 in 1972, a decrease of over half. The main reason for this steady decline was the almost constant price. It started at $3.12 in 1957, and dropped to $2.83 by 1965 (about the same it had been in 1953, twelve years previously). It rose only to $3.36 by 1972, just before the first oil shock. The increase was only 8 percent over fifteen years. During the same period, American incomes were rising rapidly, accounting for the strong drop in value.

From 1973 to 1982, world oil prices rose rapidly. Americans were sheltered to some extent by government price-freeze and roll-back policies. As a result, the price shown in Table 5.2 for this period is not the same as the world price.

In 1973, the price rose to $3.89. This increase of 53¢ was about 15 percent, the largest single-year increase since 1947. Because of accompanying inflation, the index of value rose only 3 percent, to 0.64.

Prices rose in the next five years, reaching $9.00 by 1978, just before the second oil shock. While the index of value rose sharply, during the 1973 to 1978 period its maximum was only 1.06. This was still about 20 percent less than the average of 1947 to 1957. The index dropped from 1.05 in 1975 to 0.95 in 1978.

After 1979, with the second oil shock and the loosening of U.S. price controls, the price rose strongly. It increased from $9.00 in 1978 to its all-time maximum of $31.77 in 1981, an increase of over 300 percent. The index of value rose as well, from 0.95 in 1978 to 2.52 in 1981, an increase of about 150 percent. The latter figure marked its all-time high to date. By 1981, the index of value was almost twice as high as the 1947 to 1957 average.

This provoked conservationists to claim that we had entered a new era, one in which oil prices could only increase. According to this logic, even more stringent measures to save oil should be a staple of American government. The back rooms of many energy libraries are crammed to the ceiling with studies and reports proclaiming this obvious truth.

But the high prices generated more oil exploration and decrease in energy use, both in the United States and worldwide. The price dropped from $31.77 in 1981 to $12.51 in 1986, a decrease of 60 percent. The latter year marked the price low point of the era after the second oil shock. The index of value also fell sharply, from 2.52 in 1981 to 0.73 in 1986, a decrease of over 70 percent. The latter value was about half that of the 1947 to 1957 period, generally regarded as fairly stable.

From 1986 to 1989, the price rose and fell within a range that was small compared to the 1973 to 1986 period. The index of value ranged from 0.65 to 0.86 during that time, with an average of about 0.75. This was about 40 percent less than the 1947 to 1957 average value.

We can compute the index for a long period, evening out its hills and valleys. From 1958 to 1985, the average value was 1.12, about 15 percent below the 1947 to 1957 average. From 1958 to 1985, oil prices first dropped steadily, then gyrated under the effects of the two oil shocks.

By August 1, 1990, the day before the Iraqi invasion of Kuwait, the price of oil was about $17, indicating an index of value of around 0.8. The invasion nearly doubled the world oil price for a few weeks, again pointing out the instability of prices since the decline of the Seven Sisters. However, this proved temporary. By 1993, the price was about $14, the lowest in five years. The index of value was 0.51, its lowest point in modern history.

Figure 5.1 shows five major changes in how much a barrel of oil means to us. First is the slow decline from the late 1930s to the end of World War II. Second is the post-war elimination of price controls, accompanied by a sharp increase in value. Third is the long, slow decline from the post-war era to 1973, the value dropping to its lowest point in the early 1970s. Fourth is the jagged increase from the first oil shock to 1981, when the index reached its highest point. Fifth is the almost equally steep decline since that year, the index reaching its all-time low in the early 1990s. By 1993, the index was about one-third of its value in the late 1940s, when few claimed we needed to conserve. Almost half a century had actually decreased the value of oil, in spite of claims that the tap would soon be turned off.

• • •

How many gallons of gasoline can you buy with 5 or 10 percent of annual income? Obviously, nobody will spend a year's income totally on gasoline. However, the quantity can be used as a surrogate for how much gasoline is available to us.

Of course, gallons purchasable varies over time differently from the value of a barrel of oil. The price of gasoline is set by many factors besides the cost of crude oil: the amount of capital invested in the industry, the degree of competition or monopoly between companies, profit margins, interest rates (cost of capital), and others. Traditionally, the cost of gasoline has changed much less dramatically than that of crude oil because of these cushioning factors.

From 1950 to the first oil shock of 1973, nominal gasoline prices rose very slowly, with few quick rises or falls. They mounted from 28¢ in 1950 to 43¢ in 1973, just before the first oil shock. This is shown in the first column of Table 5.3. The second column repeats the values for personal disposable in-

Figure 5.1
Index of the Value of a Barrel of Oil, 1937–1994

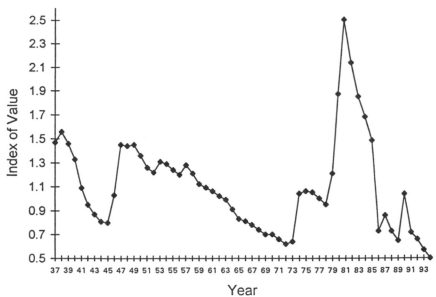

The value of a barrel of oil to U.S. consumers was lower in the late 1980s than it had been in the previous four decades, and perhaps lowest since the discovery of petroleum in Pennsylvania in the 1850s. The absolute value of the index is computed by dividing the price per barrel, in nominal dollars, by the personal disposable income of the average family, again in nominal dollars. The index of the value is computed by taking the period 1976 to 1978 as equal to 1.0. The index is proportional to the fraction of personal disposable income paid by Americans per barrel of oil.

come from Table 5.2, since these values are used in the calculations of the third column. In this table, both gasoline costs and personal income are in nominal (actual) dollars, so they are on the same basis.

The number of gallons that could be bought with one year's income, shown in the third column, rose almost continually, and is shown in Figure 5.2. Changes in the American economy from 1950 to 1973, including recessions, wars, and the like, did not seem to affect this smooth rise. Gallons purchasable rose steadily from 4,800 in 1950 to 10,540 in 1973, an increase of over two times.

In 1974, after the first oil shock, gasoline rose from 42¢ to about 52¢, a rise of 10¢ in only one year. This was about as much as it had risen in the two decades from 1950 to 1970. The number of purchasable gallons dropped at a slower rate, from 10,540 to 9,340.

Gasoline prices rose steadily after 1974, increasing from 68¢ in that year to 89¢ in 1979, just before the second oil shock. The number of gallons purchasable changed little. It reached a minimum between the two oil shocks of 8,800 in 1975, and rose steadily to 10,280 in 1978. The average for the period

Table 5.3
Gallons of Gasoline Purchasable with Total Income

Year	Cents per gallon (nominal)	Personal disposable income (in nominal dollars)	Gallons purchasable (column 2/column 1)
1950	28.2	1,355	4,800
1951	29.3	1,457	4,970
1952	29.9	1,506	5,030
1953	31.2	1,571	5,040
1954	31.4	1,574	5,010
1955	30.9	1,654	5,350
1956	32.3	1,731	5,360
1957	33.6	1,792	5,350
1958	32.6	1,821	5,590
1959	32.9	1,898	5,760
1960	33.5	1,934	5,770
1961	33.1	1,976	5,970
1962	32.7	2,058	6,290
1963	32.5	2,128	6,550
1964	32.2	2,278	7,070
1965	33.5	2,505	7,480
1966	34.3	2,597	7,570
1967	35.3	2,740	7,760
1968	35.4	2,930	8,280
1969	36.4	3,111	8,550
1970	37.6	3,489	9,590
1971	37.8	3,740	9,950
1972	38.0	4,000	10,530
1973	42.5	4,481	10,540
1974	52.0	4,855	9,340
1975	59.6	5,291	8,880
1976	61.6	5,744	9,320
1977	65.8	6,262	9,520
1978	67.8	6,968	10,280
1979	93.9	7,682	8,180
1980	117.9	8.421	7,140
1981	130.4	9,243	7,090
1982	121.5	9,724	8,000
1983	114.2	10,340	9,050
1984	112.8	11,257	10,000
1985	107.0	11,681	10,920
1986	85.7	12,496	14,580
1987	90.4	13,157	14,550
1988	86.0	14,143	16,450
1989	95.6	14,948	15,640
1990	122	15,898	13,030
1991	120	16,741	13,950
1992	119	17,616	14,800
1993	117	18,225	15,580
1994	117	19,003	16,240

Sources: Daniel Yergin, "How to Design a New Energy Strategy," *Newsweek*, 11 Feb. 1991, 43–44; U.S. Department of Energy, Energy Information Administration, *Monthly Energy Review*, various issues; U.S. Bureau of the Census, *Statistical Abstract of the United States* (Washington, D.C.: The Bureau, annual).

Figure 5.2
Gallons Purchasable with Total Income

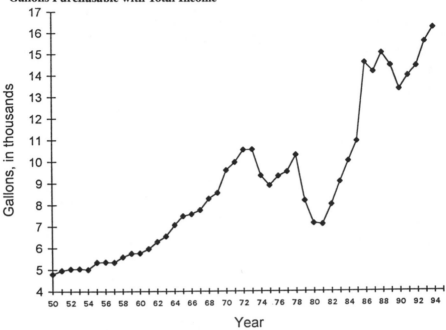

The number of gallons purchasable by an average family, assuming all its income went to buying this product, has risen since 1950. In that year, an average family could buy about 5,000 gallons. This rose gradually until 1973, when the amount was about 10,000 gallons. The oil shocks since that time made the curve much more erratic, but by the late 1980s an average family could purchase about 16,000 gallons, or about three times as much as it could in 1950.

between the oil shocks—1974 to 1978—was 9,470, only about 10 percent below the previous highs of 1972 to 1973.

In 1979, the second oil shock struck, with the fall of the Shah of Iran. Gasoline rose from 68¢ in the previous year to 94¢. This was an increase of 26¢, or about 40 percent. This increase was greater than the rise from 1950 to 1974.

The number of gallons purchasable naturally fell as well. It decreased from 10,280 in 1978 to 8,180 in 1979 and 7,140 in 1980. In spite of gasoline rising by about 50¢ in that period, the number of gallons purchasable remained higher than for any year before 1964. That is, an average citizen would have been able to buy fewer gallons of gasoline from 1950 to 1964 than in 1980.

Because the price of crude oil rose so high in the late 1970s, much greater production was stimulated. In turn, the price at the pump started to fall. It dropped from $1.30 in 1981 to $1.14 in 1983, a fall of about 16¢. This was by far the greatest decrease in modern history, admittedly from a steep level.

The number of gallons purchasable also rose, from 7,090 in 1981 to 9,050 in 1983. By 1983, the number of gallons purchasable was only slightly below the level it had reached in 1969 and 1970.

After 1983, the pump price continued to fall, and the number of gallons purchasable continued to rise. It increased to about 10,000 in 1984 and 1985.

In 1986 and 1987, it rose again to 14,500, about three times that of 1950. By 1988, the pump price was about 86¢, less than it had been in 1979. Because income had risen considerably in the interval, the number of purchasable gallons rose to its highest point ever, 16,450.

The price in 1989 increased about 10¢, to 96¢. The number of purchasable gallons dropped slightly to 15,690, still the second highest in history. Then, in 1990, Iraq invaded Kuwait, provoking the third oil shock. Crude oil and gasoline prices soared. The price rose to $1.15, a rise of about 19¢ in one year.

However, personal income had continued to rise. As a result, the number of gallons purchasable only dropped to 13,850, still more than it had been in 1985. By 1991, the gallons purchasable had recovered from the third oil shock and reached 16,600, another all-time high. In 1994, the last year shown in the table, the value was 16,240, only slightly under the all-time high of 1988.

The years 1970 to 1973 are sometimes held up as the golden age before the October 1973 oil shock and all the subsequent upheavals in the international petroleum market. The average number of gallons purchasable over those years was 10,150. The number of gallons purchasable for all subsequent years up to and including 1991 had a value of 10,800, or about 6 percent higher. In 1993, when the number of gallons purchasable was 15,580, the pump price would have had to rise from $1.15 to $3.80 to reduce the gallons purchasable to that of 1950. The golden age, if we define it as being the period in which one was able to buy as many gallons of gasoline as possible, was the late 1980s and early 1990s, not the 1950s.

What does all this mean? We consumed more gasoline in the past four decades than in all previous history. In addition, we imposed unprecedented gasoline conservation measures, such as the Corporate Average Fuel Economy (CAFE) standards.

Yet the gallons purchasable with an average income was much higher at the end of this period than at the beginning. This contradicted the assumptions of conservation advocates, which implied that the number of gallons purchasable should decrease, not increase. In common lore, we were draining a finite supply and could almost see the bottom of the tank. The imposition of conservation measures should also have made each drop of gasoline ever more valuable. This simply did not happen, a repetition of the folklore that we worry most about the things that never come about.

• • •

How many miles of travel are in your wallet? While we debate gas mileage standards and the cost of gasoline, ultimately we are buying miles of travel. This section considers how this final output is related to intermediate factors.

The distance that can be squeezed out of a gallon became one of the hottest topics of the 1970s and early 1980s. Instead of boasting about what wonderful stock market picks they had made, people at cocktail parties chattered endlessly about their car's coefficient of drag and thus increased gas mileage.

Table 5.4
Deriving Pre-1967 Average Miles per Gallon for Automobiles

Year	Miles per gallon for cars & trucks	Miles per gallon for cars	Mpg cars/mpg cars & trucks
1967	12.4	14.07	1.13
1968	12.3	13.87	1.13
1969	12.2	13.62	1.12
1970	12.1	13.52	1.12

Source: U.S. Bureau of the Census, *Historical Statistics of the United States, Colonial Times to 1970*, Series Q–148–162 (Washington, D.C.: The Bureau, 1971).

As gasoline prices crashed in the mid-1980s, the topic receded into obscurity. However, the ups and downs of miles per gallon have become a surrogate for estimating how much petroleum we are wasting, and when we will freeze in the dark.

From 1967 to 1994, average miles per gallon rose from 14.07 to 21.5.[8] The CAFE standard was set at 18 mpg for 1978, rising to 27.5 in 1985. The Secretary of Transportation, who has authority under law to lower the standard slightly, has done so on occasion.

CAFE rules apply only to new cars. By 1985, the average new car produced at least 26 mpg. It has varied slightly since then, reaching a value of 24.9 mpg in 1996.[9]

Pre-1967 mpg numbers are not easy to obtain, since that quantity was not a national concern at the time. Average miles per gallon for both cars and trucks for 1967 to 1970 are shown in the first column of Table 5.4.

From 1950 to 1966, the only data available combine information for cars and trucks. From Table 5.4, the average ratio of mpg for cars alone to that of cars and trucks was about 1.125 for the years 1967 to 1970. Since cars are generally smaller than trucks and therefore should have better gas mileage, that conclusion makes sense. We will assume this ratio holds as well for the years 1950 to 1966. With that ratio, we can estimate auto mpg for those years.

Miles per gallon from 1950 to 1990 are shown in Figure 5.3. Mpg gradually fell from 1950 to 1966, with slight variations. It held steady or even rose slightly from 1958 to 1966, with the burgeoning compact car sales of the period. The total change was small in any case.

Mpg levels dropped continuously from 1967 to 1973, the year of the first oil shock. This was primarily because of falling real gasoline prices, after inflation is taken into account. The decline was about 0.8 mpg, a larger absolute decrease than had occurred from 1950 to 1966. The relative drop in mpg was about 5.5 percent, again higher than the relative decrease from 1950 to 1966.

Figure 5.3
Total U.S. Auto Fleet Miles per Gallon

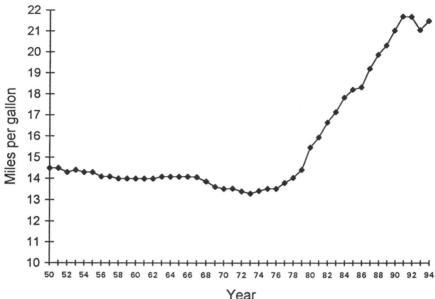

Gas mileage gradually decreased from 1950, when it was about 14.5 mpg, to the early 1970s, when it was around 13.5 mpg. The drop was around 7 percent over two decades. Under pressure of both increased gasoline prices and new federal regulations it rose fairly smoothly to around 21 mpg by 1990.

The first oil shock of 1973 impelled mpg higher, as motorists reacted to higher gasoline prices. From that point to 1978, rises in mpg were solely driven by price, since the CAFE standards were not in force. By 1978, mpg had risen to 14.04, about the level of the 1956 to 1966 decade.

Since that time, mpg has been driven by a combination of the CAFE standards and reactions to gasoline prices. The level rose to 15.5 in 1980, the first time that the previous 1950 high of 14.5 had been surpassed.[10] It reached an estimated level of 21.5 in 1994, about 50 percent higher than the 1950 level.

Now we can perform the calculations to determine how many miles of travel the average wallet contains. Suppose the average personal disposable income (after federal, state, and local taxes are deducted) is $10,000, the cost of a gallon of gasoline is $1.00, and the average miles per gallon is 20. Then the number of miles that can be driven, assuming that the entire income is devoted to travel, is

$$(\$10,000 \times 20) / \$1.00 = 200,000 \text{ miles}$$

The results of this calculation are depicted in Figure 5.4 and Table 5.5. In

Figure 5.4
Auto Miles Available from Total Income

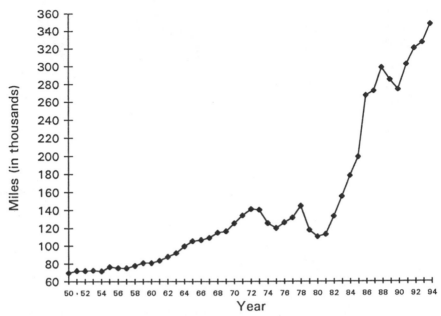

This graph shows the miles available to an average family if its total income were devoted to gasoline purchases, an obviously hypothetical case. It is assumed they drive a car with the average gas mileage for the year indicated. The distance rose gradually from about 70,000 in 1950 to about 140,000 in 1973, in spite of dropping average gas mileage. Increased family income and lower gasoline prices accounted for this. After 1973, the results are more erratic, as gasoline prices rose and fell. But by the late 1980s, the potential mileage was at an all-time high, at over 300,000 miles. Higher auto miles per gallon combined with higher family income to produce this result.

Table 5.5, the cents per gallon and personal disposable incomes are repeated from Table 5.3, since they are used in the computations.

In 1950, the level was about 70,000 miles. From then to 1973, it rose fairly steadily, doubling to about 140,000 in slightly over two decades. There were a few years when it dropped (1951–1952, 1953–1954, and 1955–1957), but the general trend was steadily upwards.

The value rose without dropping once from 1957 to 1971, a period of four-teen years. Considering the changes that took place both in the national economy—recessions in 1958, 1960 to 1961, and 1969, and the Vietnam War in the late 1960s—and the petroleum industry during that time, the steady nature of the rise was remarkable.

The first oil shock came in 1973. But the miles traveled that year were almost exactly the same as in 1972, before the oil shock. By 1974, miles traveled had dropped to about 125,000, approximately 15,000 less than in

Table 5.5
Potential Miles Traveled

Year	Cents per gallon (nominal)	Personal disposable income (in nominal dollars)	Miles per gallon (average)	Potential miles traveled, thousands (column 2 x column 3/ column 1)
1950	28.2	1,355	14.5	69.7
1951	29.3	1,457	14.5	72.1
1952	29.9	1,506	14.3	72.0
1953	31.2	1,571	14.4	72.5
1954	31.4	1,574	14.3	71.7
1955	30.9	1,654	14.3	76.5
1956	32.3	1,731	14.1	75.4
1957	33.6	1,792	14.1	75.2
1958	32.6	1,821	14.0	77.9
1959	32.9	1,898	14.0	80.8
1960	33.5	1,934	14.0	80.8
1961	33.1	1,976	14.0	83.6
1962	32.7	2,058	14.0	88.1
1963	32.5	2,128	14.1	92.3
1964	32.2	2,278	14.1	99.8
1965	33.5	2,505	14.1	105.4
1966	34.3	2,597	14.1	106.8
1967	35.3	2,740	14.07	109.2
1968	35.4	2,930	13.87	114.8
1969	36.4	3,111	13.62	116.4
1970	37.6	3,489	13.52	125.5
1971	37.8	3,740	13.54	134.0
1972	38.0	4,000	13.40	141.0
1973	42.5	4,481	13.30	140.2
1974	52.0	4,855	13.42	125.3
1975	59.6	5,291	13.52	120.0
1976	61.6	5,744	13.53	126.2
1977	65.8	6,262	13.80	131.3
1978	67.8	6,968	14.04	144.3
1979	93.9	7,682	14.41	117.9
1980	117.9	8,421	15.46	110.4
1981	130.4	9,243	15.94	113.0
1982	121.5	9,724	16.65	133.3
1983	114.2	10,340	17.14	155.2
1984	112.8	11,257	17.83	177.9
1985	107.0	11,681	18.20	198.7
1986	85.7	12,496	18.32	267.1
1987	90.4	13,157	19.20	279.4
1988	86.0	14,111	19.95	328.1
1989	95.6	14,948	20.55	322.5
1990	106	15,898	21.15	317.2
1991	122	16,741	21.69	297.6
1992	119	17,616	21.68	320.9
1993	117	18,225	21.04	327.7
1994	117	19,003	21.48	348.8

Sources: Column 1, derived from Daniel Yergin, "How to Design a New Energy Strategy," *Newsweek,* 11 Feb.1991, 43–44; U.S. Department of Energy, Energy Information Administration, *Monthly Energy Review,* various issues; column 2, U.S. Bureau of the Census, *Statistical Abstract of the United States* (Washington, D.C.: The Bureau, various years); column 3, *Highway Statistics, Summary to 1985* (Washington, D.C.: Federal Highway Administration, 1985); *Highway Statistics* (Washington, D.C.: Federal Highway Administration, annual). Data for 1950 to 1966 were estimated.

1973. The miles traveled continued its drop in 1975, decreasing to about 120,000. By then, the effect of the price rise for gasoline was being reflected in slightly higher vehicle mpg.

By 1976 to 1978, most of the effects of the first oil shock had worn off. Miles in a wallet rose to about 131,000 in 1977 and about 144,000 in 1978, about 2 percent higher than the previous crest reached in 1972. Part of this new high was due to the increase in mpg. By 1978, under the pressure of higher gasoline prices, mpg had reached 14.04, the highest since 1966.

In 1979, the second oil shock hit. This plunged the miles traveled to about 118,000, slumping to 110,000 the next year. Yet we were still in a golden age of gasoline prices. Motorists who were paying unprecedented prices at the pump (about $1.18 in 1980) probably did not appreciate this bit of news.

By 1981, the price at the pump continued to rise, reaching its all-time annual high of about $1.30 a gallon. Gas mpg continued to rise as well, reaching slightly under 16. There was a slight increase in the miles traveled to 113,000.

By 1982, higher petroleum prices generated greater exploration and production, which began to reduce pump prices. They dropped about 7 percent from their high in 1980. Combined with greater income and increasing mpg, this produced miles traveled in 1982 of about 155,000, marking an all-time high.

The years 1982 to 1988 each set annual records for miles traveled, the first time six consecutive years had done so since 1966 to 1972. However, the difference between the two sets of years was that the former was at a much higher level than the latter. The miles traveled by 1988 were around 328,000, 370 percent higher than the 1950 level.

In 1989, gasoline prices increased by about 11 percent. Due to increases in personal income and mpg, the miles traveled dropped by only about 6,000, less than 2 percent, to 322,000.

In 1990, the miles traveled dropped about 15 percent. Much of the drop was because of the increase in gasoline pump prices, which rose from 95¢ to $1.20. This was traceable to the Iraqi invasion of Kuwait in August, which disrupted international oil markets.

By 1993, after some slight dips, the miles traveled had almost reached the peak of 1988. Although 1994 personal disposable income was not available at the time of writing, it appeared likely that 1994 would set yet another record for potential miles traveled. It would be too much to claim that miles traveled has reached a permanently high plateau. Yet no year since 1982 had ever failed to top the previous high reached in 1978.

In summary, contrary to much public opinion, the true golden age of motoring, if one defines it as the period corresponding to the most travel that could be accomplished with the money in the average person's wallet or purse, is now. The miles traveled under this definition in the years 1986 to 1993 were over four times that of the early 1950s. This latter period is often regarded as a time when relative gasoline prices were low, and everyone's wallet was bulging.

More important, from the viewpoint of conservation the variation over time sketched here is the precise opposite of what was supposed to have been taking place if the theories of a fixed and diminishing oil resource were true. In those theories, the miles traveled should have been shrinking steadily as the oil was being used up. The theory of ever-smaller natural resources belongs in history's junk pile.

• • •

One of the major rationales to impose conservation regulations, rules, and standards is that they would decrease energy imports: "If we had smaller, more energy-efficient cars, refrigerators, light bulbs, and so on, we would have to import less oil. Then we would be less dependent on the Saddam Husseins, Muammar Khaddafis, Ayatollah Khomeinis—and all the dictators that will succeed them—of the world."

That argument convinces many people. One of the major aims of the U.S. National Energy Strategy, announced in 1990 by the Department of Energy, is precisely that—to reduce oil imports. This echoed the view of every President from Nixon to Clinton. The reasoning seems persuasive. If we use less energy, all other factors being equal, we should have to import less of it. Then Saddam Hussein and other oil autocrats will wreak less havoc.

The truth is somewhat different. The data are assembled in Table 5.6, which shows that greater energy efficiency will not necessarily reduce oil imports. The first column applies only to passenger cars. However, energy has a multitude of uses. The government estimates how much petroleum and natural gas, measured in British Thermal Units (BTUs), is required to produce a dollar's worth of goods and services (as measured in the gross domestic product). To avoid effects of inflation, 1982 constant dollars are used. The results are shown in column two. The numbers gradually decrease over time, as the nation has become more energy efficient. This is not a new phenomenon. Energy analysts have charted this increasing efficiency back to about 1880, over a century ago.

The national energy efficiency, shown in column three, can be defined as the inverse of column two. This column then shows the gross domestic product (output) produced per unit of energy input, in analogy to miles of travel (output) per input of one gallon. There is an almost continuous increase in both mpg and gross domestic product per BTU.

Auto mpg rises sharply after the mid-1970s. The national efficiency in terms of all petroleum and natural gas uses, including autos, of course, also rises from 1973. There are slight jiggles in the line here and there, but both overall trends are upwards. A rise in mpg is associated strongly with an increase in national energy efficiency. The trends are shown in Figure 5.5.

What has been the relationship of oil imports to energy efficiency? In Figure 5.6, the data from 1967 to 1973 are not included. During that time, the United States was not a free market for petroleum imports, which were restricted by a complicated series of tariffs and quotas. It was only by the mid-1970s that a reasonably free market emerged.

The ratio of imports to total petroleum use is shown in column seven of Table 5.6. In 1973, before the first oil shock, it was 26 percent. Although

Table 5.6
Conservation and Oil Imports

Year	Average passenger car miles per gallon	Petroleum & natural gas use (1000 BTU per 1982 dollar)	National energy efficiency, petroleum & natural gas (1982 cents per 1000 BTU)	Domestic petroleum production (in quadrillion BTU)	Crude oil imports (in quadrillion BTU)	Total petroleum use (in quadrillion BTU)	Percent imports of petroleum products
1972	13.4	20.9	4.78	19.5	6.9	26.4	26
1973	13.3	20.2	4.95	18.6	7.4	26.0	29
1974	13.4	19.5	5.38	17.7	8.7	26.4	33
1975	13.5	19.6	5.10	17.3	11.2	28.5	39
1976	13.5						
1977	13.8	19.3	5.18	17.4	13.9	31.3	44
1978	14.0	18.6	5.38	18.4	13.1	31.5	42
1979	14.4	18.1	5.52	18.1	13.3	31.4	42
1980	15.5	17.1	5.85	18.2	10.6	28.8	37
1981	15.9	16.0	6.25	18.1	8.9	27.0	33
1982	16.7	15.4	6.49	18.3	6.9	25.2	27
1983	17.1	14.5	6.89	18.4	6.7	25.1	27
1984	17.8	14.2	7.04	18.8	6.9	25.7	27
1985	18.2	13.5	7.41	19.0	6.4	25.4	25
1986	18.3	13.2	7.58	18.4	8.7	27.1	32
1987	19.2	13.2	7.58	17.7	9.7	27.4	35
1988	19.9	13.1	7.63	17.3	10.7	28.0	38
1989	20.6	13.0	7.69	16.1	12.3	28.4	42
1990	21.2	12.8	7.81	15.6	12.5	28.1	42
1991	21.7	12.8	7.80	15.7	12.3	28.0	40
1992	21.7	12.8	7.80	15.2	13.1	28.3	41
1993	21.0	12.6	7.93	14.5	14.5	29.0	44
1994	21.5	12.3	8.13	14.1	15.1	29.2	46
1995		12.2	8.19	13.8	15.6	29.4	45

Source: U.S. Department of Energy, Energy Information Administration, *Monthly Energy Review*, various issues.
Note: BTU indicates British thermal unit, a unit of heat.

Figure 5.5
Miles per Gallon versus National Energy Efficiency

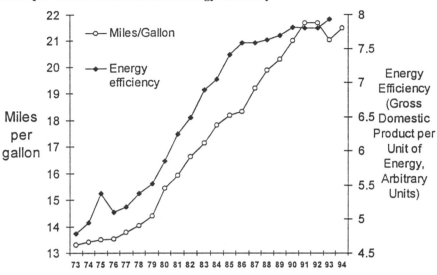

The miles per gallon for the average auto and the nation's energy efficiency went up at roughly the same pace from the mid-1960s to the late 1980s. The decrease in energy efficiency in the mid-1970s was the sole exception. The nation's energy efficiency had been rising long before the period covered by the graph.

energy efficiency improved from 1973 to 1977, the ratio of oil imports rose from 26 to 42 percent, rather than fell.

This contradicts the claims made by energy-efficiency advocates. As efficiency rose, the proportion of oil imports should have fallen.

By 1978, the proportion of oil imports was starting to fall, moving in the opposite direction from energy efficiency. So from 1978 to 1985, the graph lines ran in the "right" direction. As energy efficiency increased, the proportion of oil imports decreased.

After 1985, things fell apart again. Energy efficiency continued to increase, but now oil imports started to increase as well. The proportion rose from 27 percent around 1973 to 46 percent in 1994, an all-time high. The level of 46 percent was about 4 percent higher than the previous all-time high reached in 1978 and 1979.

As shown in Figure 5.7, there is no clear relationship between rising mpg and the fraction of American oil imports. Greater energy efficiency should lead to fewer oil imports. But all other factors, supposedly equal, are not equal. The major influence left out of the calculations of conservationists ؛ that of prices. Merely saying "increase energy efficiency and we will have to rely less on outside sources" is not according to the facts.

Figure 5.6
National Energy Efficiency versus Percentage of Oil Imports

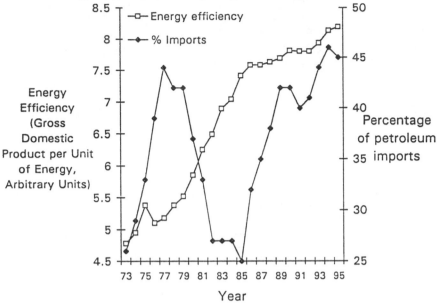

If increasing efficiency in automobiles produced lower oil imports, the two lines should move in lockstep, but they do not. Oil imports are obviously governed by many factors other than whether we drive a Geo or a Cadillac. Imports rose dramatically, for example, in the mid- and late 1970s in spite of steady improvements in gas mileage during that period.

About the same can be said about the relationship between gas mileage and the fraction of oil that is imported. According to what could be called a fundamental law of energy conservation, as gas mileage increases the fraction of oil imports should decrease. This is precisely what happened from the mid-1970s to the mid-1980s. However, around that time the law seemed to be broken, or at least slightly cracked. As Figure 5.7 shows, after the mid-1980s gas mileage continued to improve, but the fraction of oil imports also rose to even greater levels than the mid-1970s. So the conventional wisdom about the relationship among all these variables seems to be shaky at best and false at worst.

• • •

Every year, the Environmental Protection Agency (EPA) publishes a listing of auto gas mileages.[11] Cars like the Rolls Royce and Lamborghini bring up the rear, and Chevrolet Geos and some Japanese cars are at the head of the line. But if there is really not much difference in costs per year, it does not make much difference if one drives a Cadillac or a Hyundai, other than the initial costs. What are the differences?

Consider the results for 1990. The Lincoln Town Car was the most popular big or luxury car at the time. The EPA estimated a gasoline cost of $603 annually to drive 10,000 miles in padded comfort.

Figure 5.7
Gasoline Mileage versus Percentage of Oil Imports

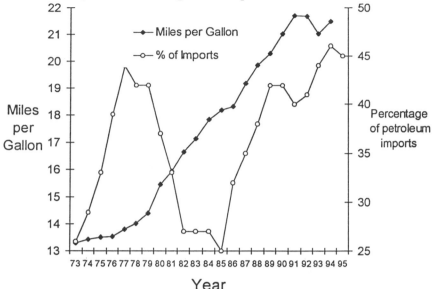

Year

The percentage of American oil imported from abroad does not have much correlation with gasoline mileage. The fraction imported jumped to an all-time high level in the mid- and late 1970s, but gasoline mileage kept chugging upward.

A typical small car was the Honda Accord, the largest-selling car of any size in the country. According to the EPA, it required $495 in fuel per year, a difference of only $108 between the large and small car. That is a difference of about $2 a week, not enough to buy a quick meal at McDonald's.

Small wonder that relative gas mileage plays little part in people's choice of cars. They may buy the Honda as opposed to the Lincoln for a variety of reasons—low initial price (although the difference between small and large cars is not as big as it once was), greater maneuverability, and so on. The amount they will have to spend on gasoline most likely does not rank high on the list.

• • •

In Chapter 2, the subject of the strange terminology in conservation-speak was addressed. A peculiar word sometimes used in discussions of this type was "negawatts," in which using more efficient appliances like highly insulated refrigerators would require less power from the utility. This saving of power capacity was called a *negawatt*, in distinction to the actual watts of power available from power plants.

One of the ways in which electrical utilities are supposed to provide negawatts to their customers, as opposed to ordinary watts, is by means of appliance subsidies. Suppose a special fluorescent bulb, designed to save energy by replacing an incandescent one, costs $10. Very few customers can be found at that price, other than those who want to conserve at any cost and have the money to do so. Under the negawatt scheme, utilities might offer to sell these high-priced bulbs for $5, or a subsidy of 50 percent. More people would be interested than at $10, although most will continue to buy Wal-Mart bulbs for a dollar. While utilities are not usually in the saving business—their main enterprise is selling electricity—regulatory agencies often force them into it.

Now consider how this might apply to automobiles. Suppose society, as exemplified by regulatory agencies, decided that "conserved" gasoline was cheaper than the cost of supplying new fuel. This is the argument that these agencies make about electricity when they require utilities to institute negawatt systems. If that were true, then Exxon should distribute rebate coupons, good for hundreds of dollars, to everyone who traded in their Cadillac for a Geo. The wealthy people who could afford a Cadillac or Buick Roadmaster would get a much bigger rebate than those who traded down from a Honda to a Geo. Inadvertently, utilities would act like Robin Hood in reverse. If any gasoline company proposed such a scheme, they would be pilloried in every newspaper in the land.

Yet this is precisely what we are doing, on a smaller scale, with negawatt schemes. We give those who have the money to buy high-priced fluorescent bulbs and other energy-saving devices even more money to buy them at a cheaper price.

• • •

In the energy crises of the 1970s and 1980s, one idea to save gasoline was accepted by almost everyone, or so it seemed: carpooling. It seemed ridiculous to have enormous traffic jams and bottlenecks on freeways when each car was carrying only one person. If everyone heads in the same direction, surely at least a few of them could get into the same car.

The Department of Energy funded massive studies on carpooling during those years. They found there are costs involved in developing large-scale carpooling, as opposed to the casual and sporadic kind. It is more than asking the person in the next office, who lives down the block from you, to share rides. Areawide carpooling requires an elaborate system of matching riders to rides, with associated computers and clerical personnel.

How did carpooling work in practice? Ride-sharing existed long before the Department of Energy came into being, and will go on long after its headquarters in Washington has crumbled to dust. It has always been in some people's interests to save time and money by carpooling. So any conclusions cannot be dramatically new.

A paper by Reichel and Geller considered what carpooling did or did not accomplish.[12] They found that when it comes to carpooling, people talk a good game but there is little action. It makes people feel good to say they support carpooling. But getting into someone else's car? That is another matter. For example, in one Iowa study, 111 people indicated a willingness to carpool. Three months later, only four people had actually formed new carpools. Of those four, three had given them up in the interval. Only one lone carpooler remained. It is not clear whether one person can constitute a carpool.

In Wilkes-Barre, Pennsylvania, about the same thing happened. Over 1,600 people expressed interest in forming carpools and were matched with potential partners. A few months later, a followup found that only twenty carpools had been formed.

In Sacramento, California, people could phone into a central service if they wanted a match. Much money was spent on advertising this service in the media. After six months, authorities collected over 5,000 names. When interviewers talked to some of these people, only about 22 percent had ever been in carpools. Of those, 15 percent had dropped out, leaving only about 7 percent still saving gasoline.

Carpooling does save energy, at least for the partners in the pool. (It cannot save energy for the nation or the world, for the reasons given elsewhere.) Unfortunately for advocates of this type of conservation, most of us give loads of lip service to the concept but we are reluctant to participate. If you search for someone saying a word against carpooling, you will be looking a long time. You will spend almost the same amount of time finding someone who really carpools.

• • •

A cartoon by Tom Toles, the Pulitzer Prize–winning cartoonist for the *Buffalo News*, appeared some time ago when the U.S. Senate debated increased auto gas mileage standards. Some Senators waved the banner of conservation, demanding that the CAFE new car standards be raised from 27.5 mpg to 40 mpg or even higher. Others thought that we had gone far enough, and that the standards were not even needed anymore. The cartoon, in a take-off on the familiar children's story, *The Little Engine That Could*, showed an auto, packed with people, inching up a line representing mileage. The line slopes upwards, presumably representing that which could be achieved with the right laws. The passengers—or is it the auto itself—are chugging, "I knew I couldn't, I knew I couldn't." The storybook little engine could do anything it wanted to, but the nation cannot even achieve greater gas mileage. It is a sad commentary.

But should we climb the mileage chart? We can conserve energy by making ever-smaller cars. Yet as we use less, there will be more available for other countries. Germans will race their BMWs down the autobahn a little faster. Chinese will buy refrigerators instead of using ice.

It seems attractive to get that car up the chart, but in the long run it will not help. The storybook little engine truly accomplished something—it delivered a load to the big city. The ever-increasing mileage standards that cartoonist Toles favors will generate little except more gasoline for the rest of the world.

• • •

Why should anyone take the advice of energy conservationists? As Jerry Taylor of the Cato Institute in Washington points out, their proposals for public policy in the past have been far off the mark.[13]

Consider diesel cars, mentioned in Chapter 4. In the early 1980s, when some claimed the last drop of oil would soon be pumped, they were all the rage. Diesel vehicles could get about 25 percent greater mileage than ordinary cars, thus conserving our dwindling—somehow the word always crept into the description—supplies of petroleum. General Motors followed the advice of the conservationists, sinking millions into diesel Oldsmobiles.

At the time, I was in the market for a car myself. I looked at the Oldsmobile and took one for a test drive. My knowledge of what was under the hood was not that great, but it seemed awfully noisy to me. While, like most people, I wanted to pay less at the fuel pump, I was not sure my next vehicle should sound like a truck. So I decided to wait a few years before plunging into diesels.

My caution was wise. The Oldsmobile had poor performance. Eventually, GM abandoned the diesel. To date, they have expended little or no effort to revive them. So much for all the money and energy that was supposed to be saved. Anyone taking the conservationist's advice in the early 1980s, as I was tempted to do, would have been worse off.[14]

Taylor gives a second example, that of the Synfuels program, which he describes as "one of the greatest boondoggles in history." In 1979, after the second oil crisis, President Carter proposed that the United States use its own resources to produce synthetic petroleum. No longer would we be dependent on malevolent Arab sheiks for this vital commodity. We would take the vast amount of coal that underlies much of the country and turn it into gasoline and other products.

Energy conservationists hailed the Synfuels program as right up their alley. Their assumption was that only a finite amount of oil existed in the world, and most of it was under the control of potentially hostile countries. So any action we could take to produce it right here was a good one, regardless of the cost.[15]

That was the governing clause: "regardless of the cost." It turned out that the gasoline and synthetic gas that was to be produced were far more expensive than the most avaricious Arabian sheik ever dreamed of charging Americans. As the plans for ever-bigger plants advanced, the costs soared into the stratosphere. Plant after plant was canceled because of these costs, until Congress finally realized that full Synfuels implementation could bankrupt the country. After many struggles between Congressmen in whose districts the plants would be built and the rest of Capitol Hill, the program was quietly buried under Ronald Reagan. It had cost billions, and little or nothing had been produced.

As Taylor points out, it was easy for conservationists to advocate these and similar programs. It was somebody else's—the taxpayers—money that was at risk, not their own. If the conservationists had had to put up the funds for these programs out of their own pockets, the schemes would never have gotten off the ground.

• • •

The American Automobile Association (AAA) is rarely described as a group of conservationists. But even they seemed to have jumped on the bandwagon. In a booklet they describe how to "conserve natural resources," among other things.[16] Some of the advice is unexceptional, such as "leave sea oats [whatever they are] and wildflowers where they are." But other suggestions, especially considering the AAA's history, are more controversial.

The AAA naturally defends motorists. They favor building more roads, keeping gasoline taxes as low as possible, and in general improving the lot of the motoring public. All these activities naturally require ever-more gasoline being produced. If the AAA has ever advocated building mass transit systems like subways to save fuel, it has escaped notice. Yet here they are, in their booklet, stating, "Use mass transit when you tour urban centers. Train and bus travel reduce urban pollution and cut travel costs."[17]

The advice makes some sense, even though it is not clear how much energy is saved. The idea of driving around the heart of European or Asian cities would unnerve most American drivers. When I drove from northern Italy down to Rome some time ago, I parked my car and took buses everywhere. I was not so much concerned about saving a few gallons of gas as finding almost nonexistent parking places after I left the one I had miraculously found.

The AAA could plead innocent to the charge of hypocrisy: "Look, this booklet saying that mass transit isn't so bad only applies to big cities. Outside New York and Chicago, we're all in favor of the car." But there is no mistaking it—the germ of conservationism has crept into that formerly pristine citadel of cruising and automatic transmissions. What will be next?

• • •

Many of the dire warnings we hear about running out of petroleum-based energy come from academics or politicians. But there is at least one energy company that sounds the alarm in their advertisements.

Archer Daniels Midland (ADM) is a large Midwestern agricultural-based firm. In early 1994 they had a series of ads on radio that said that most scientists believe that our oil reserves are disappearing. ADM had not embarked on a mission of science education. Rather, they were pushing their own product, ethanol from corn. ADM produces more ethanol from corn than any other company in the world.

The ads stated that if ethanol were used instead of dwindling petroleum, then our energy stores could last that much longer. This was, in effect, another form of conservation. Why use precious oil when ethanol would stave off the day when the wells ran dry?

What ADM neglected to say was that ethanol is probably the most highly subsidized energy product on the market. If ADM's ethanol had to compete with oil on a head-to-head basis, just about nobody would use it. Take away the subsidies, and the whole edifice collapses.

ADM, or anyone else, can promote their products on any legal basis. But when they use the familiar scare tactics of "It's all running out, so buy what we're selling," hackles rise. Many economists and scientists do not believe that we can ever run out. If ADM would tell listeners how much their subsidy is per gallon, we would have reached the promised land of truth in advertising.

NOTES

1. Based on an Internet computer posting by Bruce Hamilton of New Zealand, web location http://www.cs.ruu.nl/wais/html/nadir/autos/gasoline-faq/part1.html.

2. Bernard P. Tissot and Dietrich H. Welte, *Petroleum Formation and Occurrence* (Berlin, N.Y.: Springer-Verlag, 1978), Chapter 1.

3. Wolfgang Gerhartz, ed., *Ullmann's Encyclopedia of Industrial Chemistry*, 5th ed. (Weinheim, Germany: VCH, 1993), s.v. "resources of oil and gas."

4. *BP Statistical Review of World Energy* (London: British Petroleum) (June 1994): 2.

5. William L. Fisher, "How Technology Has Confounded U.S. Gas Resource Estimators," *Oil & Gas Journal* vol. 92 (October 1994): 100–107.

6. *1995 National Assessment of U.S. Oil and Gas Resources* (Denver: U.S. Geological Survey Information Services, 1995).

7. Mary Howe-Grant, ed., *Kirk-Othmer Encyclopedia of Chemical Technology*, 4th ed. (New York: Wiley, 1993), s.v. "alcohol fuels."

8. *Statistical Abstract of the United States, 1989* (Washington, D.C.: U.S. Bureau of the Census, 1990), 601, table 1026; U.S. Department of Energy, Energy Information Administration, *Monthly Energy Review*, Sept. 1989.

9. Anne Reifenberg and Allanna Sullivan, "Rising Gasoline Prices: Everyone Else's Fault," *Wall Street Journal*, 1 May 1996, B1.

10. However, a visit to Harrah's automobile museum in Reno, Nevada, the largest of its type in the world, suggested to me that average auto mileage in the 1920s and 1930s was probably on the order of 20 to 22 mpg. Admittedly, this was a different era.

11. "Consumers Not Yet Tilting toward Fuel-Efficient Cars," *Buffalo News*, 23 August 1990, C9.

12. David A. Reichel and E. Scott Geller, "Application of Behavioral Analysis for Conserving Transportation Energy," in *Advances in Environmental Psychology*, vol. 3, ed. A. Baum and J. E. Singer (Hillsdale, N.J.: Lawrence Erlbaum Associates, 1981), 53–91.

13. Jerry Taylor, "Energy Conservation and Coercion," *Policy Analysis* 189 (March 1993) (Issued by the Cato Institute, Washington, D.C.).

14. Ibid.

15. Ibid.

16. American Automobile Association, *Environmental Tips for World Trips* (Washington, D.C.: The Association, 1993).

17. Ibid.

6

In the Comics

Newspaper comics are sometimes a reflection of moods that are not found in editorial columns. Although polls seem to indicate that conservation is popular, a number of artists have had the temerity to poke fun at it.

In the old-time comic strips, wives like Blondie were always telling their husbands of the vast savings on their dress purchases: "It was on sale, dear. Ordinarily $100, but now just $50. Let's take the $50 I just saved for us and have a nice candle-lit dinner at Antonio's." Husbands were naturally suspicious of these savings, with cause. Their response often was, "You could have saved $100 by not buying that dress at all." (With the arrival of women's buying power, these scenes have been mostly consigned to history.)

There is a connection to the seemingly unrelated subject of conservation. Both situations are hypothetical, and bear only a slight resemblance to reality. Let us consider the conservation aspect. A typical "savings" is as follows: Someone reads an Environmental Protection Agency listing of auto gas mileages. He notes that a Chevrolet Geo gets about 50 mpg and a Buick Roadmaster about 20 mpg. He then says, "If the 100,000 people who are expected to buy a Roadmaster this year could be persuaded (or forced) to buy a Geo, the nation would save so many million gallons of gasoline."

The savings attached to the dress are about the same. If Blondie's dress had been marked down from $1,000 to $50, Dagwood and family could have taken a trip to Disney World with the savings. If the dress had been worn once by Elizabeth Taylor, it might have been marked down from $10,000 to $1,000. The fortunate woman buying it could have bought a small car with the $9,000 savings.

Of course, all the things obtained with the presumed savings—the dinner, the Disney World trip, the car—are only fantasies. They do not really exist.

The only real aspect of the transaction is the price paid for the dress. All the rest is speculation and dreams.

In the same way, the results of conservation—what would happen if we all switched to smaller cars, or used fluorescent instead of incandescent lightbulbs—tend to be castles in the air. We have trouble both in the dress example and conservation proposals because both are based, to some degree, on reality. Some dresses are more expensive than others, even before any markdowns are made. Some cars use more gasoline than others.

Where we—and Blondie—get into difficulty is in constructing a mythical framework around these solid facts. The next time you hear about the savings possible if a conservation measure is imposed, remember Blondie's plaintive cry, "But I got it on sale, dear."

• • •

Sally Forth is a strip about a young household in which the wife holds an executive job. It can be viewed as an inside look at yuppiedom. In the first of three panels of June 1990, the daughter, about ten, asks the mother if she can get a ride to the house of a friend. The mother responds that the daughter should walk. It is only three blocks, after all, and we all have to do our part for energy conservation. The second panel has no words, as the daughter stares at her mother, leaving the room. The third and final panel has the daughter bellowing, at the top of her voice, "Whose energy are we taking about?"

Energy conservation is fine, as long as it is the other guy that has to do it. When we are the victim, we think differently.

• • •

One of the rare extended critical comments about conservation was in the summer of 1990, in *Doonesbury*. Mike, the proto-yuppie with a conscience, and Zonker, the 1990s hippie, are the only two characters portrayed. In the first strip, Zonker greets Mike as the latter awakes: "Good morning, fellow spaceship earthmate," signaling the consciousness-raising that is about to follow.

Mike is grumpy. Zonker goes on, "Early to rise, early to bed! And that means energy conservation! Especially with these new screw-in fluorescents!" We see him lifting off the shade of a light fixture.

The next panel shows Zonker's hand as he screws in one of the new bulbs: "These babies are a bit expensive, but they'll last 10,000 hours and cut energy consumption by 75%! Over the long haul, they'll save you around 30 bucks a pop!" The final panel shows Mike in the shower, with just one drop coming out: "Pwit!" Zonker is calling from the next room, "Oh, by the way, I changed the shower head, too!"

Let us look at Zonker's calculations. Suppose that the bulbs last 10,000 hours, as advertised. A 100-watt incandescent bulb burning that long would require 10×100 kilowatt hours (kWhr), or 1,000 kWhr. The average national electricity cost in recent years has been about 8¢ per kWhr. Assume this rate continued into the future. Over the lifetime of the bulb, its total electricity cost would be $80 \times 100 = 8,000$¢, or $80. If the fluorescent bulbs do save 75 percent of energy consumption, this would be a saving of 0.75 × $80, or $60. If Zonker is right, he has underestimated the savings.

Assuming a typical 100-watt bulb costing perhaps 75¢, and a fluorescent bulb with the equivalent light output and lasting 10,000 hours, the $60 in these calculations would indeed be a saving. Why are people not lined up to buy them?

Zonker does not mention the price of his bulbs (other than calling them "a bit expensive"). They are almost certainly less than $60. Yet incandescent lightbulb manufacturers are not staying up nights, worrying about the new varieties.

• • •

There are three reasons for this. First, Zonker assumes that all light is the same. If we have a given number of lumens (the unit of illumination) from an incandescent bulb and the same from a fluorescent, they are equivalent.

They are not. Fluorescent bulbs have been around for about half a century. After all this time, they are used in the home to only a limited extent. They are common in kitchens and basements. That is about all. Yet fluorescents have been cheaper than incandescents, per unit of light output, for all that time.

We do not use them widely in the home because most people do not like the light it gives off. People have grown accustomed to fluorescents in the office and public buildings, but for personal reasons do not want them widely used in the home. Fluorescents are common in kitchens because that is a place of quasi-business, where food is being prepared. Nobody has ever referred to a romantic, "fluorescent-lit French dinner."

For that matter, when I was a graduate student I moved into a cheap apartment. The tiny living room/bedroom was illuminated by a circular fluorescent bulb. Even then I knew that a fluorescent cost less to run than an incandescent. But something about the light set my teeth on edge. I trotted down to the nearby Salvation Army store, and bought a small floor lamp for about a dollar. Although I probably paid a few dimes more a month, the psychological relief was palpable.

We can argue whether people are being sensible in rejecting the savings that would accrue if they replaced all their incandescents with fluorescents. That is not the point here. They have rejected a way to conserve even though the financial benefits are clear.

Second, the savings per year are very small. Assume that the average lightbulb in the house is on an average of two hours a day. This is probably an exaggeration for most bulbs. Some may not be turned on at all in a week.

If the bulb lasts for 10,000 hours, as Zonker claims, this is 10,000 ÷ 2 = 5,000 days, or 5,000 ÷ 365 = 13 years. If the saving totals $60, this is then $60 ÷ 13, or about $4.60 a year. For most people, this is so small as to be inconsequential. They are asked to lay out a much larger price for a fluorescent than an incandescent, and then recoup this at $4.60 a year. People cannot be bothered.

Third, no account is taken of the discount rate that people subconsciously apply to potential savings of all types, either energy- or nonenergy-related. For example, suppose a car were built that would last twice as long as the average vehicle. Suppose further that this was not the usual puffery of the auto manufacturers, but verified by *Consumer Reports* and other similar groups.

There would be just one little hitch—this long-lasting car would cost twice as much as regular autos. In spite of running twice as long as ordinary cars, few people would buy it. The reasoning might go as follows. Someone puts this large investment in a car. It might be destroyed in a crash, it might rust out, it could go out of style, and so on. Better not take the chance.

For a car of this type to sell, it would have to be priced not much above the price of ordinary vehicles, perhaps 1.2 or 1.3 times. This reduction from twice the value takes into account all of these subconscious feelings about longevity in autos.

• • •

The second *Doonesbury* strip is less amenable to calculations. Mike is still in the shower in the first panel. In the second panel, Zonker tells him that he installed the low-flow shower head himself. Mike is not too impressed. Zonker goes on to say that between the two of them, they should save 15,000 gallons per year from the device. Mike still is not overwhelmed. He is trying to shave with a can of shaving cream and the drips of hot water from the shower.

In the final panel, which is all black, Zonker calls out from the next room, "I also put a timer on the light!" There is a "Zip!" from Mike's razor, and an "Aiee!" as he cuts himself in the dark.

The energy savings from the 15,000 gallons is difficult to quantify. The exact amount saved will depend on the water temperature and other factors. Still, it probably is substantial.

Low-flow shower heads are not common, although they can be installed easily. You do not have to call a plumber. The reason for this is about the same as that given for fluorescent versus incandescent. In the words of the 1950s song "Constantinople," "People just like it better that way." We apparently still want a Niagara of hot water greeting us each morning.

The timer on the light reminds me of the first time I came across them in a small Loire Valley hotel in France. I saw them in the early 1970s, although they probably go back many decades. We were heading toward our room, fumbling with the keys in the hall, when the lights went out. Fortunately, it was only dusk, not night. We could dimly see where the light switch was, and flip it on again.

In France in the early 1970s, the light timer was reasonable. Energy costs as a proportion of French income had been very high for decades. The average Frenchman continually searched for ways to save energy. This applied even to hotels. Since that time, the fraction of French income spent per unit of energy, especially electricity, has gone down substantially. Back at that small hotel, the lights may now be on most of the time.

Gary Trudeau, the originator of *Doonesbury*, takes some liberty with conservation in the second strip. It is highly unlikely that even the stingiest, most energy-conserving householder would install a timer for lights in the bathroom. (There are usually timers for radiant heaters in the ceiling, though.) If the lights went out suddenly, this could be dangerous. So Trudeau is exaggerating for the sake of humor.

The artist brings out some facts, or semi-facts, about conservation. This is quite an accomplishment for a popular comic strip. He pokes a little fun at conservationists, but in a generally good-humored way. He does not go into reasons why the two devices he mentions, low-flow showerheads and screw-in fluorescent lightbulbs, have done so poorly in the marketplace. That is asking a bit much for a cartoonist.

• • •

The history of most ideas is simple. A different concept first pervades what are called the elites or intellectuals. Then it gradually makes its way down the chain until it gets to the people who never read a newspaper or magazine and hardly ever watch television news. This also applies to the comics. An idea may be tried in the more sophisticated strips, such as *Doonesbury*. Then it slowly filters down to the cruder types.

So it was with *Moose*, chronicling the exploits of some lower types. In one simply drawn strip, a truck labeled "Jungle Joe's Exotic Pets" pulls up in front of Moose Miller's house, which has a bird's nest on the roof. The second and final panel shows an obese Moose, in a flattened fedora, talking to Jungle Joe. A huge-mouthed hippo is gobbling the trash that Molly, Moose's wife, is heaving out the window. Moose says, "Molly loves her energy-conserving garbage disposal."

It is a good, if far-fetched, joke, but not too close to reality. Of the appliances in most homes, the garbage disposal uses close to the least amount of energy. While running an electric motor does use a large amount of power, the disposal is on for only a few seconds at a time. When energy analysts prepare lists of which appliances use what amount of energy, disposals often are not on the list because they consume so little. Moose may think he is saying a funny word on behalf of energy conservation. But anyone who used an animal—such as a more common goat—to save energy from garbage disposal would find they are worse off, not better.

Comic strip artists often express sentiments that are just out of public view. In the examples I have given, they struck a chord.

7

Marxism and Conservation

There may appear, at first glance, little if any connection between the philosophy of the bearded progenitor of Marxism and conservation doctrines as they are understood. This chapter points out some similarities.

Daniel Khazzoom, a professor at San Jose State University in California, has drawn a fascinating parallel between the mechanical treatment of the impact of improved household appliance efficiency and, of all things, Marxism.[1] He notes that the same question came up in the mid-nineteenth century, although in a different context.

At the time, people were concerned about the vast improvements in industrial efficiency sparked by the Industrial Revolution. Each new invention threw shoals of people out of work. Professor Khazzoom describes the situation clearly:

People asked: What will happen when the production efficiency doubles? The answer was, invariably, that half the people who worked in production would become redundant. As the efficiency triples, so went the argument, the demand for labor will drop to a third of what it used to be. And so on. The nineteenth-century theoreticians drew far-reaching conclusions from this analysis. Some, like Karl Marx, concluded that the diminishing demand for labor will create a massive pool of unemployed workers and set the stage for the final destruction of the capitalistic system. That did not happen. Why? Because the theoreticians failed to see that with increased efficiency comes a decline in the effective price of the service (or commodity) and that in the face of lower effective price, demand will increase. All one needs to do is substitute "energy saved" for "labor made redundant."

The statues of Karl Marx have come down all around the world. Soon he will be only an encyclopedia entry. While there is no statue of the conservationists who have said that saving a kilowatt hour here and there will reduce the total amount of energy we use, we should demolish their effigies in our minds.

• • •

There is another relationship between Marxism and conservation that deserves note. Over the years, I have run into a fair number of what could be termed conservation analysts. These people estimate the amount of energy that might be saved by having more insulation in refrigerators, more efficient lightbulbs, and so on. Then they multiply these values by the number of people who could or should buy these improved refrigerators, lightbulbs, and the like, yielding a global quantity of energy saving. Finally, they prove, at least to their own satisfaction, that the nation could get by just fine with 10, 20, 50, or 99 percent less energy than now. The exact number does not seem to matter all that much, as long as we cut down on waste.

My personal relations with these analysts have not been rosy. I have tried to talk to them about conservation and whether it really exists. But it seems that they have to make yet another quick calculation or rush off to the airport to attend a conference in Sweden on conservation. Thousands of gallons of jet fuel have to be burned to prove, for the hundredth time, that conservation exists—in their minds. This does not seem to bother them at all.

There was something about them that bothered me, but I could not seem to put my finger on it. They seemed to be authoritarian, with the attitude that conservation analysts really know in which direction society should be headed, and we should not pester them with our little ideas. A book published decades ago, one of the classics of political literature, had shown the portrait before: "[He] seemed to live in a half-real and half-dreamy world of statistical figures and indices, of industrial orders and instructions, a world in which no target and no objective seemed to be beyond his and the party's grasp." The description is of "the great genius and leader of the peoples," Josef Stalin, as described in one of the greatest political tales ever told, *Stalin: A Political Biography*, by Isaac Deutscher.[2] It is truly a dream world in which some of the analysts live, in which a few numbers get punched out on a computer keyboard and a world is transformed. Would that it were so simple.

These analysts have not committed the same crimes against humanity that Uncle Joe seemed to enjoy. Far from it. Yet reliance on numbers divorced from reality can lead to the same huge disasters that the late unlamented Generalissimo perpetrated.

NOTES

1. J. Daniel Khazzoom, "Energy Saving Resulting from the Adoption of More Efficient Appliances," *The Energy Journal* 8, no. 4 (1987): 85–89.

2. Isaac Deutscher, *Stalin: A Political Biography*, 2d ed. (New York: Oxford University Press, 1967).

8

Environment, Pollution, and Recycling

Energy use is clearly related to the environment. A coal-fired electricity plant, belching fumes over the countryside, comes to mind. But even a seemingly innocuous energy source like a hydroelectric dam can flood valleys and some-times destroy endangered species. How we deal with conservation affects what happens to the environment.

• • •

Recycling is tied closely to energy conservation. If we recycle more and more, we will use less and less of whatever is recycled. But recycling has been going on since the beginning of time. Some have claimed, for example, that almost all the gold ever mined is still in use somewhere. It is so valuable that it is rarely thrown away or buried.

Gold will always be recycled, and there is no need for anyone to lift a finger to make it happen. What materials should not be recycled, and when should they not? Consider a list of recycling prices, published in a report on recycling in New York State.[1] It noted the prices for different materials: Those who supplied white ledger paper to the recyclers would be paid 4½¢ a pound, steel scrap was 50¢ a pound, and so on. These materials obviously had some use to someone, or they would not pay for it.

Further down the list we start to encounter negative signs. Mixed paper is a negative ½¢ to 1¢; passenger tires are a negative $1.00 each. What does this mean? Like a broken piano, these and many other commodities have a minus value. We have to pay someone to take them away, rather than pay them to bring it to our doorstep. Their recycling prices are in the red, not the black.

All of us shell out to have garbage hauled away, but other commodities fall into that classification. The question phrased in terms of conservation is whether we should pay someone to recycle materials with a negative price.

We will always recycle gold and steel scrap, without government subsidies. Nobody would pay 50¢ a pound to discard these materials. Mixed paper with a negative price will not be recycled unless the government pays to have it done.

Here is where conservation concepts enter. William Baumol, former head of the American Economics Association and highly respected in his field, has found that it is more than a matter of yet another government subsidy.[2] If the government pays to have material recycled that would otherwise be hauled to the trash, energy is truly wasted. It is more than the actual physical energy lost as mixed paper is recycled after the market says it should not be.

The extra money spent in subsidies is what the economists call *embodied* energy. When the government subsidizes a good cause that is uneconomic, the energy that the subsidy represents is wasted. For example, the money that the government spends to recycle something that would otherwise be thrown away without the subsidy is associated with the certain amount of energy. One dollar in the economy is associated with about 13,000 BTUs of energy. (The United States consumes about 80 quadrillion BTUs per year, and has a gross domestic product of about $6 trillion.) Then each dollar of government subsidy for recycling means about 13,000 BTUs wasted, in the broad sense of the term.

While almost everyone supports recycling, we have to be careful where we draw the line. If we—or our government—have to pay extra to have some commodity recycled, we are wasting energy, not saving it.

• • •

What does sanitation have to do with conservation? Much of what is written here is to counter the notion that conservation is an unmitigated good without unpleasant side effects. Indoor plumbing has many of the same characteristics. Who could be against it? Yet as a book review notes, "In the year 1778 a device was patented by Joseph Bramah which brought death to multitudes of people. It was not a weapon of war, it was the water closet."[3]

Using the water closet, compared to the old outdoor privy, was clearly a great improvement in sanitation—for the people who were employing it. For those who had to drink water into which the toilet's wastes had been dumped, health decreased. Tens of thousands died of cholera and typhoid until, decades later, water purification systems were widespread. The moral? Devices that are claimed to confer undiluted blessings rarely, if ever, do so. The many systems that constitute what we call conservation are surely in that category.

• • •

Robert Fri, the head of Resources for the Future, a major think tank in Washington, has raised an issue about energy conservation that is rarely addressed.[4] He notes that many conservation measures add to the cost of goods and services. For example, adding greater fuel efficiency to recent cars has increased their price. When public utilities subsidize home insulation and low-energy-use lightbulbs, it is a tax on the rest who do not take advantage of these measures.

This does not bother Fri at all; society can add whatever "tax" it wants to whatever commodity it wishes. But he notes that society's antipollution measures, such as requiring sulfur dioxide to be removed from smoke stacks, also cost money.

At some point, according to Fri, the cost of these two taxes—conservation and environment quality—will become so high that we have to retreat on one. Most likely this will be under pressure of foreign competition. If we did not have to worry about it, in principle we could raise these two taxes as high as we want.

Will it be the conservation or the environment tax that falls by the wayside? Fri does not know, but he alerts us to the possibility. Until now, it has been generally assumed that if we conserved the environment would automatically get better. Fri suggests that this is not so.

• • •

The electric auto is sometimes held up as a way out of our addiction to petroleum. According to the clean air requirements for 1998 issued by the California Air Resources Board, at least 2 percent of autos in that state will have to have zero emissions of air pollutants. There is no powered vehicle that can achieve this except the electric car.

If electric vehicles were widely used, petroleum use in the transportation sector of our economy would go down. This does not necessarily mean that total petroleum use through the entire nation would fall. The release of petroleum from transportation will inevitably lower its price in other sectors, and we will find that it pays to guzzle gas somewhere else.

Regardless of how little petroleum is eventually saved as a result of government imposition of electric vehicles, they have certain environmental drawbacks. A letter to the *New York Times*, as reported by K. M. Reese, said, "What is so clean about lead-acid batteries, which must be replaced at least every two years? . . . The only contaminated waste more difficult to dispose of than battery acid is nuclear waste."[5]

The average auto on the road today has one battery which might last for four or five years. Electric vehicles might have dozens of batteries that get much more of a workout than those presently on the road. The two-year period quoted by the writer may be optimistic, given the tremendous strain that electric vehicles put on their batteries. In any case, if electric vehicles were widely used, the number of batteries to be disposed of would probably rise by perhaps a factor of ten. And the writer is correct in that the corrosive acid in batteries cannot be dumped as it used to be, in the nearest stream. It has to be carefully handled in landfills. Experience with landfills in the last decade or two shows that nobody likes them nearby.

So what looks like an ideal conservation measure to some turns out to have severe environmental consequences. As the environmentalist Barry Commoner frequently said, "You can't just do one thing."

• • •

By the early 1990s, the battle over chlorofluorocarbons (CFCs) was over. Production was to be phased out by industrialized countries by January 1, 1996. The familiar little cans of freon had already disappeared from K-Mart and other stores long before that. While it was never unanimous in the meteorological community that CFCs were directly responsible for potential global warming and the ozone hole, the weight of public policy moved like an inexorable tide.

But what could be used as a replacement in refrigerators and air conditioners? Industry came up with chemicals with equally long, if not longer, names: hydrochlorofluorocarbons (HCFCs) and hydrofluorocarbons (HFCs). But these replacements were soon attacked as also contributing to global warming, although perhaps not as much as CFCs. Taxes were proposed on HCFCs, which still carry some ozone-destroying chlorine into the stratosphere.

On HFCs, Kevin Fay, executive director of the Alliance for Responsible Atmospheric Policy, said, "We do recognize that HFCs have global-warming potential, but they also contribute substantially to energy savings in applications like refrigeration. We want to make certain [that] policy makers take into account energy efficiency rather than just looking at greenhouse potential."[6]

Putting it another way, the chemical industry could easily come up with other refrigerants which would not contribute at all to global warming potential. But much energy would be wasted in using them. For example, before freon and similar chemicals were invented, ammonia was used as a chiller. It takes much more energy to produce the same amount of cooling using ammonia as opposed to freon. So the environment butts its head on the wall of energy saving again. If we want to save as much energy as we can in the field of refrigeration, we will have to expose the environment to greater risk than we would otherwise.

• • •

In the fall of 1993, President Clinton unveiled what was announced as an "ambitious" plan for reducing the U.S. contribution to global warming.[7] Whether it would work was a matter of some debate. Government studies and proposals are notorious for gathering dust on shelves. When they are taken down from their resting place, they are studied and restudied, but nobody knows what comes of it all. When I worked at the Canadian Department of the Environment, one of my friends was studying the results and conclusions of the Stockholm environmental conference of 1973—in 1978. He may still be evaluating it today.

The President proposed to reduce the so-called greenhouse gases by the equivalent of 107 million metric tons of carbon "below what they would otherwise be in the year 2000," seven years onward. The plan was supposedly a form of conservation, in that the greenhouse gases—methane, nitrous oxides, carbon dioxide, and the like—were to decline. But "decline" might be too strong a term. Rather, they would be reduced over what they would otherwise be.

For example, suppose the United States generated 1,000 million tons of greenhouse gases in 1993. (The amount is still quite uncertain, since we do not know the volume of some greenhouse gases, like methane, too well. They are generated by creatures like cattle and ants, which resist being hooked up to meters.) If we assume normal economic growth, greenhouse gases might grow to 1,200 million tons by 2003. The government plan supposedly would slash this latter amount by 107 million tons, for a total of 1,093 million tons by 2003. Notice what has happened. The total amount of greenhouse gases has actually risen by 93 million tons, not fallen. So the touted conservation results in an increase, not a decrease.

The numbers are even shakier than they appear. First, nobody knows what the degree of economic activity will be in 2003. We may be in the midst of a recession, in which case the amount of greenhouse gases will probably be depressed. We may be in the middle of a boom, in which case we will likely be burning more gasoline and coal than ever before (fossil fuels are the source of most greenhouse gases). Not too many are likely to shout at that point, "Stop the boom, we want to get off! Greenhouse gases are going up too fast."

Even if we could predict economic growth exactly, the plan would still be built on quicksand. It is essentially based on static technology. And if there is one thing we know about technology, it is that technology changes. We may develop new ways to burn coal with less air pollution, or coal use may fall because of pollution concerns. If this happens, greenhouse gas emissions will fall. Then again, those changes may not come about. Greenhouse gases would then continue to rise at the old rate. Nobody knows which of these two cases will come about.

Plans based on "what would otherwise be" do not really conserve anything. They may provide work for government economists and the public printer, but they evade the true issue of whether conservation really exists.

• • •

Before there was energy conservation, there was water conservation. The oil shock of 1973 ensured that most of us heard about energy conservation for the first time, although the idea had bounced around academic journals before that. But the newspapers and television shows had been filled for years with stories on why water must be saved.

Headlines called out, "Experts Foresee Western Drought."[8] Canadians were put in a tizzy over something called NAWAPA—the proposed North American Water and Power Alliance. The idea was to take water from north-flowing Canadian rivers and channel it to the thirsty United States. Even though it was just the concept of a lone American engineer, Canadian politicians thundered against it from the rooftops. No question about it—we were using too much water. Those showers were taking too long, and those new-fangled dishwashers were draining the earth dry. The charts compiled by professors showed projected water use ever rising and rising. There was only one solution: conservation and more conservation.

The results, according to the *National Geographic*, were that "the total amount of water pumped out of rivers or the ground in the U.S. dropped about 10 percent between 1980 and 1985 and only slightly increased since then [to 1993]. Irrigation has declined 13 billion gallons from an all-time peak of 150 billion gallons a day in 1980."[9] It is true that part of this decrease is because of fewer agricultural acres and an increase in water cost. Yet this potential decline was supposed to have been taken into account in the rising charts of water use. The cry of impending disaster proved to be woefully mistaken.

As if this were not enough, the nation was treated, in the spring and summer of 1993, to the spectacle of unlimited water. The Missouri and Mississippi overflowed their banks, carrying away whole towns. The claims of "running out of water" were washed away and drowned in the biggest floods the nation had seen for decades.

Everyone wants to improve the environment and reduce pollution. Some of the steps we take to increase conservation may lead to precisely the opposite effect.

NOTES

1. "Markets Price Listing," *The Market: A Report on Recycling Markets in and around New York State* 1 (December 1990): 6.

2. William J. Baumol and Sue Ann Blackman, "Unprofitable Energy Is Squandered Energy," *Challenge* 23 (July/Aug. 1980): 28–35.

3. Eric Ashby, "Signature of Deadly Water," review of *A Science of Impurity*, by Christopher Hamlin, *Nature* (6 Dec. 1990): 495.

4. Robert W. Fri, "Energy and Environment: A Coming Collision?" *Resources* 98 (Winter, 1990): 1–4.

5. K. M. Reese, "Electric Cars in the News," *Chemical & Engineering News* 71 (25 Oct. 1993): 82.

6. "CFC Group Changes Name, Shifts Focus to Global Warming," *Chemical & Engineering News* 71 (25 Oct. 1993): 19.

7. Bette Hileman, "Curbing Global Warming—Clinton Unveils Ambitious Action Plan," *Chemical & Engineering News* 71 (25 Oct. 1993): 4–5.

8. *National Geographic*, Special Edition, "Water: The Power, Promise and Turmoil of North America's Fresh Water," November 1993.

9. Ibid., 32.

9

What Stanley Jevons Found

Stanley Jevons was one of the greatest economists of the nineteenth century. It is unlikely that he ever heard the word conservation used in its present meaning. However, he laid down rules that explain why so many conservation measures either fail or actually boost energy use.

• • •

In the mid-nineteenth century, concern rose about the need to conserve at virtually any cost. "Save it!" was the cry. "We will decline and fall as a power if we don't." No, it was not the United States, but Britain. And the worries were not over running out of oil, but of coal.

Britain had become the world's leading manufacturer because of its tremendous coal reserves. Even though the nation produced more coal each year, the public had the feeling that someday the mines would be emptied. Then Britain would gradually go back to the rural life it had under the Normans.

Jevons responded succinctly in 1865, at the close of the American Civil War:[1]

Many persons perhaps entertain a vague notion that some day our coal seams will be found emptied to the bottom, and swept clean like a coal-cellar. Our fires and furnaces, they think, will then be suddenly extinguished, and cold and darkness will be left to reign over a depopulated country. It is almost needless to say, however, that our mines are literally inexhaustible. We cannot get to the bottom of them; and though we may some day have to pay dear for fuel, it will never be positively wanting. (pp. xxix–xxx)

Stanley Jevons is known today mostly to economists and not the general public. However, his thoughts have great influence to this day. He is best remembered as the father of quantitative economics. That is, he used tables and figures to prove his points. Before that, economists had relied primarily on anecdotes and reasoning. For example, Adam Smith, the author of *Wealth of Nations*, employed few numbers and generally did not use them to prove laws. At the time Smith wrote (in the 1770s), almost no economic data were collected. By Jevons' time, governments and private industry were busily collecting these numbers. Jevons overthrew many of the myths about what we now call conservation. Unfortunately, these myths refused to stay dead, and sprung up again like snakes from Hydra's head. This book, in a sense, reiterates what Jevons said so long ago.

As mentioned in Chapter 5, some of the great impetuses to modern-day conservation are what could be called the *depletion tables*. Someone estimates the reserves of oil, copper, or other commodities and divides that amount by annual consumption. The result is the years that the commodity will last. For example, we are sometimes told that the world's oil will last another forty years, copper another fifty, and so on (see Chapter 5). Quoting these numbers naturally makes some people demand stringent conservation measures.

Jevons quoted a number of estimates of one giant British coal field, that of Northumberland and Durham, going back to 1792. The estimated durations of supply varied all over the map, from 200 to 1,727 years. But Jevons had little faith in any of the estimates. He noted, "These so-called estimates of duration are no such thing, but only compendious statements how many times the coal existing in the earth exceeds the quantity then annually drawn" (pp. 18–19).

Jevons is best known for noting that conservation measures often produce the opposite effect from that planned. In his words, "It is wholly a confusion of ideas to suppose that the economical use of fuel is equivalent to a diminished consumption. *The very contrary is the truth.* It is the very economy of [coal's] use which leads to its extensive consumption. It has been so in the past, and it will be so in the future" (pp. 140–141, emphasis in original).

Jevons illustrates his point by recounting the history of steam engines. We are most familiar with the one devised by Watt, but it had predecessors. The first was the Savery engine, invented by a Frenchman. Its efficiency was extremely low. By using conventional wisdom about conservation and efficiency, its energy use would have been great. As Jevons pointed out, the Savery engine was so inefficient that it was hardly used at all: "It consumed no coal, because its rate of consumption was too high" (p. 143).

The next steam engine was invented by Newcomen, and was slightly more efficient than the Savery model. The same situation existed. It required so much coal to run that it was not widely used. As Brindley put it, "Unless the consumption of coal could be reduced, the extended use of the [Newcomen] steam-engine was not practicable, by reason of its dearness, as compared with the power of horses, wind or air" (p. 143).

All the Newcomen engines put together also used little coal overall, precisely because each one was so inefficient. It was only with the coming of the Watt engine, highly efficient compared to the Savery and Newcomen models, that coal use skyrocketed. Wales and the north of England became a series of coal mines.

Jevons also used examples from the iron industry. He found that "the reduction of the consumption of coal, per ton of iron [produced], to less than one-third of its former amount, was followed in Scotland, by a tenfold total consumption [increase], between the years 1830 and 1863" (p. 154).

Jevons listed many methods by which the iron industry conserved coal: saving the waste gases to heat the blast furnace, using small gas flames instead of large coal fires, and many others. But he noted that "coal thus saved is [not] spared—it is only saved from one use to be employed in others, and the profits gained soon lead to extended employment in many new forms" (p. 155).

• • •

Jevons also anticipated the arguments of Karl Marx, who was writing *Das Kapital* around the same time. Whether the two economists ever met is not known. If the bearded German had only read Jevons a little more carefully, the world would have been spared much grief. Jevons extended his principle to labor, not merely coal and commodities: "The economy of labour effected by the introduction of new machinery throws labourers out of employment for the moment. But such is the increased demand for the cheapened products, that eventually the sphere of employment is greatly widened. Often the very labourers whose labour is saved find their more efficient labour more demanded than before" (p. 140).

Jevons anticipated and defeated most of the conservation arguments over a century ago. We are in his debt.

• • •

Stanley Jevons was buried in the nineteenth century. In the 1970s, he and his principles were buried again on Capitol Hill.

After the first oil shock of 1973, Congress passed the Energy Policy and Conservation Act, the first explicit energy conservation law. While it touched on many subjects, its most important provisions concerned what many Americans love most—their cars.

Congress determined that most autos got inadequate gas mileage. It was an average of 13.4 miles per gallon in 1974.[2] The legislators wanted to increase that value substantially. Curiously enough, Republicans went along with what was mostly a Democratic push. Observers were mystified that Republicans, usually critics of Big Brother interfering in the lives of ordinary Americans, rolled over and played dead when government bureaucrats were to decide the size of the vehicles that citizens used.

When the measure was fully in effect, the reasoning went, there would be less need for gasoline. Then the United States could avoid dancing to the tune of Middle Eastern oil sheiks.

How high should mileage be raised? A Congressional staffer was once asked how Congress chose the ultimate level, 27.5 mpg. He talked about someone who knew somebody else who had heard a story at a cocktail party. The rumor had it that one member of Congress working on the legislation drove a Mercedes Benz. Presumably he used it only in Washington, and not in his home district. He noticed that he got fairly good gas mileage, but never tried to calculate how much. He asked his staffer to help. The latter phoned up the company, and found that the Mercedes with the best mileage got about 27 mpg. His boss reasoned, "If Mercedes Benz could do it, so could American cars."

Whether this story is true will never be known. What is sure is that the ultimate goal of 27.5 mpg was enshrined in legislation. (The law gave the Secretary of Transportation a bit of flexibility, and allowed altering this value slightly.)

Because cars could not reach this level immediately, the rules specified a sliding scale. As well, cars that were already on the road in the mid-1970s were not covered by the law. It applied only to new vehicles.

The standard went up and up. It was 18 mpg in 1977, 20 in 1978, and 26 by 1981. The final standard of 27.5 mpg was about twice the typical mileage of 13 to 14 mpg in the 1960s and early 1970s. In principle, U.S. gasoline usage should have dropped by about half, all other factors remaining equal. We should have been able to thumb our noses at all the burnoosed sheiks and ayatollahs.

It did not quite work out that way, as Jevons would have predicted. Average mileage of all cars, old and new, rose under the impact of the new regulations. By 1980 it had reached 15.5 mpg, about the level of much of the 1940s and 1950s. By the end of the 1980s, in 1989, it was at 20.5 mpg, about 55 percent better than when the law was passed. Because vehicle manufacturers built engines that get better mileage in the laboratory than on the road, it remained questionable if we would ever reach the 27.5 mpg goal. By 1991, average mileage had reached about 21.7 mpg. This was about halfway between the average value of 13.4 mpg before the law was passed and the ultimate goal of 27.5 mpg.

In 1992, a curious thing happened for the first time since the law went on the books. Average mileage fell, from 21.7 to 21.6 mpg. The goal of matching Mercedes Benz gas mileage seemed to recede into the distance like a mirage. Yet most of the old gas guzzlers had departed to the great junkyard in the sky.

In spite of this, the change was impressive. If you can remember a typical American parking lot as it looked around 1975 and look at its appearance now, there is no question about the shrinking of vehicles.

As average mileage increased by about 60 percent from the mid-1970s to the early 1990s, gasoline use should have dropped to 63 percent (1/1.6) of its original level, if all other factors had remained the same. Jevons knew that they never do. From 1977 to 1979, which we can take as a benchmark, U.S. gasoline use peaked at around 7.2 million barrels per day. We can use averages over a few years, since there are year-to-year variations. The suffix "per day" is dropped in the following, for simplicity.

Under the pressure of mileage regulations and higher oil prices, gasoline use did drop after 1979. It fell to about 6.6 million barrels over 1981 to 1983, a drop of about 8 percent. While the fall was much less than Congress had hoped for when it passed its law, at least it was headed in the right direction—downward.

Figure 9.1
Gasoline Supplied in the United States, 1973–1992

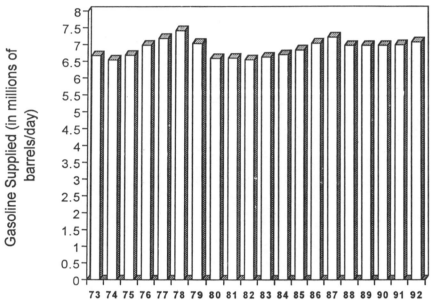

In principle, as U.S. gasoline mileage increased by about 50 percent from 1973 (its post–World War II low point) to the late 1980s, total gasoline use should have decreased. In fact, the graph of year by year variation was almost flat. Taking 1973 as a baseline, it went up slightly by 1978, but started falling again after the second oil shock of 1979. It fell back to the 1973 level by the early 1980s, and then began a slow ascent. But the total was always within the 6 to 7.5 million barrels per day range.

These fond hopes were to be dashed. By 1988 to 1990, average gasoline use was up to 7.3 million barrels. The variation over time is shown in Figure 9.1. In spite of slight dips and rises, the graph seems to be almost level. We were supposed to have slid down Mount Everest, but it never happened.

The 1988 to 1990 level was about 1.4 percent above the 1977 to 1979 level. We can take this latter period as when the mileage law was first taking hold. The 7.3 million barrels were also about 11 percent higher than the minimum reached in 1981 to 1983. All thoughts of a 35 percent or even a 50 percent decrease in gasoline use had flown out the window. Lawmakers would have been satisfied if gasoline use had remained at the level before the law was passed.

Why did this conservation measure, enacted with so much fanfare, fail so miserably in its ultimate goal? There were a number of reasons. Some of them would have applied even if the law had never been put on the books. Others were in the nature of the measure itself. Yet others were a tangle of the two factors.

Consider, for example, the miles driven each year per auto. If this goes up, all other aspects of gasoline use remaining constant, total fuel use will rise. That is what happened. From 1974 to 1989, mileage driven per car rose from 9,600 to 10,400 miles annually, an increase of over 8 percent. This result alone would have reduced the savings because of the mileage law.

As mileage standards became more and more stringent and cars shrank to European sizes, gasoline costs became a smaller and smaller portion of the total annual automobile bill. That bill consists of the purchase price, interest on any loans to buy the car, repairs, insurance, gasoline, oil, and so on, all divided by the number of years the car lasts.

For example, a typical auto used 771 gallons annually in 1973. This dropped to 506 by 1989, a decrease of about 35 percent. If you are a typical car owner, the fraction of total auto expenses per mile that gasoline represents falls in most years. Chances are you will drive more than you would have if your gasoline mileage remained constant from vehicle to vehicle. You reason, explicitly or implicitly, that most of the cost per mile is sunk in the car's initial cost, and a few more miles will not deplete your wallet or purse all that much. You then drive ten or twenty miles to visit friends rather than phone them.

The number of miles put on each car annually then is not an independent number. As the fuel used each year per car goes down, the miles driven will tend to go up. The conservation produced by the first effect will be diminished, or even completely offset, by the very results it produces. Stanley Jevons, who never saw an automobile, predicted these results 130 years ago.

• • •

Around the time that Jevons was writing, Bessemer was developing his new process for manufacturing malleable iron and steel. Although steel had long been around when Bessemer developed his idea—remember the Toledo steel blades produced centuries before—its production did not use much coal. When the world is generating only a few hundred tons of steel every year, not much coal is needed, regardless of how inefficient the process is.

Nathan Rosenberg of Stanford University recounts Bessemer's tale:

In metallurgy, for example, innovations that have drastically reduced fuel costs [by means of energy efficiency] have also led to price reductions. . . . A great innovation, such as the Bessemer process for refining pig iron into steel, brought with it a dramatic reduction in the fuel cost of steel-making. Indeed, it was this fuel-saving innovation that essentially transformed an iron industry into an iron and steel industry. . . . The Bessemer process was one of the greatest fuel-saving innovations in the history of metallurgy. . . . Its ultimate effect was to increase, and not to reduce, the demand for fuel.[3]

• • •

In the 1950s and 1960s, airport congestion grew steadily worse. Hordes of small aircraft, by present-day standards, took off and landed. They often spent hours circling the airport, waiting for a chance to descend. We have a solution to your problem, said Boeing, Lockheed, and McDonnell Douglas. It is called the 747, L–1011, and DC–10. These wide-bodied jets would carry far more passengers than existing aircraft. If they held three times more than the old 707s, then in principle one aircraft could do the work of three. Airport congestion would be greatly reduced. It might not go down by a factor of three, since there would always be a need for smaller aircraft, but it would be drastically reduced.

So we were told. The results were quite different. The wide-bodied jets reduced the cost of travel because they could hold more passengers. As the cost of flying fell, more people abandoned the train and their cars and flew. Before long, even with the new large aircraft, the airports were as congested as ever. Although the big jets were more fuel efficient than before, airline fuel use skyrocketed.

None of this was a bad thing. More people than ever before could take a fast, convenient, and safe method of transportation. But the illusion that greater aircraft efficiency—bigger planes—could reduce airport congestion and total airline fuel use proved to be only that, an illusion.

• • •

If we use energy-conserving lightbulbs, surely we will end up using less electricity. Franz Wirl, of the Technical University of Vienna, devised an example to show why this is not necessarily so, and how Jevons' teachings apply today.[4] His calculations are shown in Table 9.1.

The first column shows the relative cost of the SL–18 fluorescent lightbulb, designed to replace an ordinary 100-watt bulb. As indicated by its name, it uses 18 watts. People generally prefer incandescent in their homes to fluorescent for aesthetic reasons, but assume for the sake of this example that people are color-blind.

The SL–18 bulb costs $7 more than the ordinary bulb. This is shown in the first line of the table. Energy ratings are shown in the second line. Wirl as-

Table 9.1
Profitability of Conservation Investments

	SL–18 fluorescent light bulb	100–watt incandescent
Costs (added)	$7	
Watts	18	100
Use (hours per day)	8	5
Cost per kilowatt-hour, in cents	5	NA
Kilowatt-hours per year, at five hours per day	33	183
Hypothetical profit	50¢	NA
Kilowatt-hours per year, at eight hours per day	53	NA
Hypothetical loss	50¢	NA

sumes that the cost per kilowatt hour is 5¢. In recent years in the United States, it has been closer to 8¢. We will let this pass. So far, no mention of Jevons' ideas. He indirectly appears in the fourth line. Professor Wirl assumes that the 100-watt bulb is on for five hours a day. Because the SL–18 saves so much money, it could be on for as much as eight hours. These are only hypothetical numbers.

The SL–18 uses only 33 kilowatt hours per year. This compares to 183 for the 100-watt bulb, assuming both are on for five hours per day. The numbers are found by multiplying 5 (hours per day) times 18 or 100 (the energy ratings of the bulbs) times 365 (days in a year) and dividing by 1,000 (to go from watt hours to kilowatt hours).

The next line shows the hypothetical profit in switching from a 100-watt bulb to the SL–18, if both are used five hours a day. The SL–18 uses about 150 fewer kilowatt hours per year. At 5¢ per kilowatt hour, this is a saving of $7.50. However, we must also take into account the extra cost of the bulb itself. Wirl does this by subtracting $7 (from the first line) from the $7.50 profit, leaving a net profit of 50¢. This is shown in the sixth line. Wirl assumes that the bulb lasts one year, which may or may not be true.

Now go on to the next line, where the SL–18 is assumed to be on eight hours a day, not five. Its annual electricity use is then 53 kilowatt hours, still about 130 kilowatt hours less than the 100-watt bulb. Its electricity saving is then 5¢ times the number of kilowatt hours saved, or $6.50. When we subtract the $7 cost of the SL–18 bulb, we have a loss, not a gain, of 50¢. This is shown in the last line of the table.

The calculations pose a problem for third-party conservation programs. This is the term for when conservation is "sold" by private companies. The makers of the SL–18—or any other energy-efficient bulb—will presumably make a profit, assuming they know how to manufacture them. The conservation company that sells these lightbulbs to consumers will also presumably make a profit from the sales. Otherwise, they would go out of business. But the poor consumer, the low man on the totem pole, will be the loser if he keeps his light on longer to reap his "savings." Everyone comes out ahead except those who are supposed to profit from these innovations.

• • •

Geoffrey Greenhalgh, a British energy analyst, quotes some automobile data that again vindicates Jevons.[5] In Germany, France, Italy, the Netherlands, and Britain, new car efficiency increased by about 20 percent over the period from 1973 to 1983, the decade after the first oil shock. During the same period, oil consumption for road transport in the European Community increased by 30 percent, with an increase of over 50 percent in the number of motor vehicles. Undoubtedly, some of these increases were because of the lower running costs of these vehicles.

About the same thing happened in Danish homes. From 1977 to 1986, the electricity consumption of new washing machines went down by about 25 percent; that for freezers by 31 percent. Similar advances were recorded for other appliances. At the same time, the proportion of households with color televisions went up from about 45 percent to 80 percent, dishwashers from 16 percent to 22 percent, and so on. Again, the increase in Danes having color televisions and other appliances was due in part to the fact that they became cheaper to run.

What was the overall result? Total domestic consumption of electricity in Denmark rose from 7,200 gigawatt hours in 1978 to over 8,700 in 1986. Greater efficiency had increased total electricity use, as Jevons would have predicted.

• • •

Harry Saunders, an economist with the consulting firm of Decision and Risk Analysis in the San Francisco Bay area once made a useful analogy based on Jevons. Consider a "diesel pill." This corresponds to the gasoline pill of urban fable, which converts water to usable fuel. (According to this legend, oil companies have bought up the patent and destroyed it.) Saunders described a mythical diesel pill because it is easier to understand in the context of business use of energy. When we drive our own cars, it is a mixture of business (getting to work, for example) and pleasure (a Sunday drive in the country).

Saunders considers a fleet of tractor trailers. The marginal truck in the fleet produces $7,000 revenue per month. By "marginal" is meant the truck that produces the lowest profit, or highest loss. It could be the oldest truck, requiring more repairs than new ones, for example. The owner pays $1,000 each month toward its purchase, $5,000 for the driver's wages and benefits, and $1,000 for diesel fuel. The total payments per month are then $7,000, the same as the revenue. The truck breaks even, since revenue equals expenses. The other trucks in the fleet make at least some profit. Because this is the marginal truck, in the case of an economic downturn its driver would be the first to be laid off.

Now someone invents a diesel pill. Pop it into a tank of half water and diesel fuel and it all turns to fuel. As the economists would put it, if it existed this would be pure technical progress. The extra profit it would generate would not be dependent on economic factors such as substituting capital (more trucks) for labor (fewer drivers), interest rates, and the like.

According to the stories we hear about energy consumption every day, this diesel pill should be an unmitigated boon. The fleet owner would save $500 in fuel costs every month, because fuel costs are cut by half. The owner would use hundreds of gallons less of fuel. Our precious oil reserves in Alaska, Texas, and Louisiana would last that much longer.

But what is reality? The owner is looking at the total profit picture, not just the variations in the inputs—capital, labor, and energy. The owner's profit on this marginal truck rises from zero to $500 a month, since he or she reduces the fuel costs by that amount. If $500 a month extra profit is good, then tripling it is even better. The owner buys two more marginal trucks, ones that would earn zero profit under the previous conditions. He or she then pops the diesel pill into the tank. Now what?

Before, the fuel cost for the lone marginal truck was $1,000 monthly. The owner reduced it to $500 by using the diesel pill. This is where most discussions of energy conservation end, with a great triumph and medals being handed out all around. But the story continues. With three added marginal trucks and the magic pill, the fuel cost for the trio is 3 × $500 = $1,500. The total fuel use has gone up, not down, in spite of the fuel use per marginal truck going down. The profit from marginal trucks is now $1,500 as opposed to zero. The actions have been perfectly logical, from the owner's viewpoint. As Dr. Saunders puts it, "pure conservation" has increased energy use. Jevons must be smiling.

• • •

Stanley Jevons never saw television. But he could have predicted what would happen to its energy consumption. In 1973, before the first oil shock, there were few or no incentives to reduce energy consumption in televisions. The average nineteen- to twenty-inch set required 140 watts. By 1985, that requirement had dropped to 85 watts, a decrease of about 40 percent.[6] There should have been shouts of joy as enormous amounts of energy were conserved; but along with this greater efficiency came a drop in price of most televisions. The nineteen- to twenty-inch set became more of a toy, rather than the marvelous piece of high technology it was in the 1950s. People did not want a toy in their living room anymore. They wanted something substantial.

As a result, the market for giant televisions—thirty, forty, and even fifty inches diagonally—expanded. These televisions require much more electricity than their smaller brothers. The exact amount depends on the design.

If we look at the total amount of energy expended on operating televisions over the past two decades, we will not find the 40 percent drop we would expect on solely a physical basis. The case could be made that the total electricity used by televisions has risen, not fallen, in spite of these technological improvements. It was these improvements that made the increase possible. Professor Jevons could have foretold this without ever having seen *I Love Lucy*.

NOTES

1. W. S[tanley] Jevons, *The Coal Question: Can Britain Survive?* (London: Macmillan, 1865; reprint 1906). All quotations from this source.

2. All data from U.S. Department of Energy, Energy Information Administration, *Monthly Energy Review*, various issues.

3. Nathan Rosenberg, "Energy Efficient Technologies: Past, Present and Future Perspectives," paper presented at "How Far Can the World Get on Energy Efficiency Alone?" Conference held at Oak Ridge National Laboratory, Oak Ridge, Tenn., August 1989.

4. Franz Wirl, "Analytics of Demand-Side Conservation Program," *Energy Systems and Policy* 13, no. 4 (1989): 285–300.

5. Geoffrey Greenhalgh, "Energy Conservation Policies," *Energy Policy* 18 (April, 1990): 213–218.

6. Original paper presented at Senior Expert Symposium on Electricity and the Environment, Helsinki, May 13–17, 1991, published in *Nuclear Issues* 13, no. 5 (1991): 4.

10

Fast Forward to the Past

Conservation is a system for a future in which we use less energy, but we can draw some lessons from the past. If we do not, we are condemned to repeat our mistakes. What looked like waste to some eyes in the past really was not.

• • •

One of the main goals of alchemy in the Middle Ages was to find the "philosopher's stone." What we would now call scientists were called philosophers in those days. According to the *Encyclopaedia Brittanica*, this magical stone "was sometimes called a medicine for the rectification of 'base' or 'sick' metals and from this it was only a short step to view it as a drug for the rectification of human maladies."[1] Conservation is sometimes held up as the ultimate objective of society, as the policy that will cure a "sick" civilization. According to some of its proponents, we are wasteful and basically people with bad habits. Conservation will cure all that.

Alas for those who would resurrect the arguments of the Middle Ages, the philosopher's stone was never found. Charlatans and quacks claimed they discovered it and mulcted the masses that way. But it never existed and never will.

• • •

European visitors to nineteenth-century America noted many differences in the new country. One of the most curious was the size of American fireplaces. They were much bigger than those in Europe. If there had been any energy conservationists around in those days, they would have seen that big fireplaces are much more inefficient than small ones. Therefore, by that criterion, Americans were energy wasters.

They were not. Labor was scarce at the time, and since most people lived on the land, their lives were a constant round of chores. A large fireplace allows logs to be used with little sawing or chopping. Small ones require much more work to get the wood to fit the fireplace. Americans did not have the time for this on top of all their other work. So while the large fireplaces, in a sense, "wasted" some of the wood energy, Americans were responding logically to scarce labor. When wood prices rose as forests were depleted, householders abandoned the bigger fireplaces for the European-style small ones.

A second difference was in sawmills. By the middle of the nineteenth century, American mills used saws considerably different from those in Europe. The blades were thicker and had more widely spaced teeth than those across the Atlantic.[2] The American circular blades converted a large portion of the wood to sawdust. Why would anyone waste so much wood with these inefficient blades?

It really was not waste. The United States, with forests stretching off into the distance, had abundant wood resources. Many of Europe's trees had been cut down in previous centuries, and often not replanted. Europeans had a great incentive to save every last piece of wood. Americans did not.

Americans wanted to save money as much as Europeans. The precision blades that the Europeans used cost a lot more than the crude ones of the New World. As well, the American blades could be used for much higher-speed operations. The United States did not have enough workers to go around. Sawmill owners compensated for this by working the wood faster than Europeans. What looked to Europeans like unmitigated waste by Americans was a rational use of resources.

A third difference was in water power. There were abundant water power resources in New England, where most U.S. industry was concentrated early in the century. American water wheels before the age of hydroelectricity were inefficient compared to their European counterparts. In that sense, then, American waterpower was "wasted" in contrast to Europe. Since labor to install water wheels was cheap compared to that of Europe, it made sense in those days to build American water wheels cheaply and simply. Today, since hydroelectricity is highly valuable around the world, American hydroelectric dams are as efficient as any on the planet.

• • •

Americans could save when it was in their interest to do so. In the early nineteenth century, the cost of postage was high compared to average income. To cram as many words onto one sheet as possible and thus to save the cost of a second sheet, people used *cross-writing*. After the letter writer had filled a page the usual way, they would turn the page 90 degrees and write crossways over the previous words. The results were not easy to read, but still legible. Even the stingiest person today would not try to save a stamp that way.

• • •

As late as the 1860s, almost all the energy used in the United States was what it had been for centuries—wood based. After the Civil War, about 90 percent of American energy use was fuelwood. The other 10 percent was in the form of coal, employed in the high technology of the nineteenth century, railroads. Did energy users at that time ask themselves if they should conserve for the sake of future generations? The thought that all the trees might eventually be cut down might have occurred to some people at the time.

As the late Professor Harry Johnson once noted, let us suppose that a conservation movement had existed after the Civil War. Suppose further that strict rules to reduce tree cutting had been adopted. The tactic of allowing only so many trees to be cut down every year might have worked at the time, although politically there was not much interest in government intervention in any phase of the economy.

If all this had taken place, we might have more trees now. But that long-ago mythical conservation movement would have given us, the descendants for whom these actions were presumably taken, nothing. Trees would have been saved all right, but the use of fuelwood was beginning a long slow decline. The 1860s marked not only the Civil War and Reconstruction, but also the first commercial oil production by Colonel Drake in Titusville, Pennsylvania. At the same time, improvements in the steam engine, requiring fossil fuels like coal and petroleum, were making wood use obsolete.

If a conservation movement long ago had saved the trees because people were concerned that the forests would disappear, it would have had no impact on the late twentieth century. By now, fuelwood energy use is a tiny part of total energy and is confined mostly to fireplaces. All the trees that might have been saved in the 1860s, 1870s, and 1880s would have nothing to do with the way we live today. We do not depend any more on trees for our energy needs.

• • •

When did conservation, as we understand it, become a major issue? To answer this question, we would have to understand the complete history of energy and its ramifications. Vaclav Smil's 1994 book on the history of energy supplies some clues, but it does not focus primarily on conservation.[3]

Even the cave people used energy, presumably in the form of wood and other materials for fires. Conservation of wood probably was not a problem most of the time. However, if a forest fire burned down their wood supply, cave people would move to another area until the forest regrew. Carrying wood long distances was not possible. It is unlikely that many cave people gave much thought to ultimately running out of all wood. The forests were just too big to conceive of that.

In later times, however, scarcity of materials was common. Mines were exhausted and forests cut down completely in Roman times. But new mines were opened, or wood was transported for longer distances. The concept of a commodity disappearing, while it may have occurred to some people, generally is not recorded. There were just too few people and too small a demand on resources.

All this changed with the coming of the Industrial Revolution in the late eighteenth century. For the first time in history, enormous quantities of fuels like wood and the new kid on the block, coal, were being used. The population in Europe shot up as a result of better health conditions. Enter Thomas Malthus, an English clergyman. Malthus said nothing about energy, but his observations on food and starvation have carried over to energy and form the center of the conservation debate.[4]

Since the Malthusian prescription has carried down over two centuries to the conservation debate while many other theories of land, population, and resources have perished, it is worthwhile to devote a few words to it. Briefly, Malthus assumed that population would grow *geometrically*. Consider Adam and Eve, two people. If Cain and Abel had lived to maturity and found wives, that would have been four in the next generation. Presumably, the next generation would have doubled again, to eight. According to Malthus, populations would increase in a progression such as two, four, eight, sixteen, thirty-two, and so on. You could also have tripling between generations, or multiplying by a factor of 1.5, instead of doubling: The key point is that the previous number in the series is multiplied by a fixed factor.

Malthus assumed that the amount of land used to feed this geometrically increasing population would grow *arithmetically*. That is, in one generation or period the amount of farmland would be one unit. The next generation would use two units, the third generation three units, and so on.

A geometrically increasing series will always become bigger than an arithmetically increasing series, regardless of the two starting points. Even if there is a vast acreage of farmland in a given country and not too many people, eventually the increase in population will outstrip the growth of farmland and food supply. Malthus' predictions can be summarized in three words: We will starve.

How does this translate into conservation? The analogy is clear. Regardless of how much coal, oil, uranium, and natural gas we now have, we will run out sooner or later. We will freeze. Those in sunny climes will bake due to lack of air conditioning. Therefore we must conserve, at virtually any cost, to postpone that day of doom.

Malthus has been criticized in many ways over the centuries, in part for making up a theory out of whole cloth. It is true that his data sources were poor by modern-day standards. Still, he is either right or wrong. If he is right, then the conservationists should get even more public support than they do now. If Malthus was wrong, we should look at conservation in a more skeptical light.

Since Malthus wrote, there have indeed been mass starvations, as he predicted. Millions have died in India and elsewhere. In that sense, Malthus was right. However, Malthus did not merely say that there would be some starvation. Read correctly, his theory implies that there would be *worldwide* starvation. Only after the population was brought down by lack of food or other means such as disease would the relation between food supply and the number of people be brought into balance. That has not happened. While there have been outbreaks of starvation, the world as a whole is better fed than any previous time in history. If Malthus had been asked if the world population could ever rise to six billion, as it is now, he would have replied, "Preposterous!" So in the broad sense, Malthus' theories have not been proven correct, at least up to now.

Why did the Malthusian theories, which seemed quite reasonable to most first-time readers, prove to be off base? Economists would say they failed to take technology into account. If the average amount of food produced per acre today were the same as in the eighteenth century, hundreds of millions, if not billions, would starve. The earth could never support six billion people. Of course, the average farmer produces vastly more per acre today. This allows a well-fed nation like the United States to have perhaps 3 to 5 percent of its population on the farm.

So the Mathusian theories, a possible genesis of the conservation movement, have holes in them about as big as the one that sank the *Titanic*. Will the conservation movement meet the fate of that ship?

• • •

George Orwell's *1984* was one of the most influential books of the century. While he said little or nothing about energy conservation, one of the points he makes is applicable to the subject. That point is the rewriting of history. In *1984* and in totalitarian dictatorships like the former Soviet Union, historical figures disappeared and reappeared in books like shadows on a screen. Librarians would have pots of glue perched on their desks, to insert the latest corrections sent from the capital.

What does this have to do with energy conservation? One year we are told one thing to do, and the next year we are told something else. As Lou McClelland and Rachelle Canter of Boulder, Colorado, pointed out, setting a room temperature of 65°F is now regarded as healthful (and, incidentally, energy conserving), whereas little or no mention was made of this in the past.[5] Whether this temperature is truly healthful has nothing to do with the cost of energy or how much oil is left in the ground for future generations. It either is or it is not. Are there librarians somewhere pasting slips of paper saying that 65°F is a reasonable room temperature into older articles stating that temperatures that low would give you chills?

• • •

The Gulf War of 1990 and 1991 perhaps should not be included in a chapter on history, but Robert L. Bradley, President of the Institute for Energy Research, made a cogent observation on the relationship between patriotism and conservation shortly after the war ended:[6]

Arco [a major oil company] for political reasons decided to freeze prices in response to [President] Bush's request [a call for pricing restraint by the industry]; the policy lasted a week or a little more, and then Arco had to abandon it because every day 160 of its stations were running out of gasoline. Were the consumers who were buying gasoline from Arco at prices as much as 13 cents below the market conserving gas? Did they eliminate their Sunday drives, as the government would [have] like[d] them to do? Probably not. Such are the contradictions of government energy policy.

Drawing lessons from the past is one of the most difficult tasks for the human race. We usually fail and pay enormous penalties for our failure. The cry, "We are running out!" has echoed down through the centuries. The echoes sound remarkably like "Wolf!"

NOTES

1. *Encyclopaedia Brittanica*, 15th ed., s.v. "Occultism."

2. Analogy from Nathan Rosenberg, "Energy Efficient Technologies: Past and Future Perspectives," paper presented at "How Far Can the World Get on Energy Efficiency Alone?" Conference held at Oak Ridge National Laboratory, Oak Ridge, Tenn., August 1989.

3. Vaclav Smil, *Energy in World History* (Boulder, Colo.: Westview, 1994).

4. Thomas R. Malthus, *An Essay on Population: The Six Editions* (London: Routledge/Thoemmes Press, 1996).

5. Lou McClelland and Rachelle J. Canter, "Psychological Research on Conservation: Context, Approaches, Methods," in *Advances in Environmental Psychology*, vol. 3, *Energy Conservation: Psychological Perspectives*, ed. A. Baum and J. Singer (Hillsdale, N.J.: Lawrence Erlbaum Associates, 1981), 1–25.

6. Robert L. Bradley, Jr., "Oil, War and the Persian Gulf," *Cato Policy Report* 13, no. 1 (Jan./Feb. 1991): 6–8.

11

How Effective
Is the Government?

In principle, private individuals and the market conserve, or at least offer the opportunity to conserve, every day. We turn down the thermostat, or a do-it-yourself store offers a special deal on fiberglass insulation.

In practice, things are different. Rather than rely on the natural inclination of people to save money through saving energy, many conservation advocates want the government to do most of our thinking for us. While governments can perform a useful role in many areas, when it comes to energy conservation their mountainous efforts usually produce a mouse. This is probably in the nature of conservation itself. It is all too easy for a bureaucrat to sit in a state or national capital, manipulating energy models and proposing energy policies that do not make sense to the public.

• • •

When we talk about government, we usually think first of its spending patterns. Perhaps if we spent enough to encourage conservation, it would actually occur. We can consider conservation spending in two ways. The first is private money allocated to save energy. A homeowner decides to heed the advice of the Pink Panther on television, and buys some insulation for the attic. A businessperson does some calculations and plans a new factory with novel energy-saving facilities.

The second is how much governments spend on conservation. Most expenditures of this type flow from Washington, through the Department of Energy. Smaller amounts are spent by state governments.

Government expenditures on conservation can be divided into two parts: research and development (R&D) and direct spending. For example, the government might ask some of its researchers to develop a better or cheaper type of insulation, or ways to entice commuters from cars into buses or subways.

This is typical R&D in the conservation area. Direct expenditure would be government subsidies of insulation in slum areas.

Both of these types of government spending suffer from weak justification. If it is worthwhile to develop new and better insulation, why does Johns-Manville or another large company in the field not perform the job? Many of them, at least the larger ones, have their own research departments organized for precisely this task. It is true that the Pink Panther does not look like much of a scientist, but he may have friends who are.

As for helping poor people, who could be against that? But buying insulation for the poor may not be what they want. If poor people are starving, they want food, not a government check that can be spent only on inedible pink insulation. A case could be made for sending them a general-purpose check, some of which might be spent on insulation. Then the poor themselves, not a Washington bureaucrat, would be deciding the amount.

Just how much has the Federal government spent on conservation? From its modest beginning in 1974 as part of the Research Applied to National Needs program of the National Science Foundation, to the projected year 2000, total spending will have been over $12 billion, hardly an inconsequential amount (see Table 11.1). If we translate this to constant 1982–1984 dollars, the amount is about $10 billion. Conservation advocates often complain that the Federal government spends little or nothing on their favorite activity, but the total has been enormous.

One curiosity of the data is that spending on conservation under Presidents Reagan and Bush was much higher than common mythology suggests. According to folklore, conservation was going swimmingly under Jimmy Carter. Ronald Reagan stormed into office and cut spending on it to the bone. The data shown in Figure 11.1 do not bear that out. Spending on conservation was greater than the Carter levels (ending in 1981) during much of Reagan's first term and declined only in his second term. Carter's average from 1977 to 1980 was $296 million annually. (There are some overlaps in fiscal years here.) The average for Reagan's first term, 1981 to 1984, was $563 million. Even under Bush, from 1989 to 1992, expenditures were not too far from the half-billion level.

As a proportion of total energy outlays, conservation was higher under most Reagan years than those of Carter. In 1980, Carter's last full fiscal year, the proportion was about 6 percent. That was exceeded under much of Reagan's administration, reaching as high as 15 percent in 1988. Under Clinton, conservation spending again rose substantially, reaching a projected peak in 1997. Note that in Table 11.1, the years from 1995 to 2000 are estimates. The 1997 value of $808 million is the largest in history, exceeding the previous maximum of $730 million in 1981.

What has the Federal government gotten for its $12 billion? There is very little evidence that much has occurred, other than government checks being written. Some discoveries were made and some patents filed. In terms of real progress, however, evidence appears scant.

Table 11.1
Federal Outlays for Conservation and Energy, 1974–2000* (In Millions of Dollars)

Fiscal Year	Conservation outlays (in current dollars)	Conservation outlays (in 1982–1984 dollars)	Total civilian energy outlays	Conservation as a percentage of total energy outlays
1974	3	6	1,300	0.2
1975	48	89	2,900	1.7
1976	51	90	4,200	1.2
1977	143	236	5,780	2.5
1978	221	339	7,990	2.8
1979	252	348	9,180	2.7
1980	569	691	10,200	5.6
1981	730	802	15,200	4.8
1982	516	534	13,500	3.8
1983	477	478	9,400	5.1
1984	527	506	7,100	7.4
1985	491	456	5,700	8.6
1986	515	470	4,700	11.0
1987	281	247	4,100	6.9
1988	342	289	2,300	14.9
1989	333	269	2,700	12.3
1990	360	276	3,300	12.0
1991	386	283	2,400	16.1
1992	468	334	4,500	10.4
1993	521	361	4,300	12.1
1994	582	391**	5,200	11.2
1995*	681	444**	4,600	14.8
1996*	800	507**	4,400	18.2
1997*	808	497**	4,000	20.2
1998*	677	404**	3,500	19.3
1999*	629	365**	3,500	18.0
2000*	625	352**	3,100	20.2
Total, 1974–2000	12,036	10,064		

Sources: The Budget of the United States Government, Fiscal Year 1996 (Washington, D.C.: U.S. Government Printing Office, 1995), Table 3.2—Outlays by Function and Subfunction, 1962–2000, under categories 270 (energy) and 272 (energy conservation); column 2, U.S. Bureau of the Census, *Statistical Abstract of the United States, 1994* (Washington, D.C.: The Bureau, 1995), Table 746—Purchasing Power of the Dollar.
*Estimate.
**Assuming 3 percent annual inflation.

The claim is otherwise. In describing the fiscal year 1996 budget, it is stated that

In total, the Department [of Energy]'s energy efficiency programs are projected to save homeowners $17 billion and businesses $12.5 billion per year by the year 2005,

Figure 11.1
Federal Government Outlays on Conservation and Energy, 1974–2000

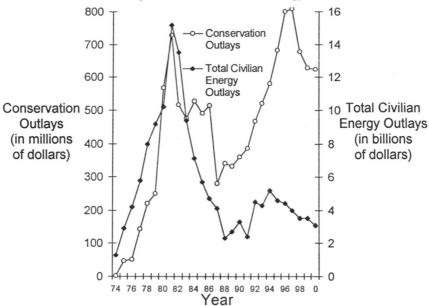

Civilian outlays for energy peaked by the late Carter and early Reagan years, and then went into a decline. They rose somewhat in the Clinton administration. Conservation outlays also went on a roller coaster, peaking around the same time as total energy spending. However, by the mid-1990s, they had reached an all-time high.

and to create almost 125,000 jobs. Energy efficiency programs for industry are projected to save U.S. firms $5.8 billion annually by the year 2000 and create 57,000 jobs. Our transportation technologies are projected to reduce oil imports by 2.3 million barrels a day by the year 2000, creating a trade deficit reduction of $47 million [it should read billion] per year.[1]

However, no specific examples or calculations are shown to back up these claims, even in an enormous document with scores of references, tables, and charts. As well, since the first date given in the quotation is about ten years after the document was written, it is fair to assume that most of its readers will have long forgotten the claims when the year 2005 dawns.

Even if new discoveries did reduce some energy use, the total effect on energy consumption will be small or zero. For example, suppose some government scientists, using some of that $12 billion, devised a cheaper or better type of insulation, one that succeeded in the marketplace.

People need less energy to heat or cool their houses, a desirable state of affairs. Less natural gas, oil, and electricity is used. Then, all other factors being equal, the price of these fuels and services will go down, as demand falls. People will use more of them than they would have at the old, higher price. The total amount of energy used remains about the same, after all that effort. Someone might say, "Alice, look at how cheap this gas grill is. It's been a pain to use those sooty briquettes. Now that our gas bills have gone way down, we can relax a little. Maybe use some of it for this grill. What do you think?"

So the "savings" computed by the analysts in the Department of Energy and the Office of Management and Budget may prove to be combustible, burnt in tens of millions of new backyard gas grills. The miraculous invention paid for it all.

There may be a role for government spending on conservation research, and other forms of conservation spending. To date, there is little proof that much of a substantive nature has been accomplished with the over $12 billion spent by the Federal government alone. Under our present economic system, it is unlikely that government can generate anything of a real and permanent nature in this area. If government produces an invention that truly saves energy, the savings it generates will be dissipated by lower energy prices for the rest of our needs.

• • •

One of the main ways that conservation becomes part of public policy is by means of subsidies to the poor. Their homes are often inadequately insulated, and they cannot afford to buy much energy-saving equipment. So the Federal government and electric utilities have, for years, bought insulation, better doors and windows to keep out the drafts, and other conservation devices for these people.

People on welfare have little ready cash. Why should energy bills eat up a big chunk of it? The way we as a nation go about answering this question reveals our attitudes toward both conservation and the poor. First, society says that it is desirable for the poor to have more money after their energy bills are paid. We do this by means of the aforementioned conservation measures.

In that sense, we are being philanthropic. Now imagine a politician advocating the same result, only in terms of cash. For example, suppose that the government's conservation measures save every recipient family $20 a month on their utility bills. These people undoubtedly save energy and money, but society as a whole does not. The politician goes on to say, "Why bother with all the bureaucracy involved in the insulation program? There are hordes of civil servants filing papers, checking applications, and writing checks. Let's get rid of them all and spend the money saved directly on the poor."

"I've calculated that all this bureaucracy costs $10 a month for each poor or welfare family. Let's take $30—the sum of $20 and $10—and add it directly to the welfare check that each family receives. The families can add the fiberglass to their attics themselves." Imagine the uproar that such a proposal might generate. "What! They'll just waste it on booze and drugs," might be the unspoken thought of many. "Better invest it in fiberglass. They can't spend the money foolishly that way."

On one hand, we want to help the poor by insulating their homes. On the other hand, we do not trust them with a dollar bill in their hand.

Some on welfare need better insulation more than anything else. They may be well fed and reasonably housed, but the utility bills leave them with a hole in their pocket at the end of the month. Others have as their number-one priority more food or clothing. The conservation program does not make a distinction between these various needs. It treats poor people as a homogeneous, faceless mass who are going to get conservation whether they like it or not.

This is not all the fault of government conservation programs, of course. Given a slight twist of events, we might have a federal program to send heavy sweaters to those on welfare, whether they lived in New Hampshire or Florida. The results, as far as those on welfare were concerned, would be about the same. Some, after shivering through frosty winters, would be overjoyed at the federal shipments containing woolly bundles. Others, sweltering in southern heat, would be mystified by the warm garments. Almost all would wish that their welfare checks were a little bigger.

• • •

Most people believe that if we spend enough money on researching any problem, we will find the solution. Does this apply to conservation?

Energy research can be divided into two parts: that performed and paid for by private industry, and that subsidized by the government. As noted, conservation research in the private sector is going on all the time. When gasoline was comparatively expensive compared to average incomes (from the beginning of the auto era to the 1950s), companies worked continuously to squeeze extra miles out of every gallon. Just go to a library and read the old *National Geographic* and *Life* magazines to see the claims for better gas mileage for the Rambler and other compact vehicles. (The builders of the Rambler devised the word "compact" to avoid the sure death of "small.") Those claims could not have been proved without at least some research.

In the same way, natural gas associated with oil fields was often flared off; that is, burnt with no benefit except lighting the night sky. Considerable research and development had to go into building pipelines to transport this gas to markets, or to ship it over the ocean in a liquefied form.

This research was performed by private companies for only one reason— they thought they could make money from it. Some did, and others failed.

Government-sponsored conservation research is another matter. The main argument for government research of any type is that governments can take long-range views that few if any companies can. For example, at the end of World War II scientists knew that they had a potentially valuable source of energy in the atom, but no company was big and rich enough to do the needed research to develop nuclear energy. Only the government could, and it did.

Is conservation of such a nature that it needs the long-term approach that only the government can provide? In most cases, no. If a car company wants to build a more fuel-efficient engine, it has the money and experience to do so. If a new type of house insulation has to be developed, Owens Corning or its foreign competitors have the resources to do it.

Very few, if any, conservation projects are of a decades-long nature. Most are short term. If there are viable conservation products lurking out there, private capital can develop almost all of them. Then the market can decide if it wants them.

The hidden assumption behind the advocacy of unlimited dollars for conservation research, whether government or private, is that with just a few more Ph.D.s, every problem worth solving can be solved. In some cases, that is true. The new products flooding the market every day, from computers to bio-engineered medicines, are testimony to the power of research. However, there are other problems that have remained unsolved, in spite of tremendous amounts of research dollars being thrown at them. Consider two examples, one related to conservation and the other not.

First, some advocates of electric cars have said their use would conserve energy, although that is still debatable. In any case, the reason we do not see them on the street is the cost and relatively short life of the batteries needed to power them. The familiar lead-acid battery was invented by a Frenchman around 1880. Although many new types of batteries have been researched and put on the market in the century since, the lead-acid battery is still the cheapest per unit of energy stored. We have more efficient batteries, such as nickel-cadmium and mercury varieties, but none cheaper. This has been in spite of millions, if not billions, of dollars being spent on research to find a lower-cost substitute. This does not mean that the research money was wasted. Rather, in this instance merely doing the research does not guarantee the results.

The other example, admittedly a slight diversion from conservation, is nuclear waste. Billions of dollars of research money have been spent on this problem in the last few decades, yet we still do not have places to put nuclear waste. The scientists say that the technical problems have been conquered, and they probably have. However, from the public's viewpoint there is no site that government officials can point to and say, "This is where the waste has gone."

Because research can solve many scientific problems, we unconsciously believe that it can solve all problems. It cannot. The same maxim applies to conservation. Perhaps one of the biggest flops in conservation research came about with the "super-insulated" houses built in the 1970s and 1980s. These houses had enormous amounts of insulation, triple-pane windows like those used in Siberia, and all types of other energy-saving devices. They had been carefully researched to produce the maximum amount of energy savings possible.

The super-insulated houses worked. The amount of energy used was tiny compared to that needed in the average house. Unfortunately, their cost was much higher than that of ordinary houses. Occupants also complained about the tremendous moisture condensation on windows and the stuffy smell of the air. Because close to no heat and air was exiting the house, people had the feeling they were living in a closet.

Research is clearly a part of conservation. Yet we should not imagine that if we pile up enough money at the doors of scientists, all our conservation and energy problems will soon be over.

• • •

In February 1991, when the Bush administration National Energy Strategy was unveiled, the Federal government made some reasonable observations on conservation.[2] The exact wording of the title deserves some notice. During the Reagan administration, considerable effort was devoted to keeping the word *plan* out of anything the government suggested about energy. The words *proposal, program,* and others were considered, until some unknown bureaucrat picked *strategy.* This was believed to be much less redolent of government dictates. By then, Reagan had been succeeded by George Bush. Such are the ways of government.

Regardless of the exact title, the document made some sense. The concentration was on energy production, not conservation. According to one news report, "Some conservation measures were considered, then deleted, including standards and tests for lighting, a government fund that federal agencies could tap for energy conservation, and tax benefits for production of renewable energy sources such as wind and solar energy."

All these aborted proposals sound reasonable on their face, but they were bound to fail. Most of them had been tried in the 1970s, with a conspicuous lack of success. If they had been promising, they would have been picked up by the private sector when they scented profits. There was no scent, and no pick-up.

The administration's emphasis on energy production bothered some environmentalists. Daniel Becker, on behalf of the Sierra Club, said that the policy "is to put a gas guzzler and a nuclear power plant in every garage." Hyperbole aside, the administration clearly realized that the failed conservation policies of the past flopped not because of maladministration, but because they were unworkable. Some governments do learn lessons, albeit painfully.

• • •

One of the ways that many governments promote conservation is by subsidies, either direct or indirect. But William Baumol, former head of the American Economics Association, has said these subsidies are more than just a waste of money.[3] As noted previously, in his opinion, subsidized energy is wasted energy.

In addition, as Wetzler writes,

To the extent that subsidizing energy conservation by energy-intensive industries lowers the price of products produced by these industries, the energy saving impact of the subsidy will be diluted and the subsidies could act perversely to increase energy consumption. Similarly, subsidies for energy-conserving investments by homeowners [such as wood stoves] can backfire by encouraging energy-intensive activities such as turning up thermostats or adding new rooms to the house.[4]

There may be cases where some subsidies are needed. However, the fact that investors will not put their money in certain energy systems shows that these methods of generating or saving energy are inherently money or energy losers.

Consider a few examples taken from energy production, not energy conservation. In the 1930s, hydroelectricity was a proved technology. It was well known that some hydroelectric sites in the Tennessee Valley, the Pacific Northwest, and elsewhere could produce enormous amounts of electricity, if they were developed. There was a political stalemate on these sites between advocates of private power development and public (government-owned) power. Even if the sites had been sold to private utilities, there was doubt that they could be developed in a short time. The Great Depression had cut most construction budgets close to zero.

The sites themselves were on public lands. Private investors wanted to buy the sites and develop them. Yet they could give no guarantee when or even if the dams would ever be built.

The situation was then a worthwhile subsidization scheme. Private investors were willing to go forward, but economic conditions prevented them from developing the resources promptly.

The Federal government, through the Tennessee Valley Authority (TVA) and other agencies, built the hydroelectric dams in the 1930s and early 1940s. Was this a subsidy, wasting energy rather than producing it? It would have been if the money spent on the dams had never been recovered from electricity users, but the dams were tremendous money-makers for the government. The economic judgment made by President Roosevelt at the time was correct. To this day, almost six decades later, hydroelectric power from TVA and other federal installations is still the cheapest way to produce electricity. In this case, then, while the Federal government built the dams, the projects were not subsidies in the ordinary sense.

The solar projects of the 1970s and 1980s were different. The Federal government, which paid out most of the subsidies (some were spent by state governments) never even claimed that it would get back its outlays. The purpose was to develop a new industry and to reduce reliance on fossil fuels. While there was—and still is—considerable public interest in solar technologies, it was not high enough to develop substantial private investment. Once the subsidies were removed with the passage of the Tax Reform Act of 1986, the industry shrank considerably.

The case of nuclear power is between hydroelectric and solar. Until 1954, with the passage of the Atomic Energy Act, private development of this energy form was prohibited. Private contractors operated the energy laboratories in Oak Ridge, Los Alamos, and elsewhere, but until 1954 public policy was to keep the eventual profits of nuclear power in government hands. Government expenditures on nuclear research from 1945 to 1954 were therefore subsidies, but only because private investment was forbidden by law.

After 1954, some subsidies were continued, down to the present day. Arguments range over how large these subsidies are. Many are indirect. One example is the study of the biological effect of radiation. This has little to do with the development of better and cheaper reactors. Much of the cost of developing new reactors, the so-called "inherently safe" ones, has been shouldered by private firms, like ASEA in Sweden and Westinghouse in the United States.

Whatever the true size of these government subsidies to nuclear power, the ratio of these payments to the size of the nuclear industry's revenues has decreased substantially since 1954. That is, the amount of government payouts compared to the billions of dollars of revenues generated by reactors is small.

Originally, most of the revenue of the Nuclear Regulatory Commission (NRC), the watchdog agency over nuclear power, came from the government. It was then a subsidy to the industry. In recent years, almost all of the NRC's funds have come from taxes on the industry. So the subsidy to the industry for its patrolling has dropped close to zero.

When the government spends money to conserve energy that would not be otherwise spent by the marketplace, by Baumol's definition it is wasted. As noted in Table 11.1, the Federal government has spent over $12 billion in recent years in this area.

As well, the government can set conservation regulations that cause people to spend money that they otherwise would not have spent. The government can require higher levels of insulation, smaller cars, and so on. These may all be worthwhile, but only a small number of people would have spent the money without the government requiring it. This is then wasted money and energy, by Baumol's definition.

We are all acquainted with government waste of money—junkets to the Riviera by Congressmen, projects that are never completed, and the like. When the government subsidizes conservation, it is not only wasting money, but the very energy it is trying to save.

• • •

The words *wasted, squandering, spendthrift,* and *needlessly polluting* took up a goodly portion of an article on government spending on conservation in *Science*, the most widely read scientific journal in the world.[5] But nowhere in the article are they defined. *Waste* implies that the government—the culprit identified in this report—has deliberately thrown energy out the window. This may be proved in the report on which the article is based, but the article itself never manages to do so.

The only evidence of these disgraceful practices is illustrated in Figure 11.2, which shows that government spending on energy efficiency improvements declined from 1985 to 1989. This in itself proves nothing about wasting. It merely shows that spending for certain items in the federal budget has dropped. The items comprising the spending numbers were not specified in the article. Let us suppose that they include such items as insulation, research on more efficient furnaces, and the like. Let us suppose further than the numbers depicted are accurate. It is well known to those who plow through government budgets that supposed shifts in spending are often because of accountants moving items from one category to another. The underlying expenditures do not change that much. In that way, a bureaucrat can point to a budget and say,

Figure 11.2
Federal Spending on Energy Efficiency Improvements

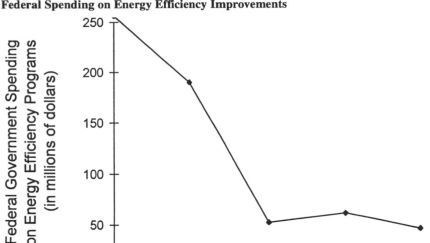

Federal spending on energy efficiency improvements dropped from about a quarter of a billion dollars per year in the mid-1980s to about $45 million per year in the late 1980s. There was a certain logic to this. Since we, as a nation, were continuously improving our energy efficiency ratings, there was less and less reason for the Federal government to subsidize these actions.

"We have eliminated 90 percent of the terrible spending on project X," without noting that most of it appears in another line on a later page.

What then does Figure 11.2 show? Spending on insulation and other items did decrease from 1985 to 1987, from which time they held about constant. But the slide occurred during a large decrease in fossil fuel prices. These fossil fuels supply the heat for most government buildings.

If the price of these fuels rises, then it is reasonable for the government— or anyone else, for that matter—to spend more on greater energy efficiency. Similarly, if the price drops, it is equally reasonable for the government to spend less on this area. The government acted logically, not illogically, in reducing expenditures in this area. No doubt the Alliance to Save Energy, the group that compiled these figures, would like the government to have a continuously rising rate of spending on insulation. But if the government has to act contrary to its best interests in so doing, should taxpayers pay for it?

Another point to consider about the table is the time factor. Suppose you have already installed rolls of pink insulation in your attic, improved the furnace, put in a timed thermostat, and so on. Suppose further you had plotted on a chart all the money you had spent on these devices. You would see large expenditures for the last few years as all these improvements were installed.

Now someone comes along and says, "Why don't you consider changing all the windows in your house to double-hung? It'll cost only a few thousand." You may very well respond, "I've spent all I'm going to for the next few years on saving energy. If I get my hands on some money, it's going toward a trip to Bermuda, not on windows."

If that was your decision, your chart on conservation spending would show zero spending for this year and the next few. This would not mean that you were a waster or spendthrift. It would indicate only that you had reached the point of diminishing returns on energy saving. Is it not possible that the government, in some admittedly haphazard way, had reached the same conclusion?

That is, perhaps most of the insulation, new furnaces, and the like that would make much difference in energy use had already been installed in government buildings by the mid-1980s. Have officials in the Office of Management and Budget, required to oversee programs like this, ever made a specific calculation of this type? If they had, they might have reached the same conclusions of the homeowner who turns down a chance to change all his fairly energy-efficient windows to even more efficient ones. Enough is enough.

• • •

One of the suggestions of the Alliance to Save Energy mentioned in the article does make some sense—allowing federal facilities to retain two-thirds of any energy cost savings they implement. Business retains any financial savings from energy efficiency spending. Conversely, if they guess wrong, they suffer a financial penalty. Heads roll. If they spend beyond the point of diminishing returns, the extra expenditures come out of their profits. There are companies, swept along on a wave of energy efficiency enthusiasm, that have spent thousands to save a few dollars. Whether they come out ahead or behind, the money involved is real. It either adds to their profits or decreases them.

That is not true for government. If a manager saves energy by a simple action like caulking windows, he or she gets little beyond a certificate at the end of the year. On the other side of the scales, if a manager of a government building thinks that workers should have more fresh air in summer and raises the windows with the air conditioner on, he or she will not get much of a penalty. There will just be a request for the agency to allot more money for cooling next year.

So allowing an agency to collect some of its savings seems reasonable, on the face of it. The problem lies in the implementation of such a worthy goal. Specifically, who is going to pay for the improvements that will yield these savings?

Suppose we implemented the Alliance to Save Energy proposal, and Agency X wants to take advantage of it. Consider two simple examples dealing with energy use in buildings. (Of course, the government uses energy in many other ways, such as in vehicles.)

In the first case, Agency X has a new building. To determine how much energy it will save and thus how much money it will receive at the end of the year from the treasury, it needs to know its baseline energy use. The higher the baseline, the greater the potential for improvements in coming years. Thus, the agency will not be much concerned about saving energy in the first few years, all other factors remaining the same. This will demonstrate in later years that it is "saving" energy. For example, it might keep the windows open, summer and winter, in the first few years as the baseline is established. Then, in later years, it shuts the windows and adds a bit of insulation. Lo and behold, energy and financial savings abound. Send two-thirds to Agency X, please.

But who should pay for the insulation? This is the second of the two problems. The agency submits a bill for the insulation in its annual budget, and the treasury approves. Should the agency get most of the savings it accrues as a result of this insulation as a bonus in next year's budget? To be fair, they should get the money only if the cost of the insulation or other energy-saving systems it had installed came out of this year's budget. Just as in private industry, those who want to reap the benefits of the savings should have to pay for the capital equipment to produce them. If that were true, each agency would have to decide just how much energy-saving equipment was cost effective for its buildings and vehicles.

If someone could get a car for free, exactly the same as the one they now own but using only half the gasoline per mile, they would jump at the chance. If you and other taxpayers had to pay for it, you might not be quite as enthusiastic as the recipient.

The agencies that would get most of their energy savings back as a bonus might be eager for the plan that the Alliance to Save Energy advocates. All taxpayers would have to foot the bill for the insulation, smaller cars, and so on that these agencies would buy to produce all these wonderful savings. The taxpayers would not be quite as joyful as the agencies.

To summarize, it can be logical for the government to spend less on energy-saving equipment as more and more is installed. The nature of government spending precludes most agencies from making a serious effort at conservation.

• • •

Governments work in more ways than collecting and spending tax dollars. What else they can do was brought home painfully to Ronna Brooks, an environment teacher in suburban Buffalo, New York.[6] Ms. Brooks was taking her glass, tin, plastic, and newspapers to a recycling center. Along the way she came across a truck from the city dog patrol. Most people would not have paid much attention, but Ms. Brooks did. The truck's engine was running while the driver talked to an employee of the highway department.

Conservation advocates sometimes tend to be judgmental in their attitudes toward the rest of us dissipators. Ms. Brooks walked over to the offending driver and told him that the energy she saved by recycling was being wasted through his truck idling. She asked him to turn his truck off. His reply was recorded as "We all got to die sometime."

Ms. Brooks was not satisfied with this rebuff. She went over to the highway department truck and asked the driver why *his* truck was idling. The response she got was no more polite: "Lady, what is your problem? My feet are cold and I am running the heater." (Remember, this is Buffalo.)

At first glance, these two uncivil civil servants appear to be the epitome of waste. They idle their engines, using gasoline paid for by taxpayers, neither with much of an excuse.

Look a little closer. Let us suppose that, as a result of her run in, Ms. Brooks was appointed head of the Energy Police, devoted to rooting out waste everywhere and anywhere. Her letter to the *Buffalo News*, describing her experience, makes it seem that she might be interested. Then she would have the right to pull the keys from the ignitions of idling cars. She would be in a strong moral position with taxpayer-funded vehicles, since we all hate government waste.

But what about the tired businesswoman out for a leisurely drive in the country after an exhausting week at work? What about the teenage boys cruising past McDonald's and Arby's, hoping to pick up nubile young girls? What about all the other activities involving cars that could be called waste in one form or another? Would the zealous Ms. Brooks race after them (wasting energy in the process), give them a tongue-lashing, and switch off the engine?

Even if the Energy Police were set up with the earnest Ms. Brooks at its head, they could accomplish little. They might be able to crack down on government employees who waste energy, but the energy that Ms. Brooks and her cohorts would "save" would simply provide more gasoline for the rest of us to use, either wisely or unwisely. The Energy Police would undoubtedly file reports on all the energy they had saved, but they would plow the sea in terms of conservation.

• • •

James Wetzler made some cogent observations on why well-meaning government conservation measures usually flop.[7] They deserve to be quoted here. The first deals with the problem that conservation in one area frees up energy to be used in another. He evaluated a proposal that public transportation facilities should be exempted, wholly or partially, from federal or state taxes on gasoline and petroleum products. This, in the view of its advocates, would encourage more public transportation and thus reduce total energy use. Wetzler notes the following:

Exempting buses [from the federal gasoline tax] encourages conservation to the extent that it shifts people from autos to buses with lower fuel use per passenger-mile; however, it also discourages conservation to the extent that it provides an incentive to buy less fuel-efficient buses and encourages trips by lightly traveled buses whose fuel use per passenger-mile is high. Which of these two effects predominates is unclear as a theoretical matter. This sort of indeterminacy arises again and again in evaluation of energy-related tax incentives.[8] (p. 146)

Wetzler goes on to discuss a familiar proposal for government, the "gas guzzler" tax. This has been proposed on cars that get less than so many miles per gallon, with the goal of either getting them off the road or encouraging their manufacturers to improve their gas mileage. The Federal government has enacted such a law, but on the basis of the cost of the car, not its mileage. Wetzler says,

It is impossible to prove *a priori* that a larger [gas guzzler] tax would significantly reduce fuel consumption. Such a tax would give consumers who plan to buy a car an incentive to buy a more fuel-efficient model, but other consumers who respond perversely to a higher tax, either by keeping the old gas guzzlers on the road for a longer period of time [than they would have otherwise] or by buying a less fuel-efficient pickup truck [since trucks with gross vehicle weight of 6,000 pounds or more are exempt].

The number of cars that would be affected by such a tax would be, almost by definition, small. If the cut-off were 20 mpg, for example, many cars and light trucks would be affected. Millions of consumers would rise up in wrath. Thus, while punishing gas guzzlers sounds stirring issuing from the mouth of a politician, it would achieve close to nothing. In any case, those wealthy enough to afford one of these gas guzzlers would think nothing of paying the tax.

In summary, while governments can solve, or at least alleviate, certain social problems, their records on the conservation front are dismal. This is not because of the incompetence of the bureaucrats who have administered the many programs. Rather, the nature of energy use suggests that even if a program were successful in reducing energy requirements in one sector, that very success would increase energy use in another.

NOTES

1. *The Budget of the United States Government, Fiscal Year 1996* (Washington, D.C.: U.S. Government Printing Office, 1995), 440.

2. *National Energy Strategy: Powerful Ideas for America* (Washington, D.C.: U.S. Government Printing Office, 1991/1992).

3. William J. Baumol and Sue Anne Batey Blackman, "Unprofitable Energy Is Squandered Energy," *Challenge* 23 (July/Aug. 1980): 28.

4. James W. Wetzler, "Taxation of Energy Producers and Consumers," in *Free Market Energy: The Way to Benefit Consumers*, ed. S. Fred Singer, (New York: Universe Books, 1984), 149.

5. "Uncle Sam, the Energy Spendthrift," *Science* 251 (22 March 1991): 1424.

6. Ronna Brooks, "Idling Trucks Negate the Savings from Recycling," *Buffalo News*, 21 December 1991, C2.

7. Wetzler, "Taxation of Energy," 144–171.

8. Ibid., 146.

12

Crime and Conservation

Conservation, whether it exists or not, has nothing to do with crime. It is perfectly legal everywhere. However, there are aspects of crime prevention that seem to have some relationship to conservation. Here are two examples.

In the 1980s, a wave of auto thefts swept across the United States. Previously, owners who were concerned about the possibility used electronic devices to stop the thieves. These would emit a loud beep or wail if somebody tried to break in.

These devices had a nasty habit of failing. They would give off their yelps when nobody was around or, even worse, when the legitimate owner tried to open the door. As a result, some entrepreneurs saw their chance. They devised a locking device in the form of a bar fastened to the steering wheel. Only the owner had the key. Since there were no electronics to the systems, no embarrassing screeches would be heard when the owner entered the vehicle.

Manufacturers of the devices, sometimes known as "The Club," were confident that it would work. In their ads, they said they would pay an owner's expenses if his or her car were stolen with the device attached. They said, in effect, "Put yourself in the position of a car thief. If he sees our device on your car, chances are he'll go to the next one, where there is no device. Why should he go to the trouble of unfastening our device?"

So far, not a word about conserving energy. But suppose the number of cars stolen each year is a quantity like energy use. Reducing that number is a "good thing," just like using less energy. Who, except the "League of Thieves," could be in favor of auto theft?

So buy a locking device for your steering wheel. You will drastically reduce your chances of coming back to a lonely oil stain in the parking lot instead of your car. The ads are correct in that sense.

They are also right in another way. The thief, unless he has his heart set on your particular model and year, will go on down the row to the next attractive vehicle. The total number of stolen cars will not go down. The only thing that will change is the distribution of pilfered cars.

In the same way, when someone adopts an energy-conserving device, he or she usually does reduce energy use. But overall energy use changes little, if at all. The distribution of energy use is changed. That is all that happens.

• • •

Let us take this analogy one step further. You do not really need to buy the Club to keep your car out of the clutches of crooks. You can absolutely prevent theft by simply hauling your engine out of its compartment and hanging it from a tree. It is not completely out of the question. Shade-tree mechanics do this all the time. When they do, nobody steals the cars they are working on.

Completely and utterly ridiculous, you say. You do not want your car stolen, but taking out your engine every time you park it is unreasonable. This is using a piledriver to crack a peanut shell. But suppose that the government mandated taking out the engine. If it ever did—for the commendable goal of reducing car thefts—it would not stay in office for more than a few seconds.

This is what is happening in the conservation field. Governments, to "save" energy, impose outlandish and impractical goals. Saving energy, just like reducing car thefts, is probably a reasonable goal of society, although many others, such as reducing poverty, are much more important. If extreme measures, like stringing up car engines, are used to pursue reasonable goals, then those objectives will lose all meaning.

13

Public Utilities

For many of us, our main dealing with energy, other than the gas station, is the utility bill we receive each month. It comes from a mysterious corporation, whose workings are cloaked in darkness. What they do—or do not do—about energy sources and saving of energy has profound implications. Conservationists have focused much of their energy on public utilities, hoping to get them to adopt rules mandating energy saving.

Since some points covered here deal with demand-side management (DSM), a few words about it are in order. Briefly, its purpose is to reduce the total amount of energy used by utility customers and to transfer it to those times of the day when there is less use. If consumer electricity demand never rises, the utility will not have to build new plants to meet increased demand. All they will have to do is replace worn-out old power plants. Electricity demand is much less during the night compared to the day. If some electrical or gas tasks, such as heating hot water, could be transferred to the night, fewer new plants would be needed.

Related to DSM is the idea of the energy audit, similar to a financial one. Its purpose is to determine where a homeowner might be wasting energy, and point out what steps could stop the problem. The ultimate purpose of all this conservation activity is to lower utility rates and bills to the consumer. Whether it does so is the subject of this chapter.

• • •

Under force of federal and state laws, many utilities have tried to set up conservation programs for their customers. With few exceptions, they have been micro-successes and macro-failures. The utilities can point to many water heater blankets sold or given away and many brochures sent to their customers. In some cases, the ratepayers even read the brochures.

But the graph of electricity use keeps rising. This is in spite of these successes, trumpeted to the rooftops and the state public utility commissions. Why is this so? Larry Condelli and his colleagues, from the University of California at Santa Cruz, have explained.[1] Condelli's words deserve to be reprinted in full:

Suppose people were shown an advertisement for Crest toothpaste in which clear data are presented that it produces fewer cavities than other toothpastes. Suppose these viewers were then interviewed and asked how they feel about Crest's effectiveness. Social psychological research suggests that most of the viewers would have increased their respect for Crest. Probably a substantial (but somewhat smaller) number would also claim to use Crest. Only a small percentage of those who intend to use Crest, however, would subsequently buy it. Nonetheless, an ad campaign for Crest might be cost effective since the barriers to switching to Crest, habit and loyalty, are minor. Toothpaste is something a person buys often and the prices are comparable among various name brands. So, while in the supermarket, the consumer might just as easily reach for Crest as for Pepsodent.

Energy conservation behaviors are different. It is much easier to try a new brand of toothpaste than it is to curtail a sharply pleasurable activity (such as keeping one's home comfortably warm in the winter). Considerably more expense is required to retrofit one's home or install solar water heating. Such behaviors require changes in lifestyle and behavior patterns, changes made with far greater difficulty.

Since the electric utilities apparently thought they were selling just a slightly different version of Crest, the results of their vast conservation campaigns— Condelli and his colleagues note that $200 million was spent in California in 1983 alone—were inevitable. According to one article in the *San Jose (Cal.) Mercury*, promotional and advertising costs to install energy-saving measures in low-income housing were greater than it would have cost simply to install the insulation in the targeted housing. To draw a toothpaste analogy, if it cost more to advertise Crest than to give it away, the advertising agency would be fired.

• • •

In recent years, ads on the radio for energy conservation, sponsored by utilities, have proliferated. Some of them were by Niagara Mohawk, which served the area in Buffalo where I once lived. The booklets they kindly supplied to every ratepayer had more of the same: Put in more insulation, turn back the thermostat, wear sweaters in the winter, and so on. Who could be against that?

The problem comes when we try to base public policy on these suggestions. Consider the viewpoint of the state public utility commission (PUC), which regulates and thus sets policy for electric utilities. The PUC members have read stories saying that conservation is the answer to most or even all of the nation's energy problems. The state legislature may even have passed laws telling the PUC to require conservation measures from the utilities they regulate. These laws tend to be vague, leaving the precise conservation steps to the PUC.

   The formlessness of the state laws on conservation foreshadow what is to come. State lawmakers can write precise laws if they want to—the exact sentences lawbreakers are to serve in prison, the tax rates down to the nearest penny. Yet in a matter that almost everyone claims is vital, the legislators could not define conservation or exactly what steps they should take to bring it about.

   Let us get back to the PUC. A talk between them and a fictional electric utility they regulate, Enormous Electric Power (EEP), might go as follows:

   "Ladies and gentlemen of EEP, we at the PUC have this mandate from the state legislature to enforce conservation, expressed in law 97–110. As you know, they've thrown the ball in your laps. Precisely what steps do you propose to take?"

   "Well, we can have energy audits, advertise appliances that use less energy than others on the market, sell insulation at half price, and so on. All these steps were proposed in the 1960s and 1970s, so there's nothing new here. Many other utilities around the country have taken one or more of these steps. We'll follow in their path."

   "This sounds fine. Go to it. All we need from EEP is an annual statement saying how many homes you have audited, how much insulation you have installed, and a listing of all the other measures you have taken. Finally, tell us how much you have spent on the entire program."

   "This talk of money raises a key point. Are we going to be able to include these expenditures on the rates we charge our customers, or will they have to come out of the pockets of our shareholders?"

   "Not to worry. The legislature has said that the money any utility in this state spends on conservation is 'reasonable and proper,' to use the legal phrase. Whatever you spend is an allowable expense, according to the law. So you can charge your customers whatever you allocate to conservation."

   While the participants talked about conservation, there was no mention in this fictional example of how the PUC or the utility would measure progress. To use economics terms, the PUC and the utility would know the input of the conservation measures—the number of energy audits, the quantity distributed of thermostats with timers to turn them on and off, and the total cost of the program—but what is the output, the actual and verifiable amount of energy or electricity saved? That remains a mystery. It is much easier for the PUC to go back to the state legislature and say, "We are following your law to the letter. We've gotten the electric utilities to spend $100 million annually on conservation. Here's the report certifying all this. Conservation is a done deal in this state."

   Or is it? Consider what might happen if an electric utility went before the PUC with a proposal to build a coal-fired or nuclear power plant:

   "Here are the drawings, ladies and gentlemen of the PUC. They sure look beautiful, don't they?"

   The PUC is naturally more practical minded:

"We've sat through three hours of this presentation. In all this time, you haven't told us just how much electricity this plant will produce. Are you ever going to supply us with the numbers?"

"Well, we admit we're not too sure about this right now. Don't worry, all will be revealed in due course. In the meantime, what do you think about Chinese red for the front door?"

Any utility executive who went before the PUC not knowing how much electricity his proposed new plant would produce would be regarded as only slightly better than an idiot by the regulators. Five minutes after he left their offices, the PUC would be discussing legal action against his company. Similarly, any PUC that did not ask the utility proposing a new plant just how much energy would flow down its cables would be equally incompetent. It might take a little longer for the truth to come out, but eventually the public would know that the agency designed to guard their interests was staffed by bunglers. Contrast this with the chat about conservation. Chances are that the subject of results or outputs did not even arise.

Does this mean that PUCs and electric utilities are bunglers when it comes to conservation and wise when the subject is electricity production? The answer depends on whether we can really measure conservation. If it does not really exist, then of course there is no way of putting its results down on paper. If it does exist, then state legislatures, PUCs, and electric utilities are sorely negligent in fumbling such an important matter.

Consider the PUC's viewpoint. Suppose that electricity production by EEP went up 3 percent last year. Suppose further that the utility never had a conservation program until that point. Of course, its customers had always conserved over the years in ways that seemed appropriate to them. Some had installed fiberglass in their attic to save energy. Others had not bothered, because it was too expensive or too much trouble. Now EEP goes before the PUC with its conservation program, and puts it into effect. The next year, the utility records a 2 percent increase in electricity use.

Is the 1 percent drop (in the increase, not in the total amount used) because of the conservation program, or have other factors intervened? The utility wants to be able to charge its conservation expenses to its customers, so it will crow that the 1 percent decrease was because of its noble efforts. The PUC, which does not want to be accused by the state legislature of promoting a botched program in an area of much public concern, will just as naturally go along with the utility's claim. And state legislators, who want to tell their constituents that one of their laws is working, will also point with pride to their handiwork.

Is it the truth? There might have been a recession in the second year. Drops in economic activity usually accompany decreases in energy use.

Another explanation of the drop is a continuation of the national trend toward greater energy efficiency. This greater efficiency can be defined as a decrease in the ratio of energy used to produce the national total of goods and services, divided by the economic value of those goods and services, known as the gross domestic product. As the nation moves from steel mills to computerized offices, we need less energy to produce a dollar's worth of output, regardless of any conservation programs by utilities or others. By this definition, energy efficiency has been increasing for decades, with a few aberrations here and there. This alone could account for the observed decrease.

If you asked EEP flatly, "Can you prove just how much energy you saved by your conservation program?" you would get squirming, not defensible answers. At best, you would be told, "Well, we conducted 5,000 energy audits, and installed 30,000 shower head flow reducers." That again would be the input to the program, not the output.

It is tempting for the utility to take credit for the 3 percent to 2 percent drop in the annual increase. Recall that this is a decrease in the increase, not an absolute decrease in electricity use. Partisans of conservation would like to see an absolute decrease, not a decrease in the increase. "It is all due to our diligence and energy audits," the utility might say. "You can pin that gold medal right here."

What happens if a big new industry, one that uses loads of electricity, moves into the area served by EEP? In this scenario, electricity generated goes up by 4 percent over last year, compared to the 3 percent expected from past changes. This is a result devoutly wished by the utility, at the same time that the conservation program is going full blast. Most of us have read ads by utilities in national magazines, suggesting that industries build new plants in their area. The utility might say, "Look, our conservation program really works, in spite of the increase in electricity use. Without it, the increase might have been 5 percent, not 4 percent. Okay, we may not deserve a gold medal. But at least don't criticize our conservation plan."

Now we are beginning to enter the realm of metaphysics and conjecture, a dangerous domain. If energy use decreases, it is because of the conservation program. If it increases, it would have risen even faster if it were not for the program. Framed this way, any conservation program is, by definition, an unalloyed good. No matter what happens—a slump in the economy, the opening of big new energy-guzzling industries—there can be only one interpretation: The conservation program is effective.

A radiology professor named Ernest Sternglass made some startling claims about the effect of radiation in the 1960s and 1970s. He had noticed that infant mortality rates had decreased nationally for many years, because of better public health, improved nutrition, and other factors. Sternglass also noticed that, after this long decrease, infant mortality rates had leveled off in certain areas. That is, the expected decrease, year by year, had vanished in some counties.

A few of these counties contained nuclear reactors. The professor said that the radiation emitted from these plants was the cause of the leveling of infant mortality. In effect, the reactors were causing baby deaths.

This surprising assertion might have been accepted by the scientific community if infant mortality had flattened out only in the places with nuclear reactors and had continued its downward trend in nuclear-free towns and counties. Alas for Sternglass, things were not quite that simple. The numbers were a jumbled mixture. Some towns with nuclear reactors did indeed have a constant infant mortality in recent years, as he claimed. Others with nearby nuclear plants showed a continuing downward plunge. Some towns that had never had an atom split inside the city limits also had a leveling off in infant mortality. Yet other communities devoid of uranium continued to be part of the downward national trend. In short, the data on infant mortality were so mixed up that their relation to radiation and nuclear reactors, if any, was almost completely obscure.

What does all this have to do with conservation? Some utilities with conservation programs will be able to point with pride at the decrease in the increase. Some may even have an absolute decrease in electricity generated. They will inevitably say that these programs were the cause.

In other parts of the country, utilities may not have a conservation program in place. Yet precisely the same decrease in the increase, or an absolute drop in electricity consumption, has taken place. Assuming we really want to know if conservation programs work, a logical question poses itself. Have these efforts really accomplished anything, if we can achieve about the same results without them?

Some readers might say, "Don't be silly. The extra insulation, the turning down of thermostats, and all the other conservation steps must have accomplished something. Insulation works regardless of our feelings about it. Lowering the thermostat saves energy whether we think that conservation programs are the greatest thing since buttered toast or a complete boondoggle." Of course insulation works. That does not mean that overall conservation takes place after the pink stuff is installed in the attic.

Consider an example. After the insulation is stuffed between the rafters, suppose that the homeowner expects an average saving of $20 per month from this action. Possibly the homeowner is going to think subconsciously, "My energy bill will be going down, at long last. So if I turn up the hot water temperature to make the dishes come out of the dishwasher a lot cleaner, I'm still ahead. And I've been considering installing night lights all around the house for security. With the money I'll save from the insulation, I can do it." The savings from insulation and other conservation measures are real. That does not mean that total electricity (or energy) consumption for a given household will drop. The family may make the mental calculation that since they have saved in one area, they can loosen up or expand their energy consumption in another. After a conservation measure taken in good faith and with the best of intentions, total electricity use may actually rise. This is precisely what many utilities have found.

Now suppose that for a given household, total energy use decreases. That is, if the attic insulation saves them $20 per month, they do not dissipate these savings by increasing their energy use in other areas by more than $20 monthly. Suppose further than there are thousands of families like this, all saving some electricity or energy because of the wonderful programs of the utility. For these families, total energy use has definitely dropped.

There will be thousands of other families who have not participated in the conservation programs. In the Tennessee Valley Authority program discussed later in this chapter, one estimate was that only 6 percent of their residential customers had taken part in even the smallest way, such as by having an energy audit performed.

Even when the audit had taken place, not every family whose home was inspected took an actual conservation measure. Many just read what the auditor had written and threw it in the trash. An auto mechanic can point out problems with a car, but for a variety of reasons the owner may not buy new parts to replace the worn ones.

For almost all utilities, the fraction of families that participate in the conservation programs is small. The fraction that takes concrete steps to reduce energy use is smaller still. What happens to the rest? That will depend, to a large degree, on whether the cost of electricity goes up or down as a result of the conservation program. If it rises, chances are that many of the nonparticipants will conserve in spite of themselves. If it drops, it is highly likely that the nonparticipants will use more electricity than they would have if its price had remained the same.

Consider a simple example. If you found out that the price of your electricity was going to be cut in half tomorrow, would you be tempted to spend just a little longer in the shower? In this hypothetical case, the extra electricity nonparticipants use could well wipe out the savings by those who take part in the conservation program.

Will the overall price of electricity rise or fall as a result of the program? To answer that, we have to know if there will be any overall savings. A case can be made why there might not be any effect at all. In that case, the price per kilowatt hour should remain about the same.

To make matters a little easier on conservation proponents, let us assume that the cost of the program itself is a small proportion of the utility's revenues. So the cost to all consumers, both those who take part and those who avoid the conservation program, will not be large.

As a specific example, suppose that the cost of the conservation program is $10 million, and that the utility's revenues are $1 billion. Suppose further than the program itself does not change the cost of electricity at all. The price of electricity per kilowatt hour under these assumptions will rise by 1 percent, if the utility's cost is passed on in higher electric bills. Most consumers would hardly notice this increase, since their electricity consumption varies by a much higher fraction from month to month.

All this dances around the question: Will the cost per kilowatt hour rise or fall as a result of the conservation program? To that question there is no easy answer. There are at least three possibilities.

There are some factors that suggest a lowering of costs. A utility may be based mostly on fossil fuels, such as coal or gas. About half of all U.S. electricity derives from coal. A true conservation effort will generate a lower requirement for these fuels. The total annual bill to the utility from coal and gas companies will decrease. In principle at least, this could lead to a reduction in cost per kilowatt hour.

On the other side of the ledger, the utility's plants have been (or will be) paid by ratepayers. If some of these plants stand idle because of lack of demand, the bills to pay off the bonds for these plants still come due. Less electricity is being produced because of conservation under our assumptions, but these fixed costs continue. The price per unit of electricity under this scenario would rise, not fall.

The third possibility is that it all could be a wash. The conservation program effects that cause a rise or fall in electricity price would balance each other out, leaving the price about what it was before the program began.

Which will it be? Nobody really knows, although one 1994 study stated that "DSM programs often increase electricity prices slightly."[2] One thing is certain: The utility, when it makes its presentation to the PUC, will claim that the price will fall, not rise.

To understand why, imagine yourself as a utility president sitting in front of the PUC. You could say, "Our economists have determined that this conservation program will be wonderful for those people who take part. Unfortunately, for the 95 percent we estimate will sit it out, their rates will go up."

The response comes back in a flash from the PUC: "Mr. President, this doesn't sound like a very good program for the bulk of your customers. Are you really sure you want to go ahead with it?" The discussion will likely end around there. Now consider the case where the overall result would be about a wash:

"Mr. President, we at the PUC would like to hear about your proposed conservation program."

"It will definitely provide benefits to those who take part. As for the rest, well, they'll come out about the same as at the beginning."

"Mr. President, how much did you say this program will cost your ratepayers?"

"Oh, about $50 million."

"Seems like an awful lot to lay out to get back to the starting point for most people, doesn't it?"

With thoughts about interchanges like this in the back of his mind, the typical utility president might say something like,

"Members of the PUC, we have determined that this conservation program will lower electricity costs for almost everyone in the region we serve. It's a win–win situation for practically all ratepayers."

Given the pressures on a utility president, chances are he will say this, regardless of what his economists calculate.

The conservation program now begins. In terms of price to consumers who stay out of the program, two events can happen. First, the utility president's prediction of lower electricity prices could be proved false. The price remains the same or even rises.

Second, there is a chance he could be correct after all. The price of electricity drops, as he optimistically predicted it would.

Consider what happens next. Electricity bills drop, and the inevitable takes place—electricity use goes up, as people relax whatever informal conservation rules they set for themselves in the past.

While some ratepayers, those who have participated in the conservation program, are saving energy, others, who notice that their electricity bills have gone down, use more. The overall effect may well be an increase in total electricity use by utility customers. After all, there are far more people outside the conservation program than inside. Whether the increase will take place depends on many factors. There is, nonetheless, a clear possibility that a well-meaning conservation program could promote, not decrease, energy waste.

None of the above suggests that utility conservation programs should never go forward. In some cases, they may indeed save electricity and energy. In other instances, they would produce an effect opposite to what the conservationists wanted; that is, an increase in energy use.

Conservation programs would join a long, dreary list of well-intentioned social devices that have produced the wrong result. Welfare programs were originally intended to help the poorest. But now they have inadvertently produced so many problems that even their advocates usually defend only the funding levels, not the programs themselves. Even President Clinton, long a defender of welfare rights, had to accept a sharp reduction in spending and government commitment for this program in 1996, under congressional pressure.

Getting a handle on what conservation programs have achieved is not simple, and often close to impossible. If consumers boost their electricity use by 3 percent and the utility had previously estimated a 4 percent increase, is the conservation program a success? The 3 percent is a real figure, but the 4 percent is predicated on a host of assumptions, some buried in computer software. If next year the increase is 4 percent, is that because of the new factory that opened, or has the conservation program been a failure? Once we get into details like this, we become so entangled in a web of "what ifs" that we can draw almost no real conclusions about the success of utility-sponsored conservation programs.

• • •

We often do not read anything even mildly critical of conservation in the major media. But a Mr. Brown of Georgia ventured where others feared to tread.

The media present various viewpoints on just about any topic, but when it comes to conservation, they are close to united behind one stand: "It is a good thing, and don't you forget it." Thus, it was a surprise when an E. Brown of

Martinez, Georgia, criticized the concept. Georgia Power, the local utility, had persuaded the state public utility commission to allow it to set higher rates in the name of conservation, apparently charging a dollar extra a month for all residential customers.

Mr. Brown was not having any of it. His brief letter follows:

Like most folks who are contending with today's economy, I am desperately trying to survive on what I have in retirement without looking to already over-laden agencies. For example, I conserve electricity by keeping my air conditioner at 80 degrees on summer days and turning it off at night. I wash only two loads of clothes a week and dry them outdoors, weather permitting. I don't use the dishwasher at all, and I retire at 9 p.m. to save on lights.

What good has been accomplished? Georgia Power is going to charge an extra dollar per month!

Of course, I can recover the loss, Georgia Power says, by further cutbacks. Where? I don't know! Why? So it can charge us even more the next time! When? Maybe in the next world![3]

Mr. Brown was evidently hot under the collar, and may well have used asbestos-lined paper to write his missive. But there is truth in what he says. Those who have already taken energy conservation measures got little or no benefit out of the Georgia Power initiative. Those who have dawdled and postponed profited.

It is a little like the legend of the ant and the grasshopper. The ant worked hard, storing food for the winter. He warned the grasshopper that the snows of winter were coming, but to no avail. The grasshopper played his violin and sang all summer. When the weather turned cold, the grasshopper begged the ant for the food he had stored. The larger insect was turned away and died. Righteousness triumphed.

In the fable as rewritten by Georgia Power, the grasshopper would still be as lazy as ever. But when the cold winds came down from the north, he would get a government grant or rebate for what he needed. Where would the money come from? There would only be one source—the hapless ant. It is not clear if Georgia Power really intended to rewrite Aesop's fable, but that is the moral of their proposals.

It is true that a dollar a month, as Mr. Brown describes, is not much of a tax these days. Nonetheless, any tax, if it is put to the wrong purpose, hinders rather than helps economic prosperity. Rewriting the fable of the ant and the grasshopper is worth a lot less than a dollar a month.

• • •

The late Professor Petr Beckman of Czechoslovakia was one of the true gadflies of energy. Moving to Colorado, he became publisher of one of the most provocative newsletters in the field—*Access to Energy*. Thinking the calls for demand-side management by the electric utility was madness, he devised an analogy to demonstrate its foolishness. According to him, the shoe industry would never advocate people resoling their shoes and perhaps even going barefoot when they can make more money by producing new shoes.[4] Yet the equivalent of this is precisely what is advocated by proponents of DSM programs.

If DSM applied to footwear, the shoe companies would stop making as many shoes as demanded and go into the shoe repair business. They would tell their customers, "Look, you don't really need new shoes. The old ones you have aren't really all that bad. If you'll just step this way, you can be taken care of in our shoe repair department. What? Don't have enough money for resoling? Have you considered going barefoot? They say it's really better for the feet."

Until recently, public utilities made all their money from selling energy. They had no other source of income. Now, along comes DSM. Under it, the utilities can earn profits in a new way, in addition to the old method of producing electricity and piping natural gas. They are allowed to make money by selling conservation. The utility is to sell insulation, fluorescent lightbulbs to replace incandescents, and so on.

But conservation products are usually expensive. If market forces were allowed to operate, the utility would incur a loss on each sale it makes. To allow for this, the utility is allowed by the public utility commissions, which regulate them, to levy a special charge on all customers. This charge is added to all bills, whether you buy the special conservation products.

Will the utility make more money from the old style of doing business, selling electricity and natural gas? Or will the new style, selling conservation products and recouping the losses through higher rates, in addition to the old energy products, be more profitable? Beckman says that it is better both for the shoe industry and society at large for them to truly stick to their last and make new shoes. Once they get into the resoling business, they will tend to make less money. He thinks the same thing will happen with public utilities.

Conservationists hold out the carrot of greater profits for utilities under DSM, hoping that this will make the new direction more palatable. Just like an ocean liner may require miles to turn around, it is difficult for any firm to launch into new products, regardless of the merits of the innovations. Conservationists might say to the utilities, "Don't worry. You'll make more money under DSM than you did under the old ways. Your stockholders can sleep soundly at night."

Where does the truth lie? The profits of utilities are regulated. Whether a utility is efficient or not, it will tend to earn about the same percentage on the capital invested in its business. The proportion is usually 12 to 15 percent. For example, if a utility has about $100 million invested in plants, transmission systems, and office buildings, the PUC will let it raise its rates until it earns about $12 to $15 million in profits annually.

Conversely, if a utility comes up with a wonderful invention that allows it to cut its fuel costs by half, it will not be allowed to charge the old rates for electricity and gas. If it did, its profits would soar out of sight. The PUC will demand that it lower its rates until it earns about the same profit per dollar of investment as before its miraculous invention.

All this may sound somewhat unfair. But it is in reaction to the way utilities behaved in the 1920s and earlier, when there was little or no regulation. They could raise their rates overnight, and nobody could stop them. They were a natural monopoly, to use economic jargon. In response to these abuses, PUCs were set up to regulate rates.

In spite of conservationist claims, nobody really knows if utilities will be better off under DSM than before. It will all depend on the rate the PUCs allow, and nobody can predict what that will be. The carrot that the conservationists hold out may turn out to be a stick.

Let us get back to Beckman's analogy of the shoe companies. Right now, shoe manufacturers make shoes, and independent cobblers repair shoes for those who do not want or cannot spend the money for new shoes. The market, without regulation, adjusts the relative prices of new and resoled shoes. Many people, including myself, have their shoes resoled. There is no sense throwing them out if all they need are soles.

Beckman is right. If any company tries to artificially lower demand for its product, it could find itself on the ropes financially. The old saying, "Shoemaker, stick to your last," also applies to utilities.

• • •

Demand-side management is sometimes held up as the panacea for all the electricity ills plaguing society. Companies affected by it do not see it that way. Supposedly, there are no losers. That is, everyone must gain, or at least not lose, from increased energy efficiency. This might be the case in a perfect world. Unfortunately, these goals have to be translated into policy set down by the bureaucrats in public utility commissions. Something tends to be lost in translation.

Some examples were given by John Hughes of the Electricity Consumers Resource Council in Washington, and Barbara Brenner, an attorney in Albany, New York.[5] Their results apply only to New York State, but similar ones could be dredged up from other states where DSM has been instituted.

DSM comes with its own set of surcharges on all, or most, customers. Thus, if a customer pays more in surcharges than he or she gets in rebates, they are a loser by any standard. Camden Wire received only $740 in rebates from 1990 to 1992, yet it estimates it will pay over $150,000 in DSM-related surcharges annually. This company is one that has made great investments in energy conservation in the past. But the rebates apply only to new investments, not old ones.

The Blue Circle Cement Ravenna plant will pay $683,000 in surcharges, but will get only $100,000 in rebates. The Bristol-Myers Squibb plant will pay over $700,000 in surcharges, but will get back only $2,000 in rebates. The list could be extended indefinitely. So the claim that there are no losers clearly is a false one. Many other claims made for DSM are equally false.

Some might say that some of the companies named are large corporations, staffed mainly by fat cats. Who cares if they pay out much more than they take in? They deserve to be punished. If we want to levy high taxes on corporations—or anybody else for that matter—why not just use the tax code? Punishing companies by means of a complex and roundabout method is a peculiarly inefficient way to proceed.

In any case, some of the companies noted are far from large. All companies, large and small, are subject to the DSM surcharges. And if company taxes get too high—regardless of the motive behind those levies—some firms will go out of business. Employees, hardly fat cats, will be thrown out of work. The motives behind the DSM surcharges may be as pure as the driven snow, but their effects can harm innocent bystanders. There are losers, and some of them may already be poor.

● ● ●

In 1986, Ronald Reagan put through some fundamental reforms of the tax code. Among other things, he made it much more difficult to use tax shelters based on accelerated depreciation of real estate and other resources.

In previous decades, helpful legislators had made these provisions ever more generous. A commercial building might last perhaps fifty years in the real world, depending on many factors. But the code might allow it to be written off, for tax purposes, in perhaps fifteen or twenty years. This naturally produced many more investments in these buildings than would have been the case if the true lifetime had been used by the IRS.

The buildings were not torn down after fifteen or twenty years. They kept on producing revenue for decades after they had disappeared in the eyes of the taxman.

Economists were almost unanimous in decrying this practice. They pointed out that investments in other areas of the economy, such as manufacturing, dropped off as more and more money went into building commercial structures.

For years, nobody listened to them. Gradually, Washington realized that it had distorted national priorities. When President Reagan proposed a massive overhaul of the tax structure in the mid-1980s, these tax shelters largely fell by the wayside. Now investment in commercial structures has to compete on a level playing field with other potential investments by companies and individuals.

What does this have to do with conservation? In DSM, one of the goals is to retire so-called energy-inefficient appliances before their time, using tax incentives. For example, a refrigerator built a decade ago might use $100 a year of electricity. Suppose there is another model on the market that would use $80 annually. According to DSM, the old one should be junked and a new one bought, because it is more efficient. Most people would not do that for a long time, because the device is still working, and it would cost hundreds or even a thousand dollars to replace it.

Not to worry, say the demand-siders. We will give you a check for the amount, if you will just replace your old refrigerator with a new one. According to the rules laid down by public utilities in many states, the check would soon be in the mail.

This is just a repeat of the old tax shelters abolished in 1986 under a new name. We retire a useful resource before its time. This makes no economic sense. If a refrigerator's electricity use zoomed upwards, or it was on its last days, most people would replace it without urging from the public utility commission. Since the utility regulated by the PUC has to send a check to do what would be done in the normal course of events, something is fundamentally flawed here.

• • •

God generally does not play a role in discussions about conservation. But in order to solve some of the problems these programs create, we may need Him (or Her).

Larry Ruff, writing in *Electricity Journal*, points out how He can be useful.[6] In utility DSM programs, all sorts of prices are set by these companies. For example, they may offer to give customers a $25 rebate if they replace an old electric heater, $2 on special energy-saving lightbulbs, and so on. But where do these numbers come from? In essence, they are plucked out of the air by the utility. Somebody thinks that a $20 rebate for a hot water heater is too low, and $50 is too high. So they settle on $25.

This way of proceeding is quite a bit different from that of the market. If a manufacturer of hot water heaters sets his price too high, he will sell too few and go out of business. If he sets it too low, he will sell many, but incur a loss on each. He will again face bankruptcy. Only by paying attention to what economists call market signals can the manufacturer stay in business and make a profit.

There are no such signals in DSM. The utility guesses at the rebates that will produce the most amount of conservation, and crosses their fingers. If they are wrong, they do not have to suffer like the star-crossed manufacturer. Their losses come out of the pockets of ratepayers who did not take advantage of the rebates.

This is where God comes in. Only He will have enough knowledge to say the most reduction of energy use in water heating will be achieved if you offer a rebate of $27.83 on water heaters.

Unfortunately for conservationists, God is engaged in more cosmic matters, and does not spend much time thinking about water heaters or DSM. As a result, DSM attempts will often be wrong and wasteful. The bill for all these mistakes and confusion is paid by the lowly ratepayer.

• • •

Many of us have picked wild fruit—apples, cherries, or peaches—at some time. We all instinctively follow the same pattern. We pick the lowest and easiest-to-reach ones first. If we are still hungry, and want some more, we look for a ladder. Very few of us would use the ladder first and then pick the low-hanging fruit.

So it is with DSM programs. The easy conservation programs are instituted first, and the harder ones left for later. What this means in practical
terms is that the initial programs cost little, and later ones cost more. In the
same way, picking the low-hanging fruit does not take much effort—just reach
up and there it is. Looking for a ladder or a tree-shaking machine takes a lot
more work, and the devices may not even be available.

All this was brought home in a study by Brown and White of the Bonneville
Power Authority (BPA) in the U.S. Northwest.[7] Their data were analyzed by Paul
Joskow and Donald Marron of the Massachusetts Institute of Technology.[8]

BPA started energy conservation measures, mostly in terms of home insulation and other weatherization measures, in 1980, and has continued it to the
present day. This makes it the winner in utility program longevity, in the
United States at least. As a result, they have a lot more data than do Johnny-
come-lately utilities. The results of the study are shown in Figure 13.1 The
cost per kWhr saved doubled from 1980 to 1982 to 1989, less than a decade.
There was a slight dip in 1982–1983 compared to 1980–1982, but the trend
was otherwise upward.

Figure 13.1
Bonneville Power Authority Residential Weatherization Program Results

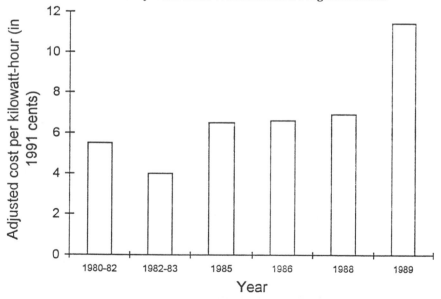

Source: Paul L. Joskow and Donald B. Marron, "What Does a Negawatt Really Cost? Evidence from Utility Conservation Programs," *Energy Journal* 13, no. 4 (1992): 41–74.
This shows the "picking of low fruit" phenomenon at Bonneville Power Authority. In the first
few years of the energy conservation program, the cost per kilowatt hour saved ranged between 4 and 6¢. However, by 1989 the cost was over 11¢. This indicates that all the easy
projects were done, and saving energy had become harder and harder as time progressed.

By 1989, the cost per kWhr saved was almost 50 percent greater than the average price paid per kWhr in the United States in recent years, which was about 8¢. It was about twice the amount used by the BPA itself (5.9¢) in estimating what is or what is not cost-effective. That is, something that costs more than 5.9¢ per kWhr in the BPA region is deemed, on its face, not to be worth the effort.

These results should not be surprising. We did not have to know that much about the BPA or conservation to have predicted the results long before the first roll of fiberglass was laid down in an Oregon attic.

When you lay that first roll of fiberglass down, you will probably save a certain amount of heating and cooling energy. (Chances are you will probably blow the savings by keeping the house warmer in winter and cooler in summer with your new-found savings, under the bounce-back or snapback effect.)

Now, imbued with the conservation ethic, you want to save even more. You rush out to the hardware store and buy another roll. But after it is installed, you find that you have much less energy saving than the first roll produced. Undaunted, you lay down a third roll. Results are even worse. You may not be able to detect any savings at all. The law of diminishing returns has taken over.

About the same considerations apply to other conservation forms. Install double-paned glass and you might save a certain amount of energy. But triple panes might not yield a detectable difference over double panes.

So it was with BPA. They clearly picked the low-hanging fruit first, in common with human nature. The fruit in the form of energy savings that remained was much higher in terms of both effort and cost to gather it. The proof is shown in Figure 13.1. When people say, in effect, "the demand-side management programs of utilities are just getting underway. It's no wonder some of them are ineffective. In the future, energy savings will get ever greater," remember the low-hanging fruit. Electric utilities into demand-side management are just like the rest of us in that respect—they look for the easy way.

• • •

Politics, it is said, makes strange bedfellows. One of the most peculiar examples of this came about in the fall 1993 debate over the North American Free Trade Agreement (NAFTA). Pat Buchanan, ultra-conservative columnist and two-time presidential candidate, allied himself with Ralph Nader, ultra-liberal consumer activist and 1996 candidate for president, in opposing NAFTA. Whether Buchanan was observed in public hugging Nader and whether Nader wrote the columnist "Dear Pat" letters has not been recorded. But they were pals, at least for a little while.

About the same thing happened in conservation as practiced by public utilities. Ordinarily, environmental and consumer groups snarl whenever utilities propose an increase in electricity rates. "Gouging the hapless consumer," they cry, and often go to court—or even take to the streets—to prevent the price rise. If Ralph Nader ever threw a bouquet to utilities, the flowers have long faded. In utility board rooms, there is little good said about environmentalists.

Conservation is another story. Utilities pay for DSM programs the same way they pay for everything else—through charges to their customers. Environmental groups not only do not object to this, but even applaud.

This was brought out in a recent lawsuit in Georgia, where electricity-using companies sued to prevent a DSM charge being added to their Georgia Power Company bills.[9] Curiously enough, the exact amount of the surcharge was not shown separately on the bills. Again, in the past, environmental groups demanded that each surcharge—to build nuclear plants and to pay for out-of-state power—be shown in bold print on every consumer's bill. In that way, the reasoning went, ratepayers would know how much of their money was being spent in various areas, and could protest if they thought the charges were unwarranted.

The amount collected as a result of the surcharge was not that large; on the order of $1.3 million a month. That is chicken feed for a company like Georgia Power, which has revenues in the order of hundreds of millions. Still, if DSM had not been instituted, presumably the surcharge would not exist.

In the Georgia case, a judge held that Georgia Power could not just add the surcharge at their whim, but had to go through a rate review just as with any other rate change. The utility, according to one news report, planned to appeal. In bed with them were two consumer groups, the Southern Environmental Law Center and the Campaign for a Prosperous Georgia. The two groups were not arguing (as they had in the past) for a rollback of utility surcharges, but rather for their continuation. Demand-side management also makes strange bedfellows.

• • •

The late 1970s were the heyday of all sorts of energy legislation promoting solar power, conservation, and a host of other goals. A decade and a half have passed since bills were frantically tossed into the legislative hopper to head off the catastrophic energy crisis then believed to be looming. One of the more important studies of this phenomenon was by Glenn Blackmon, then a Ph.D. candidate at the Kennedy School of Government at Harvard. He analyzed what Washington State did to promote conservation.[10]

Washington's 1980 law targeted electric utilities. Federal laws already provided benefits for conservation measures undertaken by homeowners, but provided nothing for utilities. Washington State moved to fill in this omission.

The law expired at the end of 1989. Rather than renew it as written or provide even more benefits to utilities, the legislature restricted the scope of the conservation investments qualifying for state money. If the law had been a success, it is almost certain that the legislature would have extended it, or even expanded its provisions. It apparently accomplished little, so the legislature swung the ax.

How did it work? Since the legislature felt it was close to impossible to measure the outputs of conservation, it handed out bonuses based on the inputs, not the outputs. Those two ideas are not the same.

In the United States, as mentioned earlier in this chapter, almost all electric utilities are regulated based on a fixed percentage of return on investment. How did Washington State handle the problem of how to reward conservation investment? They said they would allow a certain rate of return on investments by utilities they regulated for power production, and do the same for conservation investments. But they allowed a higher rate of return on conservation as opposed to production investments to insure that the utilities spent money on conservation.

The legislators called the extra rate of return the "equity kicker," and it was set at 2 percent. For example, if a utility could earn 14 percent on its production investments, it would earn 16 percent on conservation investments. The utility would then have an incentive to invest more in conservation. The equity kicker allowed them to do better than ordinary: Stimulate investments in conservation, and results are bound to flow. But they did not.

As Blackmon noted, utilities continued to invest 80 to 90 percent of capital funds on projects that did not qualify for the extra 2 percent. If the utilities were interested in boosting the value of their stock at any price, they would have reversed the proportions.

This suggests that utilities did not believe that they would get the extra money from the utility commission, even though the kicker was enshrined in law. Otherwise, why would they forego the chance to make easy money?

If the equity kicker is allowed by the PUC, where does the extra 2 percent come from? There can be only one source—the users of electricity. They have to pay more than they would have if conservation investments had the same rate of return as ordinary, power-producing investments. So the concept of a "free" good proves to be illusory.

Besides the equity kicker, the legislature provided for utility tax relief. For each investment in "alternative resources"—conservation measures were included in this—the utility could deduct a fixed percentage from its state tax bill. The exact calculation of the tax reduction was complicated, but Blackmon estimates it as about half the size of the equity kicker.

Stockholders of the utilities should have been sitting pretty. They got a special conservation bonus, as well as a reduction in their taxes. The lack of a rush to abandon power-producing investments in favor of conservation ones shows that there were severe problems in the law.

The main problem with the legislation, from the global viewpoint, was that there was no way of telling if any conservation was achieved. The legislation defined the input carefully enough, but not the output. Consider pumping gasoline into a car gas tank. This is the input. If we could not determine the output—how far the vehicle had gone on that gasoline—we could not say much about the energy in the liquid or the vehicle's gas mileage.

There was also a fundamental flaw in the reasoning behind the legislation. The more the utility spends on conservation, the more extra profit it can make. The temptation is to spend wastefully. This is precisely the opposite of the conservation ethic. As Blackmon writes, "Installing triple-paned windows in a house might save $3,000 in costs of a new coal plant. The normal cost of installing these windows might be $2,000, but the utility can get the most extra profits if it can increase the cost to $3,000." Yet the whole purpose of conservation is to save, not to waste. The legislation as written was a great incentive to spend money as if it were going out of style. As Blackmon notes, the biggest rewards go to the worst projects.

A third problem lies in just who is performing the work. Electric utilities are usually efficient at providing power to their customers, but not so effective in new areas such as conservation. This is reflected in their performance in the conservation realm. If homeowners are the ones to benefit from conservation, ideally they, not a bumbling though well-meaning organization, should have control of what happens.

In 1989, the law was revised. The only way that utilities in Washington State can now qualify for the increased return on investment is for new residential construction and programs for the elderly and low-income people.

But the essential problems still remain: It is more profitable for a utility to waste money and energy than it is to truly conserve under the program. And nobody can tell if any lasting results were produced. As Southey wrote about the Battle of Waterloo, "What good came of it all? Ah, that I cannot tell."

• • •

We may think that utility DSM is confined to the vicinity of that particular electric company. If the Montana PUC decides that utilities in that state have to institute costly DSM programs that have little or no benefit, that is for Montanans to decide, and has nothing to do with Iowans.

However, the Federal government also plays a part in DSM. Figure 13.2, based on the 1996 U.S. budget, shows how. Some utility DSM expenditures are deductible from their federal taxes. In 1994, the revenue loss to the federal treasury was estimated at $100 million, rising to almost a billion in the year 2000. The total from these seven years is expected to be almost $2 billion.

In addition, revenue losses can be considered as tax expenditures. For example, the deductibility of the interest on American home mortgages (not often found in other industrialized countries) is not a direct payment to homeowners, but is the equivalent in terms of money. Based on federal tax rates, the revenue loss from these indirect conservation subsidies can be multiplied by about 1.4 to yield what the budgeters call the "outlay equivalent." This is what the Federal government would have had to spend to achieve the same level of subsidy. This outlay equivalent will be about $2.7 billion over the seven-year period.

Thus, all the taxpayers, not merely the ratepayers in those states and utilities with DSM programs, are paying for brochures, radio ads, fiberglass, computer programs, consultants, and the rest. A rancher in Wyoming, whose electricity derives from his small generator, is contributing to a roll of insulation jammed into the rafters of a million-dollar house in the Hamptons on Long Island.

One of the major energy conservation measures proposed in the 1970s was the energy audit. According to the script, electric utilities would no longer

Figure 13.2
Losses to U.S. Treasury Because of Conservation Subsidies to Public Utilities, 1994–2000

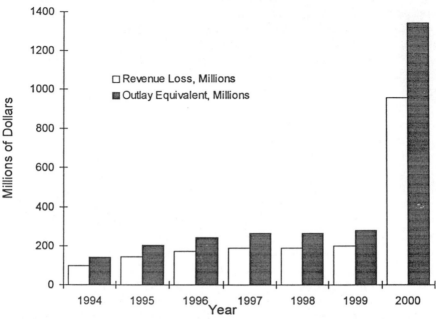

Source: Budget of the United States Government, Fiscal Year 1996 (Washington, D.C.: U.S. Government Printing Office, 1995), Table 5–1, Total Revenue Loss Estimates for Tax Expenditures in the Income Tax; Table 5–4, Outlay Equivalent Estimates for Tax Expenditures in the Income Tax.

When the Federal government subsidzes energy conservation, it appears to some people to be a complete freebie, with no cost to anyone. But the Treasury accountants have added up their losses. By the year 2000, they will be on the order of $1 billion, not counting secondary effects.

push more appliances on their customers. They would send out auditors who would advise ratepayers how to decrease, not increase, their electric bills. What could be more reasonable?

The customers could accept or reject the advice of the auditors, trained to look for inadequate insulation, leaky windows, and the like. They would have complete freedom to install as many conservation measures as they wanted or could afford.

That was the way the script read. The practice was different. Steve Pickels, of Houston Light and Power, described some of the pitfalls.[11] First, the U.S. Department of Energy (DOE) heavily bureaucratized the program. DOE specified that the only way that customers were to be notified of the program was by mail. Phone calls and personal visits to the utility were out. Pickels thinks this proved expensive and time-wasting. All this paperwork could have been justified if the response rate had been as high as DOE predicted—about 7 percent. Customers responded at a rate of about one-fourth of the prediction—1.7 percent. This means that if each of the customers who requested an audit had gone berserk and torn down the wires leading to their house—the ultimate electricity conservation measure—less than one part in fifty of all the electricity produced would have been "saved."

Pickels noted another important fact about those who wanted an audit. At the time, many of them had just installed energy improvements (better insulation and perhaps a more efficient refrigerator) and wanted to get an estimate of what they would save. They were not in the market for further energy improvements. Yet that was the entire purpose of the auditing system.

Another significant group of audit requesters did not want to know about conserving energy at all. They simply wanted to compare their electricity bill to those with similar homes and lifestyles. As Pickels writes, "They didn't know if last month's $150 utility bill is comparable to, higher than or lower than what families in similar homes paid last month." Unfortunately for this curious group, the auditors generally could not answer this question.

So in Pickels' opinion, the highly touted audit program accomplished little, mostly because of almost total lack of response. It cost a lot, almost $150 per audit. That is not much of a recommendation for future energy conservation programs.

• • •

We have been assuming that all audits are accurate. What if they are not? Suppose, for example, that you were not satisfied with an energy auditor's advice, and sent for a second one. Ordinarily, this would cost the householder more than a hundred dollars, and few would take this step. In almost all cases, the utility pays the full cost of the first audit, under order from a regulatory commission. All the householder has to do is request to have the auditor come around.

Suppose further that a second audit, and even a third to verify the results of the first two, produced a different result. Auditor #1 says, "Double the thickness of your attic insulation." Auditor #2 says, "Not worth the trouble and expense. No matter how long you live, you'll never recoup the money."

Auditor #3 says "Replace your refrigerator. It's a real energy waster." On to auditor #4, who states, "Don't bother. What you really must do is replace all your windows. They're leaky."

By this point, most people would be close to insanity. They would be tempted to toss out all the auditors and go back to big, roomy refrigerators and overheated rooms.

Could this happen? There is some evidence that it is not too far from the truth. Scientists at a research center run by the European Community in Ispra, Italy took the role of the hapless homeowner.[12] They commissioned four different consulting firms to do audits on a set of buildings. The scientists themselves also did a thorough audit, as a check on the outside auditors.

The results were as muddled as our hypothetical example. The scientists noticed significant disparities among all four of the outside audits, as well as major differences from the presumably accurate study they conducted themselves.

What were these differences? While it would take too much space to list them all, one was the actual size of the buildings being audited. You would think that a company claiming to be energy consultants would at least know how to use a ruler, but apparently this was not so.

Other discrepancies between the audits were matters as simple as the length of the heating season, which could be determined by a quick trip to the library.

The audit performed by the scientists turned up many potential energy-saving measures, some of which were completely overlooked by the commercial audits. Overall, the results showed that the commercial audits disagreed both with each other and the scientific baseline audit.

Is this just a dispute between scientists and commercial auditing firms, who were perhaps just interested in making a quick buck? It is much more than that.

The essence of any scientific experiment is *replication*. If scientist A in Tokyo performs an experiment and gets certain results, scientist B in London should get the same results. If he or she does not, then something is wrong.

So the fact that four auditing companies all got different results is more than a commercial difference. It suggests that the assumption underlying audits—that there is a reasonable set of recommendations for a given house or building that most people would agree on—is shaky. In turn, the panacea for most household energy problems that audits are claimed to be is a mirage. If nobody can agree on what steps to take to reduce energy consumption, why bother having an audit in the first place?

• • •

This story suggests that energy audits accomplish little, in spite of their noble goals. What do the numbers show?

Ray Hartman of Boston University measured some of the effects for the Portland General Electric Company.[13] He did not rely on what consumers told him, but rather on a computer model that could separate the wheat from the chaff.

He found that the average yearly usage by consumers in that area was about 23,700 kilowatt hours before the conservation program went into effect. The utility offered not only a free audit but a zero-interest loan—what I would call "home-aloan"—for improvements that were identified as a result of the audits. This was about the only place that ratepayers in that area could get a zero-interest loan for anything.

What were the actual savings as a result of these elaborate and expensive programs? Hartman presented the results in terms of statistical distributions. For simplicity, we can concentrate on the average household. That household saved about 390 kWhr annually as a result of the audit and zero-interest loan. This was less than 2 percent of the annual bill, not exactly a huge saving. In most households, the variation from month to month would have swamped this tiny reduction in electricity use.

But this combined the audit and the loan for improvements. When just the audit itself was considered, the savings were about 200 kWhr annually, or less than 1 percent of the total electricity bill. Again, this is so minuscule as to be hardly visible.

The size of the average loan was not specified, so we cannot tell whether the energy improvements that were made—better insulation, tighter windows, and so on—were cost effective. But we can do this for the audit itself.

The average cost of an audit was about $150, taking into account the cost of the auditor and administrative costs.[14] The average savings attributable to it were about 200 kWhr. Assume that the average cost of electricity is about 8¢ per kilowatt hour, the recent national average. (Actual costs in Portland are lower, because of its great dependence on cheap hydroelectricity.)

If we divide that number into the cost of the audit itself, we get the following:

$$150 \text{ (dollars)} \times 100 \text{ (cents per dollar)} \div 8 \text{ (cents per kilowatt hour)}$$
$$\times 200 \text{ (kilowatt hours saved per year)} = 9.4 \text{ years}$$

That is 9.4 years to pay back the cost of the audit. The householder whose home was audited did not have to pay back a penny, of course. The utility bore the entire cost. The rest of the utility's customers had to pay it back. They might not have been too happy if they had known that it would take nine years to recoup these highly touted investments.

Nine years is a long time, but how about two decades? Suppose the homeowner had to pay for the audit himself. The "opportunity cost" for the $150 might be at a rate of about 6 percent, the money he would have earned if he had left it in the bank. (The exact value will vary by year, of course.) This means that the homeowner would have lost $9 a year if he had paid for the audit himself. He then gains 200 kilowatt hours, at 8¢ per kWhr, for a total annual saving of about $16. From that, subtract $9 for his lost interest for an annual net savings of $7. The audit cost $150, so it would take twenty-two years to pay back the audit's cost. Not too many people are willing to wait that long.

• • •

Because of federal and state laws, many electric utilities have undertaken conservation programs. For example, in the early 1980s, the TVA gave free energy audits to their customers. I had one done for my own home. The man knocked at the door, looked in the attic and basement, checked the windows, and generally inspected the place thoroughly from top to bottom. He came up with a list of conservation measures I could employ, along with an approximate cost for each.

Some were simple and cost almost nothing, such as stuffing insulation around my electrical outlets. I had not thought that cold air could leak in from there. He told me that it could. Within a week, I had bought and installed the inexpensive kits to prevent this. I presume I saved a few dollars in heating and cooling bills in subsequent years.

Sam, the energy auditor, admitted that some of the conservation steps he suggested were expensive: "I see that you've got only single-hung windows in this house, although most have double-panes with air between them. If you really want to save money, install double-hung ones. Of course, it won't be cheap. You've got a lot of windows, so I estimate $2,000 to $3,000. Think about it." I did think about it—for about a microsecond. At the time, my heating and cooling bills were averaging about $40 to $50 a month. Tennessee, where I lived, has a mild climate. So I would have had to live to the age of Methuselah to pay back the investment on these double-hung windows. Since none of my ancestors ever lived past 100, I decided to pass on the window-changing suggestion.

• • •

Phone companies are public utilities as well, whose rates are regulated by public utility commissions. While they clearly do not produce energy, a conservation analogy can be drawn with the savings promised by long distance phone companies.

In late 1990 and early 1991, AT&T ran a television advertisement showing why people should switch from phone companies that offered lower-priced service back to "Ma Bell." The advertisement depicted unsatisfied customers of another unspecified phone company trying to get credit for a wrong number and waiting for lengthy periods to get an operator.

From the viewpoint of conservation, the scene that most interests us is the one where a young woman looks at a sheaf of phone bills and complains, "They [the competing phone company] promised big savings. But where are they?"

What does this have to do with conservation? Homeowners buy many devices—insulation, more efficient refrigerators, double-hung windows—to save energy. But consumers do not have an electricity meter attached to each of their appliances showing how much each has used during a day or month. All they get is a monthly bill from the utility, covering all their electricity uses.

They very well may have saved $2 that month because their new refrigerator uses less electricity than the old one. At the same time, they may have forgotten to turn the lights off that month as much as they did before. As a result, they may say, in chorus with the unfortunate phone user, "Where are the savings?"

The disappointment faced by many energy conservers reflects what is said here: Conservation, in a broad sense, is nonexistent. The new refrigerator, taken by itself, could be called a conserver compared to the old one. Yet all the lights and appliances in a household cannot be called conservers, since they are a mixture of the old and the new. As well, how much energy we use is a function of our varying attitudes toward energy saving.

So the frustration displayed by the woman in the telephone commercial is not too different from what might cross our minds when we get our electricity or gas bill. She may have decided to chat with her sister across the continent for an hour. During the palaver, she anticipated wonderful savings, but when the long distance bill comes, it is higher than she expected. In the same way, we often ease up on energy frugality in other areas after we buy a new energy-saving appliance. It is no wonder we cry out in bafflement, "Where's the savings?"

NOTES

1. Larry Condelli, Dane Archer, Elliott Aronson, Barbara Curbow, Beverley McLeod, Thomas F. Pettigrew, Lawrence T. White, and Suzanne Yates, "Improving Utility Conservation Programs: Outcomes, Interventions and Evaluations," *Energy* 9, no. 6 (1984): 485.

2. Eric Hirst and Stan Hadley, "Price Impacts of Electric-Utility DSM Programs," report ORNL/CON-402, Oak Ridge National Laboratory, Oak Ridge, Tenn., November 1994, 27.

3. E. Brown, *Augusta* [Ga.] *Chronicle*, 21 Jan. 1993, 4A.

4. Petr Beckman, "Belongs to All of Us," *Access to Energy* 1 (April 1991).

5. John P. Hughes and Barbara S. Brenner, "DSM: When Should Industrials Just Say No?" in *Proceedings of 6th National Demand-Side Management Conference* (Palo Alto, Calif.: Electric Power Research Institute, 1993).

6. Larry Ruff, "Equity vs. Efficiency: Getting DSM Pricing Right," *Electricity Journal* 5 (Nov. 1992): 24.

7. M. A. Brown and D. L. White, "Evaluation of Bonneville's 1988 and 1989 Residential Weatherization Program: A Northwest Study of Program Dynamics," report CON-323, Oak Ridge National Laboratory, Oak Ridge, Tenn., Dec. 1992.

8. Paul L. Joskow and Donald B. Marron, "What Does a Negawatt Really Cost? Evidence from Utility Conservation Programs," *Energy Journal* 13, no. 4 (1992): 41–74.

9. Frank LoMonte, "Utility Appeals Surcharge Ban," *Augusta* [Ga.] *Chronicle*, 25 Nov. 1993, 19B.

10. Glenn Blackmon, "Conservation Incentives: Evaluating the Washington State Experience," *Public Utilities Fortnightly* 127 (15 Jan. 1991): 24–27.

11. Stephen J. Pickels and Philip Audet, "Second Generation Programs with an Increasing Utility Initiative," *Public Utilities Fortnightly* 120 (24 Dec. 1987): 9–13.

12. G. A. Heicke, "A Detailed Comparison of Energy Audits Carried Out by Four Separate Companies on the Same Set of Buildings," *Energy & Buildings* 14, no. 2 (1990): 153–165.

13. Raymond S. Hartman and Michael J. Doane, "The Estimation of the Effects of Utility-Sponsored Conservation Programmes," *Applied Economics* 18 (1986): 1.

14. Pickels and Audet, "Second Generation Programs," 9–13.

14

The Question of Waste

Defining "waste" exactly is perhaps the most difficult task in the field of energy conservation. It has proved more than merely troublesome—it has been almost impossible. You may think that an electric backscratcher is a waste of energy. Someone else may counter that it eases the itch, and thus helps them be more cheerful and ultimately more productive. Who will draw the line?

• • •

If conservation truly existed, we could define "waste" carefully. And since just about everyone is against waste (usually someone else's), this could provide needed revenue for the government if it were taxed.

Fereidoon Sioshansi, an economist with the electric utility Southern California Edison, has proposed what he calls an energy inefficiency surcharge (EIS).[1] In principle, it would impose a financial penalty on electricity wasters. Considering this tax in detail shows why the energy conservation schemes proposed by utilities usually fall on their faces.

He considered a typical ratepayer with three appliances: A, B, and C. A uses 50 kilowatt hours per month on average; B uses 100; and C uses 10. A 100-watt bulb burning for one hour would use one-tenth of a kWhr. Dr. Sioshansi's idea was to levy a tax on energy use above a target level.

We immediately run into difficulties in calculating the tax. How do we know appliance A uses 50 kWhr per month? Ratepayers get one bill at the end of the month, adding up all the electricity they have used. Nobody has a separate meter for every lightbulb and appliance in their house. So even here there is a problem in calculating the EIS.

Let us suppose that this brave ratepayer agrees to have meters clutter up all his rooms, and he is able to determine average electricity use for each appliance. To calculate an EIS, we have to estimate a target level of consumption for appliances A, B, and C. But who is to do it, and on what basis?

Table 14.1
Calculating a Potential Tax on Energy Waste

	Current consumption level (kWhr)	Target level (kWhr)	Difference (kWhr)
Appliance A	50	40	10
Appliance B	100	80	20
Appliance C	10	10	0
Total	160	130	30

Sources: Fereidoon P. Sioshansi, "The Myths and Facts of Energy Efficiency," *Energy Policy* 19 (April 1991): 231–243.

Table 14.1 shows a target of 40 kWhr for appliance A. This appliance, using 50 kWhr a month, is thus above the target, and its owner should be penalized in some way. The target of 50 kWhr is only Dr. Sioshansi's opinion, of course. If we were casual about energy conservation, we might use a target of 70 kWhr instead. In that case, there would be no penalty assessed against the owner of appliance A. On the other hand, if we had a philosophical orientation against wasters, we might place a target of 30 kWhr in the second column for appliance A. In that case, the difference between the first and second columns would be 20 kWhr, or twice what Dr. Sioshansi specified. All this illustrates that, just as beauty is in the eyes of the beholder, so is energy conservation. Because there is no definition of what it is, the last two columns of the table can be whatever we want.

The problem is not too far from the ancient tale of "Belling the Cat." A houseful of mice, having had too many of its members eaten by the prowling feline, call a meeting. "It's really quite simple," one of them pipes up, "We get caught because we don't hear him coming. If he had a bell around his neck, we would hear him. So one of us has to fasten a little bell to him." The oldest and wisest mouse replies, "Fine for you to say. Exactly who is going to perform this wonderful feat?"

In the same way, who is going to draw the boundary between waste and appropriate energy use? The economist Sioshansi, with his degrees, experience in the electricity industry, and knowledge of the scientific literature on conservation, could not and would not. Then who among us is so wise as to have this amazing capacity?

The reason an energy inefficiency surtax could never work, either at the philosophical or practical level, is simple. Consider the first column of Table 14.1, showing current levels of consumption. Suppose appliance A is a washing machine, something that many American's own.

In principle, the electric company could attach meters to every washing machine in the land. Then some type of average usage is established. Suppose, for example, that it is 50 kWhr per month for this appliance A.

Consider a bachelor who sends most of his dirty clothes to the dry cleaners. He might use his washer once every two weeks, producing a usage of 5 kWhr per month. He would never be subjected to a tax on electricity waste, even though he drove a huge car from the 1970s.

His next-door neighbor has three young children, and runs her washer almost continuously. Her usage might be 200 kWhr, and she has to pay a huge "wasters" tax. She explodes when she gets the bill: "Are you kidding? Do you think I run the washer a minute more than I have to? If you had three little ones, you'd be at the washer all day, too. Whoever came up with this wasters tax has to be crazy." So ultimately a tax on energy wasters cannot be implemented. We all use energy so differently. One person's waste is another's dire necessity.

• • •

An experiment once suggested who might be wasters, but came up with surprising conclusions. R. A. Winett and his colleagues measured energy consumption in households after a rebate program was instituted.[2] The experimenters also determined energy consumption before the subsidy was offered.

In a survey of this type, there would inevitably be some statistical variability. For example, a family may have their in-laws move in for the duration of the experiment. There would then be much more energy used for showers, cooking, and the like.

Experimenters are familiar with this phenomenon, and allow for it in their calculations. They know that in any experiment designed to save energy, there will be a few that, for various reasons, actually increase energy use.

In Winett's experiments, the explanations were different. The wasters, that is, those who increased their energy consumption, were mostly those who had instituted energy-saving measures before the experiment had begun. These were the people who should have been getting gold medals for trying to save energy *before* the rebates began. Instead, they could be condemned as wasters.

They were not. They were probably part of the bounce-back or snap-back effect. This is where people who install energy-saving appliances like highly efficient refrigerators gradually take longer showers, lengthier car trips, and so on. They slowly increase their energy use in other areas, counting on the vast energy savings they imagine they are getting.

Who are the true wasters? On one hand, we have the people who, for noble or other reasons, tried to save energy before the rebates were sent out. Because of the bounce-back effect, they used more energy than before the experiment began. On the other hand, we have those—probably the vast majority—who did little or nothing until money crossed their palms. Which of the two groups are the true wasters?

• • •

Waste is more than a statistical phenomenon, of course. If it exists, it is generated by people. John Horn of the Associated Press once wrote a revealing article on the relationship between Hollywood figures and conservation.[3] In the article, celebrities were criticized for leaving their limousines idling at a fundraising party for the environment. Many arrived in Mercedes, BMWs, Rolls Royces, and the like. The 1,000 or so guests at the Beverly Hills party raised $1.2 million for environmental causes.

From the viewpoint of conservation, the key point is not that these celebrities burn up more gasoline in their cars than the average person. They do, but the difference in terms of conservation is small.

Suppose that each of the celebrities drove to the party in his or her own Rolls Royce, getting six miles to the gallon, and each drove twenty miles to the party. This is probably an overestimate of the gasoline used. Many of them lived right in Beverly Hills, where the party was held. Even eliminating this fact, the combined trips would use up 3,000 gallons at most. To get this figure, we multiply the number of attendees (1,000) by twenty to get the total miles driven, yielding 20,000. Many will have gone in groups of two or more. Divide the 20,000 by the number of miles per gallon that a Rolls gets (six) and we get about 3,300 gallons.

The important point for conservation is that these celebrities earn large incomes on average. The amount they spend on items other than gasoline is ultimately reflected in energy use. For example, if they buy a house worth $1 million, a large amount of energy is embedded in its materials and construction. The extra amount they spend to heat or cool the million-dollar home is a small part of the total energy expenditure. The same principle applies to their other spending. The proportion spent directly on energy like electricity, gasoline, and so on is a small part of their total indirect energy expenditures.

Bob Hattoy of the Sierra Club, quoted in the article, had it about right: "It's great celebrities are getting involved. But it's not about doing lunch. It's about changing the way we live." He adds a moral judgment: "Lifestyles of the rich and famous are often lifestyles of the wasteful and indulgent." Wastefulness is clearly in the eyes of the beholder. Hattoy delivered the statement from his lofty moral perch, but the lesson to learn, after the solemn pronouncements are ended, is that total earnings and expenditures, not the size of their car, indicate how much energy is ultimately used by a person.

There are wealthy people who earn as much as these celebrities. Some of those on the *Forbes 400* list have much more than many of those who turned up at the Beverly Hills party, but their names and faces are hardly known to the general public.

Can it be demonstrated, taking account of their expenditure patterns, that the total energy use of the noncelebrities at the same income level of the celebrities is less? For example, if real estate mogul R makes $1 million a year, the same as movie star M, does he use less energy because the man on the street has no idea who he is? Noncelebrities probably use about as much energy overall as celebrities at the same income level. But we do not read statements that Bill Gates, Warren Buffett, Michael Milken (before he went to jail), or Sam Walton idled their engines excessively while at a party.

Suppose that one of these celebrities makes $1 million a year. The average U.S. family income in recent years has been about $25,000. The celebrity earns as much as forty average families. A good case can be made that the celebrity's overall *direct* energy use is less than forty times that of the average family. Putting it another way, the celebrity uses less energy per dollar of income than the average family. After all, very few if any of the celebrities own sixty cars—perhaps the number of cars owned by a group of forty average families—that they drive every day. They would have to do this to equal the gasoline consumption of the forty average families.

Because of their extremely high income, celebrities probably save more per dollar of income than average families. Saving is generally associated with less energy use per dollar than spending. So on these two points alone, celebrities probably expend less energy per dollar of income than average families. Even if they idled their Rolls Royces and BMWs day and night, that statement would be true.

• • •

Willie Nelson is a country-and-western singer with a difference. Famed for his "outlaw" style, he has taken a serious interest in the decline of the American family farmer. As opposed to the casual interest of many stars, who merely lend their names to the letterheads of charitable organizations, Nelson has held numerous concerts to raise money for small farmers. He has spoken on many occasions on their plight.

One of those times was on Capitol Hill in Washington. Nelson was testifying before a congressional committee on some forthcoming legislation. Like many touring stars, he travels with a luxurious bus, rather than flying from place to place. Apparently his driver parked the bus near the Capitol but left the motor running. An alert District of Columbia policeman noticed this and gave Nelson a ticket. The event made headlines in papers around the country.

There are presumably two violations in tickets of this type: air pollution and waste of resources. Let us deal with air pollution first. If Nelson's bus was in compliance with the federal air pollution laws that govern just about all motorized vehicles, then the emissions he was producing were below legal limits. Nelson's bus driver could have circled Capitol Hill all day without breaking any laws.

The waste of resources is a more prominent issue. Here we had a wealthy man (he has never claimed to be as poor as the farmers he supports) using up the gasoline that the rest of us require. This is hypocrisy when he comes to testify on behalf of the needy. Or so it appeared.

The amount of gasoline that Nelson's driver (nobody ever accused Nelson himself of ordering the idling) wasted could not have been more than a gallon or two, hardly making a dent in the income of a man who sells millions of records. That amount of gasoline would be consumed in a tiny fraction of a second in the huge rush hour streaming into Washington each morning. By that comparison, the waste was on a microscopic level. The gasoline, in the words of Gilbert and Sullivan's *Mikado*, "would hardly be missed." The headlines implied that Nelson was single-tonguedly slurping up the petroleum resources of the world, but an hour or two of idling still leaves lots in the ground.

• • •

While many of us try to save energy at home, we may imagine that waste occurs frequently at the industrial level. Appearances may be deceiving. In most houses, when a lightbulb burns out people replace it, sometimes after considerable delay. Few change one before it gives that little pop that indicates the end of life in bulb world.

Now consider a factory, with perhaps hundreds or thousands of fluorescent bulbs. Wait under a bank of them long enough, and you will see workers coming to replace both the good and the bad. "Just a second," you might say, "You're replacing perfectly good bulbs. Look at them; only about half in this area are burned out. Why not just replace the ones that are gone? If ever there was a waste, this is it." It is not really wasteful, from the company's viewpoint. Their costs have two parts: the price of the bulbs and the labor required to replace them. Many companies have found that it is cheaper for them to replace whole banks of bulbs, even when many of them have not burned out.

How could this be? Consider a janitor wandering through a factory and peering up at the ceiling. He spots a burned-out bulb and puts up his ladder to replace it. All this takes time. As well, in so doing he is disrupting the work of those nearby, which also costs the company money.

Contrast this with changing bulbs at the end of their advertised life, or some such regular interval. The janitor goes directly to the bank of bulbs and replaces them all. The disruption of productivity happens just once, not frequently as in the case of the "when they're burned out" procedure. The janitor spends less time per bulb as well.

When companies add up the costs of these two approaches, the answer is obvious. Replace on a regular schedule, even if that means throwing away perfectly good bulbs.

What about the waste of resources? True, working bulbs are discarded, so there is a waste from society's viewpoint. But the firm's accountants will say, "We can show it's much cheaper to replace bulbs on a fixed schedule, not one by one. The company's money can be put to better uses, like creating more jobs." This waste would never happen in a house, because people's leisure time is not paid. Nobody pays householders to change bulbs. As a result, it will always be cheaper to replace them when they burn out, and not a minute before.

Waste is in the eye of the beholder. What seems like waste to someone touring a factory and watching perfectly good bulbs being tossed into the garbage is true conservation from the company's viewpoint.

• • •

What if most of a valuable energy source was burned to heat the great outdoors, or used to provide light where nobody would see it? Surely everyone would agree that this was a waste. This is precisely what happened to the natural gas often discovered when Americans drilled for oil in the 1930s. Unless there was a nearby town where the gas could be piped and burned, it was simply flared off. The practice continued in countries like Saudi Arabia until the 1980s.

Flaring gas was a waste. How did it enter into energy statistics? Not at all. Since it was never bought or sold, there was no record of how much once lighted Texas skies.

The invention of high-pressure pipelines, such as the Big Inch of World War II, allowed gas to be moved from the southwest to consumers in the north. Flaring gradually diminished until it was negligible. Almost all the waste ended, as consumers employed the gas for home heating and other useful purposes.

Or has the waste really stopped? Look at the energy statistics. Use of natural gas goes up, up, up. The nation is then lectured about the untrammeled waste of energy. But the true waste took place long ago, as millions of cubic feet of gas were used to toast marshmallows for gas field roustabouts. It is true that the world uses much more gas than in the past. Global consumption rose 8 percent annually from 1950 to 1970. In spite of this increasing demand, the proportion wasted is much smaller than before.

All this shows that the definition of "waste" is often based on a speaker's philosophical inclinations. There are some who look at a rising graph of energy consumption and equate it with waste. The true waste, however, once illumined Texas heavens.

• • •

To produce aluminum requires much more energy, mostly electricity, per unit weight than competitors like steel or copper. Thus aluminum is an energy waster. Why would we use it? For a very good reason. At the same time it is wasting energy in its manufacture, it is saving it in transportation. In cars, the rise of gasoline prices and federally mandated mileage standards have led to a skyrocketing of aluminum use. Billions of gallons of gasoline have been saved because of these lighter cars, with steel being replaced by aluminum.

By considering only the tremendous energy requirements of aluminum manufacture, we would condemn it as a waster and banish it to the materials equivalent of Siberia. When we look at the bigger picture, we see that on balance it promotes energy efficiency. We have to consider the entire system, not just isolated parts.

NOTES

1. Fereidoon P. Sioshansi, "The Myths and Facts of Energy Efficiency," *Energy Policy* 19 (April 1991): 231–243.

2. Richard A. Winett et al., "Effects of Monetary Rebates, Feedback and Information in Residential Energy Conservation," *Journal of Applied Psychology* 63, no. 1 (1978): 73-80.

3. John Horn, "Some Celebrities Miscast in Environmental Role," *Buffalo News*, 22 April 1990, A14.

15

The Economic Aspect

Discussions of conservation rarely consider the cost of things. Hand wringing over running out of oil usually does not evaluate how much petroleum is available at what price. Economics helps to put it all in perspective. The beauty is that one need not have taken Economics 101 to understand.

• • •

Many people think that conservation exists when it does not because of their mental model of energy use. This model corresponds to an image of a laboratory we have in our mind.

In a lab situation, an experiment excludes all extraneous factors, such as the temperature outside, whether the sun is shining, and so on. However, factors outside the laboratory determine if conservation occurs.

For example, suppose we have two gasoline motors in the lab, each using the same amount of energy per minute. Suppose further that there is a gallon of gasoline available. No more can be brought in from the outside. The objective of the experiment is to have the motors run as long as possible on that gallon of gas. We can easily calculate just how long that will be at the start of the experiment. Call it an hour.

Then we make one of the motors more fuel efficient by installing new spark plugs or some other improvement. It uses less gasoline per minute after we are through with the modifications. We then find the two motors will run longer, in total, than before. Call it seventy minutes. This "proves" that conservation exists. Of course it does, if life were confined to laboratory settings. It is not.

Alert readers will have noticed that two motors, not one, were specified. Why not perform the experiment on just one? Surely the second one does not prove anything. After all, there were no claims that it was more (or less) fuel efficient than the first. It merely consumed gasoline at its usual rate.

It was included in the experiment to show how economics determines what happens in proposed conservation measures. Economics takes account of both people and money. In the experiment, no people were involved. As well, the cost of the gasoline was not mentioned. This is fine for a lab setting, but matters change once you leave its confines.

Now step outside the lab, into a real world setting. The first difference we note is that people operate and own the motors. They have a vital concern about how much running the motor will cost them. Conservation is favored in a general way, as long as it confers some benefits on them.

Now repeat the experiment, this time taking account of people. We again start off with two standard motors. Call the owner of the first one Joe. For Joe, we again improve the spark plugs so he uses less gasoline. He is overjoyed, since his cost of operation has dropped. For him, energy conservation works, no two ways about it.

What about Kevin, the owner of the second motor? We have made no improvements on his device, so it uses the same gas per minute as before. He is as interested in conservation as Joe, but he is unable to improve his motor's efficiency.

By leaving the laboratory, have we merely attached owners to the two motors, with the results about the same? We have done more than provide ownership certificates. We have also indirectly provided a price mechanism, one that was missing in the lab.

With his improved motor, Joe finds that he does not need to use as much gasoline as before. What is the effect of Joe's reduced energy use on Kevin? Recall that there was a fixed amount of gasoline available, one gallon. So now the supply of gasoline to Kevin is greater than before.

When the supply of anything goes up, the price usually goes down. Then more is used. For example, suppose there is a flood of fresh melons into the market and the price drops from $3 to $1. The result is obvious—people eat a lot more melons.

So now Kevin has to pay less for his portion of gasoline. Suddenly, conservation does not seem so important to him anymore. He may decide to run his motor in ways he might have regarded as wasteful before Joe's spark plugs were changed. Kevin may, for example, decide to put hot-rod attachments on his motor so it can run faster than ever. He does not worry too much about its cost, since gasoline is suddenly so cheap—because of Joe's new spark plugs.

Joe uses less energy, but Kevin uses more. The total amount of energy use by both Joe and Kevin will be about the same as if the experiment had never been held. What has happened is substantially different from the lab experiment, where real conservation did occur. Things turned out differently in real life because economics—the cost of gasoline—now plays a role. It did not in the lab. To use a bit of jargon, economics mediated the transactions between Joe and Kevin. There was no such mechanism in the lab. Only motors, not people, were involved.

• • •

The real world is vastly different from the lab, especially when it comes to conservation. In the lab, conservation truly exists. Unfortunately for its proponents, we do not live there. When we enter the real world, economics plays a role. Conservation disappears like a block of ice in the sun.

Some of the arguments for why conservation does not exist can be made clearer to readers by means of diagrams adapted from Economics 101. The graphs may look complicated, but in reality they describe a simple process.

Consider Figure 15.1. Begin at point A, where supply curve S and demand curve D intersect. Curve S tells us what happens to the supply of energy as the price and quantity vary. When it slopes down to the left, the quantity supplied—by an oil company, for example—will decrease as the price drops. Curve D tells us the same about demand; that is, how much energy society (or an individual) wants and can use. As the curve drops off to the right, the quantity demanded increases as the price falls.

At point A, the quantity of energy used is Q_A, found by dropping vertically down from point A. The horizontal axis is quantity Q, and the vertical axis is price P. Supply curves slope upward to the right, and demand curves slope downward to the left. Supply curve S′ and demand curve D′ are merely supply and demand curves, respectively, for different conditions from S and D.

Figure 15.1
Demand–Supply Curves Show Why Conservation Does Not Exist

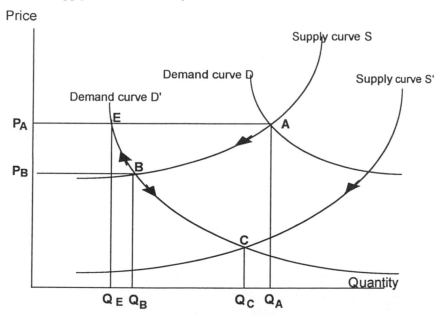

If demand for energy drops from curve D to D′, for any reason, then the amount used drops from Q_A to Q_B along curve AB. But since the price has fallen, from P_A to P_B, there is a tendency for the quantity used to rise along the curve BC. Whether the total energy use is greater or smaller after the demand changes will depend on whether Q_C is greater than Q_A. In this graph it is greater, but this may not always be the case.

Suppose that the demand for energy drops from D to D´ because of ethics, government regulations, attempts to save money, or any other reason. Then the old supply and new demand curves (S and D´) intersect at B. The quantity used is now Q_B, again found by dropping vertically down from point B. Q_B is less than Q_A, since it is closer to the left-hand side of the graph. The quantities Q start at zero on the left-hand side. In that sense, conservation has worked.

However, while the quantity of energy Q used has dropped, so has the price P. Before the change, the price was P_A. Now it has dropped to P_B, found by moving horizontally to the left from point B.

The price–quantity intersection can move up or down the revised demand curve D´. This is shown by arrows pointing in two directions. If it moves up the curve to point E, this implies that the price rises toward the initial price P_A, and the quantity of energy used falls to Q_E. Q_E is even lower than Q_B. But there are no economic forces impelling the price to rise again. After all, demand has fallen.

The more logical way for the price to move after it gets to point B is *downward*, from point B to point C, again along the demand curve D´. The price has fallen from P_A to P_B, so the quantity demanded increases from curve S to S´. Specifically, the amount used goes from Q_B to Q_C along curve D´. The lowered price generates *increased* use.

Is Q_C more to the right of the graph than Q_A, that is, is Q_C greater than Q_A? If it is, then the conservation efforts have produced greater, not lesser, usage of energy. If it is not, then conservation has worked to some degree. However, the effect is smaller than the initial conservation of going from Q_A to Q_B.

There is no a priori method of answering this question. It can be answered only with full knowledge of the elasticities (or slopes) of the demand and supply curves at the point in question. While we know the slopes in some cases, there is no general rule for computing them.

However, one conclusion that can be drawn is the existence of a "rebound" effect, that is, the move from Q_B to Q_C. If Q_C minus Q_B is about equal to Q_B minus Q_A, then conservation does not generally exist. If Q_C minus Q_B is much less than Q_B minus Q_A, then the rebound effect is small, and conservation does exist. If Q_C minus Q_B is greater than Q_B minus Q_A, any effort at conservation produces greater, not lesser, energy use.

• • •

Economists have debated for years the cost of conservation programs. They have concentrated on those organized by electric utilities and governments, because those organizations have to answer to the public service commissions that regulate them, or to the taxpayers, respectively.

In so doing, they may have lost sight of a larger issue. The total cost to society of conservation programs may be much higher than the amounts that electric utilities or governments spend. They can transform society in ways that nobody wants or likes.

Friedrich Hayek, the Nobel laureate in economics, pointed this out in *The Constitution of Liberty*, issued a generation ago. He wrote, "Industrial development would have been greatly retarded if 60 or 80 years ago the warning of the conservationists about the threatened exhaustion of the supply of coal had been heeded; and the internal combustion engine would never have revolutionized transport if its use had been limited to the [then] known supplies of oil."[1] Hayek put his finger on the main assumption of conservationists: There is a finite supply of oil, coal, gas, or anything else for that matter, and we should base our policies on this fact.

Consider the situation around 1860 when Nikolaus Otto—wonderfully named—and others were developing the first crude petroleum-based engines. Fortunately for these tinkerers, there were no government agencies with a vast array of economists and geologists around to estimate petroleum reserves. If there had been, as Hayek notes, their conclusion would have been unanimous—there simply was not enough petroleum around to support the vast fleet of vehicles that the inventors hypothesized.

"Why waste your time in the workshop?" the inventors would be told, "Even if you come up with a useful horseless carriage, there won't be enough fuel to power more than a few thousand vehicles. And the little that exists will be gone in a few years. You have invented a temporary toy for the super-rich."

No government agency conveyed that message, but undoubtedly the inventors in Europe and the United States heard it from others. What did they do? They ignored it. True, petroleum reserves at the time were small. The inventors had faith that when their machines were used widely, more reserves would be found. There would never come a time when millions of cars would be by the side of the road, stalled because of lack of fuel.

The rest is history. The claim of the long-ago conservationists proved to be false. The spread of the automobile triggered the greatest investment in minerals—in this case, petroleum—that the world had ever seen. It swamped, in money and effort, all the combined gold rushes of the past. The search made a burgeoning field out of geology, which before that time had been a lonely pursuit of a handful of professors.

If a government agency at the time had said, "There's not enough petroleum around to power cars. Better forget the whole thing," the world would be a poorer place. The unparalleled mobility that hundreds of millions now have, once only granted to kings and potentates, would never have appeared. Horses and streetcars would fill our cities as they once did. Is there anyone who wants to go back to those times? We would, if the conservationists of those days had had their way.

• • •

There are other economic tools we can use to analyze conservation. One way we can determine how people really feel toward potential energy savings, as opposed to the lip service that is usually employed, is to consider the discount rate. This is a calculation employed mostly by economists, but it can illustrate some of the questions about how people act toward conservation.

While the mathematics of discount rates can get complicated, the principle is simple. If something has a high discount rate, usually expressed in percentages, it means that its value decreases quickly over time. Its use to someone will drop rapidly. One example sometimes used is that of an ice cream cone. A discount rate for it will be high, even though it is desirable. In a few minutes, whether it is eaten or not, the ice cream will be gone. On the other hand, if something has a low discount rate, its value will only slowly decrease over time.

Discount rates will be used to discuss a specific conservation example—energy ratings on refrigerators. By federal regulation, all these appliances have to have a big label attached to them stating how much electricity they would use under normal conditions. The label is only an approximation to the truth, of course. Each family will use a refrigerator—or any other appliance for that matter—in a different way. There is thus some variability that should be attached to the single number on the label. For the sake of argument, assume that the number giving the refrigerator's annual electricity bill is perfectly accurate.

There is another number attached to each refrigerator in the showroom—its cost. My tour of an appliance showroom suggested that the lower the estimated electricity bill, the higher the cost of the refrigerator. To produce greater energy savings, there must be more insulation, perhaps a more expensive design for the motor, and so on. There are exceptions to this rule, but not many.

Let us take a specific although hypothetical example. Refrigerator A costs $600, and is expected to run up a $100 electric bill annually. B costs $700, but will cost only $80 in electricity every year. Assume that A and B are exactly the same in every other feature—size, color, arrangement of shelves, and so on.

Now you have to decide: A or B? If B saves $20 a year in electricity compared to A, then it will take five years to recoup the difference in initial cost.

Suppose you have a low discount rate in your mind. (Few people other than economists take the time to work out the mathematics.) You would then go for B, the energy-saving model. You are expecting to use it for more than five years. You will get back the extra outlay since you are so patient.

But suppose that you have to buy a new refrigerator in the same week that you discover that your roof is leaking and that your daughter has been accepted into Harvard. Finances are tight. In that case, the initial cost is just about everything. You would tend to ignore the energy label on the refrigerator's side. You would reason, "I might not own this appliance in five years, so why should I worry about its energy use? Besides, I really can use the extra $100 right now." Economists would say that in this case you would have a high discount rate. You would be living only for the moment, or close to it.

Consumers are a mixture of those with high discount rates when it comes to energy conservation, those with low discount rates, and most somewhere in-between.

What do consumers buy when they have a chance to save energy? Professor Kenneth Train studied this with real prices paid by consumers for appliances and other hard goods.[2] He found that, for many appliances and automobiles, discount rates (allowing for inflation) were often very high, ranging up to 20, 40, and even 100 percent. Unless most consumers can get their extra outlay for energy conservation within one (corresponding to a discount rate of 100 percent) to three (a discount rate of 33 percent) years, they will not spend the extra money needed. As a result, many energy saving innovations that look good on paper or in the lab flop in the marketplace.

All this is in great contrast to what we read, see, and hear in the media. According to press reports, consumers are champing at the bit to use energy conservation measures. It is only the oil companies and electric utilities that are holding them back. Neither of these two statements is true, based on Train's research.

The exact value of consumer energy savings discount rates are not of importance here. What is significant is that study after study shows that they are high. Conservation is not worth much in the eyes of consumers. What they say outside the showroom door and what they do while inside are two different matters.

• • •

A number related to discount rates is the rate of interest. We tend to worry about interest rates primarily when we make a payment on a credit card or look for a mortgage. The rest of the time they are confined to the financial pages, but interest levels strongly affect how much conservation we will pursue. As Nathan Rosenberg, of the Economics Department at Stanford University, has said, "A society in which the cost of capital is low will thus find it worth while to pursue improved energy efficiency much further than one in which the cost of capital is high. It is astonishing that this consideration does not receive much more explicit and prominent attention in discussions of prospects for greater energy efficiency."[3]

The reason is not difficult to find. Many, though not all, conservation measures are capital intensive, with a long payback time. We can spend hundreds of dollars to put insulation in the attic, but it may be many years before we recover the investment. If we pay 1 percent interest on a loan for the insulation, we will get our payback much sooner than if the rate is 10 percent or 15 percent. We do not have to be bankers to figure that one out.

So if we want to spread conservation measures, we have to pressure the Federal Reserve Board, urging them to keep interest rates at the lowest levels.

Alas, this creates a countervailing pressure to *increase*, not decrease, the use of energy. When interest rates are low, business will boom. New factories will spring up. Consumers will rush out to buy new cars, houses, VCRs, and trips to Bermuda. It will be Christmas in July and all the other months.

What will happen to energy use? With all this frenzied economic activity as loans become almost interest free, there is only one way for it to go—up. The added investment in conservation measures due to the low interest rates will slow the increase somewhat, but there is little question that more energy than ever will be consumed. The lure of low interest rates will not accomplish its goal of cutting down total energy use.

• • •

Talk about economics often leads, directly or indirectly, to talk about taxes. One of the major ways that conservation was boosted by government actions during the 1970s and 1980s was by means of tax credits. Companies could take a direct tax credit from either the federal or state government for saving energy. Most of the publicity for these energy laws went to the solar- and wind-powered aspects, but conservation spending was also included.

A tax credit is much better than a deduction, from the taxpayer's viewpoint. Using a tax deduction, if someone spends $100 to save energy, they subtract that amount from their total income. If they are in the 30 percent marginal tax bracket, they reduce their taxes by $30. On the other hand, if they have a tax credit for $100, they can subtract this amount directly from their taxes. Since most people pay more than $100 in income taxes annually, almost everyone, in this example, will save $100.

There is no need to detail all the various conservation tax credits and initiatives that were offered in the past. They changed from year to year and state to state. Describing them all would take up too much space.

One of the major distinctions between tax credits and deductions is that lawmakers only give the former to the most important societal goals. For example, home ownership is clearly a major national objective, but interest paid toward mortgage interest is only a deduction, not a credit.

Conservation of energy apparently is an issue that was even more important to lawmakers. It often got tax credits, not deductions.

Do these laws accomplish anything? Remember that some types of conservation are going on all the time. New inventions that save energy are patented and put on the market. People are not going to use more energy than necessary to perform a specific task if they can get the same result using less energy and money.

So determining exactly what these conservation tax credits have accomplished is a tricky statistical task. Michael Walsh, of the Chicago Board of Trade, has performed the feat.[4] He found that energy tax credits do not lead to more widespread or extensive energy conservation activities. About the same degree of conservation took place before the tax credit laws were passed as after. The main difference is the U.S. Treasury and state governments were out billions of dollars for these credits. They had to make up the difference by taxing the rest of us that much more. Walsh's work is only one of many studies to come to this conclusion.

The conservation tax credit laws were based on a false assumption: that conservation as defined in the laws really exists. It does not. The result was inevitable as the night following the day. Billions were wasted, and the amounts had to come out of the pockets of those who did not get the credits. It would be wonderful to say that lawmakers have learned a lesson from all this, but few have.

• • •

We can go from tax credits to how conservation is affected by tariffs on energy. Many people have advocated taxing foreign oil heavily to conserve supposedly dwindling resources. According to William Baumol, demand–supply curves applicable to tariffs look like Figure 15.2.[5] These curves are used by economists to plot the relationship between what we want and what we can obtain.

In Figure 15.2, the quantity of energy supplied is the horizontal axis, and the price is plotted on the vertical axis. We will start with demand curve D and supply curve S, which intersect at point O. Dropping a vertical line from that point to the horizontal axis yields a quantity used Q_0. In the same way, the price P_0 (of the curves D and S) is found by drawing a horizontal line from point O to the vertical price axis.

The demand curve D slopes upward to the left. When the price of any commodity rises, we demand less of it. Starting from the right-hand side, the supply curve S slopes downward to the left. As the price drops, producers will supply less and less of a commodity.

Figure 15.2
Effect of Tariffs and/or Taxes on Demand–Supply Curves

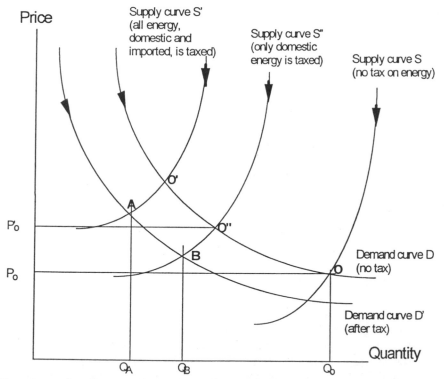

From time to time, Washington proposes a tariff on foreign oil, but putting a tariff on that oil would drain domestic supplies first. The difference per year in the quantity of U.S. oil used would be $Q_B - Q_A$. The amount comes about from moving the supply curve from S, its original shape, to S″, after the imposition of a tariff.

Consider the effect of tariffs or levies on imported goods. Suppose that all energy is imported, and a tariff is placed on it. This will produce the new supply curve S′, somewhere to the left of the original curve S. How far over curve S′ is compared to curve S will depend on the level of the tariff. If it is small, S′ will be close to S; if it is large, S′ will be much to the left.

The equilibrium point, or where demand meets supply, moves up the demand curve D to point O′. The quantity demanded decreases as the price increases. To put this another way, point O′ is to the left of point O.

The increase in price will eventually reduce demand to curve D′, below the original curve D. This is borne out by historical evidence. In the 1960s and early 1970s, electric companies projected an annual growth of about 7 percent. They forgot that the price of electricity might rise. When it did, as a result of the oil shocks and other factors, annual growth slumped to 2 to 3 percent, and sometimes zero.

The intersection of the two new curves, S′ and D′, is point A. The new quantity used is then Q_A, found by dropping a vertical line down from point A to the horizontal quantity axis. The amount of energy "saved" as a result of the tariff is then Q_o minus Q_A, the difference between the original and final quantities. Quotation marks are used around the word "saved" because, as noted elsewhere, there is no global saving. The country imposing the tariff may use less energy, but the world as a whole does not.

In the United States, almost all electricity is generated internally. A small amount is imported from Canada, a tiny proportion of the whole. About the same conclusions can be drawn about natural gas and coal.

Oil is different. In recent years, the United States has imported about half of the petroleum it uses.[6] The proportion will likely increase in future decades. The United States, in petroleum industry jargon, is a well-developed province. It is highly unlikely that new giant fields will be found, at least in the lower forty-eight states.

If a tariff is imposed on imported oil but U.S. oil is untaxed, the resultant supply curve will be S″, somewhere between S and S′. Recall that the second supply curve, S′, was based on the assumption that all energy is subject to a tariff or tax. Thus, curve S″ will lie to the right of curve S′. The distance that curve S″ lies to the right of curve S′ will depend on the level of oil imports and tariffs.

The equilibrium point after the tariff on imported oil is applied is now point O″, with an equilibrium price of P'_o. The price P'_o is found by drawing a horizontal line from point O″ to the vertical price axis. Because the new price P'_o is greater than the initial price P_o, demand will fall. For simplicity, we will assume that the final demand curve D′ is the same one as used in the previous example, when we assumed that all energy had a tax.

Then, the final point of demand–supply equilibrium is point B. The price at point B is lower than the price at A, as expected. The quantity used is Q_B, found by drawing a vertical line down from point B to the horizontal axis.

Quantity Q_B is greater than Q_A. The difference in quantity used between the two scenarios is then Q_B minus Q_A.[7] This implies that if we tax only foreign oil, we must supply Q_B minus Q_A units of oil compared to the situation where we tax all oil.

Where would the extra oil come from? Foreign oil has been made more expensive than domestic because of the tariff on imports. The extra oil can come from only one source: American wells. So, as Baumol writes, "Putting a tariff on foreign sources would indeed drain domestic supplies before the time they would disappear without a tariff. In turn, reliance on foreign supplies will come sooner than would be the case without a tariff."[8]

While tariffs on imported oil have been proposed to aid conservation, Figure 15.2 shows conclusively that they would only deplete American oil faster. This is another example of well-meaning efforts having the result opposite to that intended.

• • •

Until the 1970s, anyone trying to sell electricity to the power company might as well have tried buying a ticket for a moon flight. It just was not done.

Congress changed all that with the arrival of PURPA—the Public Utilities Regulation and Planning Act. Under this law, independent power producers—those not affiliated with the large utilities that had supplied almost all power—can sell electricity to those utilities. The latter have to buy it from their new suppliers.

There is one catch as far as independent electricity producers are concerned. Suppose the utility needs a new capacity of X kilowatts, and a variety of independent producers want to sell them 2X kilowatts. The utility does not want to buy more than it needs.

Which companies should the utilities choose? The law requires utilities to sell the lowest-cost power, consistent with other requirements such as reliability. One way of choosing which independent producers to use would be to have an auction.

For example, suppose there were ten companies bidding for the right to sell power to a utility. Some produce their power by wind, others by natural gas, hydroelectric, and a variety of sources. The utility president says, "Who can sell us power at 3¢ per kilowatt hour?" Someone in the corner pipes up, "I can supply power of 50 kilowatts at that price."

The utility responds, "You're in. Mark him down for 50 kilowatts at 3¢ per kWhr. Now who else can supply us with electricity at 4¢ per kilowatt hour?"

Someone else speaks up. The auction goes on until the needs of the utility have been satisfied. By economic definition, it has received the lowest-cost power and energy for its customers.

What does all this have to do with conservation? The key to the existing system, as far as some environmentalists are concerned, is its emphasis on production. Only producers of energy enter the auction. Conservers of energy, such as those who might produce a more efficient lightbulb, are excluded.

The solution, from their viewpoint, is to have conservers as well as producers take part. It would then proceed as follows: The utility president would again enter the room and start the bidding. It would sound a little different: "We're starting the bidding again at 3¢ per kWhr. We'll entertain bids for either energy production or conservation this time. Any bidders? That lady in the corner? You will save energy by installing conserving hot water heaters, and you can do it for 3¢ a kWhr. Just how much capacity will you save? 100 kilowatts? Good. That's the first bid, and now we'll take bids at 3½¢ per kWhr."

That is the way a conservation auction would work, in principle. What could be fairer? Why should utilities and their customers pay 4¢ for production if they can conserve the same amount of electricity for 3¢?

One question looms over this rosy picture: Does it have any relation to reality? Not really. If conservation does not really exist in the popular sense, then the offer of 3½ or 4¢, or any amount per kWhr, does not mean anything. If conservation does not exist, then the price per kWhr of energy conserved is not a few cents, but infinite.

Let us see why this comes about. Suppose the head of the "conservation company" has a new lightbulb that produces the same illumination as regular lightbulbs but uses less energy. Anyone who visits a hardware store has seen floodlights that use 120 watts but are claimed to have the lighting ability of 150 watts.

She says that if the utility gives her a contract, she will ensure that a million of these lightbulbs are installed. She will do this by posters, brochures, advertisements on television and radio, and everything else that Madison Avenue has dreamed up.

So far, all this is plausible. Some lightbulbs and appliances require less energy than others. If you go into an appliance store, you will see labels on refrigerators, stoves, and the like stating how much energy they use in normal operation. Some use more than others.

Now comes the tricky part. The executive of the conservation company says, "My lightbulbs, on average, will use 50 kWhr each year less than the ones they replace. If I install one million lightbulbs in this region, consumers will save 50 times one million, or 50 million kWhr in one year. These are the savings I am claiming. It forms part of the contract we have signed."

But this claim takes no account of the bounce-back effect, where people use more energy because of their new-found savings. Even if that new lightbulb does save 50 kWhr per year, for many people the overall electric bill remains about the same. As far as the utility is concerned, nothing has happened, except they have paid the conservation company a bundle to install their lightbulbs.

The second reason why the conservation may not work as advertised is the overall economic effect. Suppose that the region's energy use is insulated from the rest of the world. That is, no energy flows in and none flows out.

Now the thousands of lightbulbs are installed throughout the region. Suppose further that the bounce-back effect does not take place. Ratepayers actually save 50 kWhr annually per new lightbulb on their electric bills.

On this basis, it would seem the conservation company has really earned their money. Energy use by ratepayers has indeed gone down. But this means that there is more energy for other uses, such as transportation, industry, and so on. When there is more energy available, its price will go down. So people will buy bigger cars and industry will use more energy to produce their products. The utility will need less energy to generate its electricity, as the conservation company predicted. However, energy use in the region by everyone except the utility will go up. Putting it another way, the utility will produce less energy. Everyone else will use more. Society as a whole will be about the same as before the new lightbulbs went in.

When the conservation auction was first proposed, utilities were skeptical, but cautious. Criticizing conservation can sometimes lead to accusations of being an unholy combination of Attila the Hun and Adolf Hitler. Eventually, however, the utilities threw cold water on the conservation auction. And underwater it has remained ever since.

• • •

If conservation truly produced something of value, then at least some individuals should be getting fabulously rich from it, just as when some useful new product or service is introduced. Consider the state of personal computers around 1976. While computers had been developed in World War II they were huge and complicated. Only the largest companies, like Univac or IBM, could manufacture them. They were used only by giant government agencies, like the Social Security Administration, or mammoth companies like General Motors.

Yet many articles had been written over the years, prophesying that one day almost everyone would have their own computer (the phrase personal computer had not been coined). It still seemed impossible by the mid-1970s, about three decades after the first clumsy computer, run by thousands of vacuum tubes, had been installed. It still took a massive amount of training to operate one, as well as a wallet stuffed with enormous amounts of cash. Computers were housed in special air-conditioned rooms and approached by white-coated technicians like an altar in a Gothic cathedral. The goal of everyone having their own computer seemed as far off as the post–World War II objective of an airplane in every garage.

But the computer buffs around San Francisco Bay had not given up on the dream. By stringing together bits of tape recorders and other electronic equipment from Radio Shack and Heathkit, they were able to put together the first crude personal computers (PCs). These simple models did not work much faster than a hand-held calculator, but they allowed an individual to do something on a computer for himself, rather than waiting on a computer operator.

Some of those developing the first PCs concentrated only on producing a new and fancy toy. Others, perhaps more selfless, were interested in bettering the lot of mankind. Yet others, in the capitalistic tradition, realized that enormous amounts of money could be made by producing better software or hardware.

One of the early computer whizzes, Bill Gates, head of Microsoft, later emerged as the wealthiest man in America according to some surveys. PCs and their associated software proved to be enormously profitable. In the process, they changed worldwide business more than any other recent invention.

One aspect of the PC revolution which is rarely noted is that little of it was done through government regulation or subsidies. The first giant computers were developed mostly through government. World War II raged, and Washington dominated most activities. The first computer bought commercially went to a big government agency, the Census Bureau.

All this may seem to have little to do with conservation, but where are the conservation millionaires corresponding to the computer millionaires? Conservation is held out by some people as an unparalleled opportunity for new and innovative businesses to make money. Build novel and more efficient lightbulbs, cars, and the like, and your bank account will have untold numbers of zeroes. Even better, there is no need to rely on the heavy hand of government bureaucracy doling out contracts to its favorites. Just invent ways to save even more energy, and the pot of gold at the end of the rainbow will be yours.

It did not quite happen this way. If there are any conservation millionaires around, they have managed to keep off the *Forbes 400* list. And a large proportion of conservation measures have been sponsored by governments at every level.

To illustrate the dearth of new conservation millionaires, the largest expenditures on conservation have been in the field of home insulation using fiberglass and other simple materials. But these were invented years ago, and the field was dominated by large firms, such as Dow Corning. Money was made for stockholders by the sales upsurge because of greater emphasis on conservation. But no inventor appeared on the scene to make fiberglass at half the price and with twice the insulating qualities.

About the same thing happened with the fluorescent lightbulbs that were designed to replace incandescents at a great savings in energy. The field is dominated by companies like General Electric that have been making lightbulbs since the turn of the century. If an inventor has come along with a magic bulb that uses no more current than a flashlight but can light a baseball stadium, he has not made many headlines.

So all of this indicates that in spite of the talk about a conservation revolution, it has not taken place. If it had, we would be seeing conservation millionaires who made their money saving energy using a bit of it as they ride around in their Rolls Royces.

• • •

In the spring and summer of 1993, national debate raged on the merits of President Clinton's five-year budget proposals. Economists and politicians battled over whether the new taxes proposed would retard the economy or help it in the long run.

Along with the tax increases went budget cuts. The idea was that the American people had the will to sacrifice, as long-time government programs were reduced or even eliminated.

Economists soon noticed something peculiar about the proposed budget cuts. Most of them had one of two features. First, many were to be instituted after 1996, when President Clinton's first term would end. Thus, if these cuts were to be carried out, the first Clinton administration would not feel the heat. In the view of most politicians, the next administration seems to be a lifetime away. The second feature, for those programs slated to be cut promptly, was a decrease in the rate of increase. For budget purposes, this was counted as a cut.

By way of example, suppose there was a program costing $2 billion annually, and rising at the rate of 10 percent a year. The administration might propose that it rise at the rate of 6 percent annually. The difference of 4 percent of $2 billion, or $80 million, would be counted as a cut under their budget. Forget that spending for this program would be $2.12 billion the next year (an increase of 6 percent), $2.25 billion the following one, and so on. A budget cut is a budget cut.

This is not the place to discuss whether the President's budget was right or wrong. Some observers felt that the President had taken a few baby steps toward solving the seemingly perpetual budget deficit (it has not been in balance since 1969), although his accounting methods were a little strange.

There is an analogy here with the equally odd accounting methods used for conservation programs. We say that so many fuel-conserving cars are to be on the road, or a given number of electricity-saving lightbulbs are to be screwed into sockets. We can easily calculate the savings on the back of an envelope, and thus the savings must be real.

Most of the "savings" are fictional at best, and the process may increase, rather than decrease, energy use. As explained before, a reduction of energy use in one area will likely boost energy consumption in another. Yet some energy planners continue to use as gospel the numbers they have calculated, without looking into them. In both the fiscal year 1994 Clinton budget and the analogous energy savings budgets beloved of energy bureaucrats, the cuts are airplanes taking off on flights of fancy. Were they taking lessons from each other?

• • •

Some conservation measures require new capital spending by consumers, and others apparently do not. When the government imposes electricity usage standards on new refrigerators, for example, the new refrigerators may cost more than previous less efficient models. Of course, if a consumer rushes out to buy a new, more efficient refrigerator primarily to save electricity, this would count as a capital expenditure.

Other measures do require capital outlays to achieve energy savings. The prime example is that of adding insulation to existing houses. The homeowner must spend money in the hope of recouping it over the years in reduced energy costs.

Where should this money come from? D. J. Miller, the Director of Engineering with a British electric utility, discussed this some years ago:

The problem of insulating houses is primarily that of finding the capital. It has been estimated that to insulate a typical post World War II semi-detached house [in Britain] would cost between £1,500 - 2,000 [about $2800 to $3800]. Not many people can raise such sums of money, however cost-effective the measures might be. The fervent advocates of conservation are quick to suggest that the Government should give financial incentives to householders. But there are more important demands on the money available.[9]

We replace refrigerators when they wear out. When we go to the show-room, we see a wide range of models. Some use more electricity, or so the labels claim, than others. Nobody suggests that there be subsidies to help people buy the refrigerators that consume the smallest amount of electricity. If such a proposal were enacted, it would involve the outlay of considerable capital by the government. Yet such a proposal has been made—and in some states, implemented—for home insulation. Some utilities have been required by the public utility commissions that regulate them to lend their customers money for insulation at low or zero interest rates.

The utility must raise capital for distribution to the small proportion of their customers that plan to install insulation. While the government itself is not supplying the money, the utility would never do it if the government, either in the form of a public utility commission or Washington, did not re-quire it. Utilities are generally in the business of supplying electricity or gas, not money lending.

Utilities, like any other business, have only a limited amount of capital they can raise. If they are lending it out to homeowners to buy insulation, there will be less capital to build new power plants, or even to repair the existing ones. Conservation advocates say that the amount of energy saved by the insulation that the utilities are subsidizing will be much more than energy that would have been produced by the power plants that will never be built. Everyone will come out ahead.

This is just a claim. If there is any proof behind it, the numbers have not seen the light of day. As noted elsewhere, it is far from clear that conserva-tion, which in this context can be defined as a decrease in the total amount of energy used by a utility's customers, really exists. The energy that some homeowners save because of their new insulation will be used by other homeowners who leave the lights on a little longer than before. The utility will find that the amount of energy it supplies will be about the same.

Their financial picture will be gloomier, however. The interest they could have earned on the money they loaned out to some homeowners will be lost forever. The conservation subsidy program is a method for ensuring that all of us pay higher electricity and gas rates.

• • •

Some time back there was a report on National Public Radio (NPR) about a "religious mutual fund," sponsored by the Mennonites, a pacifist group. Its spokesman said that it avoided investing in defense-related stocks like McDonnell-Douglas. It is not clear what could be called "peaceful stocks," but presumably these were everything outside the defense industry.

If someone invested in this fund, the money would not go to building tanks and missiles. If he or she was a pacifist, or someone uneasy about large de-fense budgets, this decision about what to do with the money would make them feel good.

But what would the overall effect be? This fund is tiny compared to the giants like Fidelity Magellan. The behemoth funds do not draw moral conclusions, at least in terms of defense, about which stocks they should buy. So unless the religious funds blossom, their effect will be like ripples on the ocean.

If religious funds did receive a sudden influx of billions, this would mean that many Americans wanted the defense budget to be slashed substantially. Defense stocks would plunge to the basement. So the religious funds by themselves will not affect matters that much. They would only be a mirror to changes in our attitudes toward defense spending.

The same results apply to conservation efforts. Someone may feel good in putting up more insulation and flicking a light off. Smugness will fade as they realize that somebody else now has more energy to waste. Those who do not invest in religious mutual funds will tend to treat defense stocks like other investments. If they imagine they can make money from them, their dollars will head there. If they think that defense will be a money-loser, they will invest in Microsoft or Wal-Mart.

The religious funds may satisfy their owners. In terms of overall effect on defense stocks, that is about all they will accomplish.

• • •

One of the phrases that economists often use is *input factors*. To produce a certain good or service takes inputs: raw materials, the cost of borrowing money, the cost of labor, and so on. One of these factors usually is the cost of energy.

To build a car, we have to factor in the cost of the raw materials: the iron ore, coal for steel, petrochemicals for plastics, leather if it is a luxury model, and the like. Then we add in the cost of paying the auto workers. We keep going down the list. We come to the cost of borrowing the money to build the factory, and the cost of land for the factory and other buildings. Finally, we add the cost of energy.

One way to reduce energy cost to the industry is for the government to impose conservation rules. The government would then be doing for automakers what the latter should have been doing all along, reducing the waste of energy. That way more jobs will be created in the domestic auto industry, and we will all come out ahead.

This rosy picture is not quite what it appears. First, if we produce more cars in this country, we will use more energy in the long run. Presumably those cars are produced for transportation, not to sit immobile in someone's garage.

The second point gets to the meaning of input factors. Why should the government reduce the cost of one input factor, energy, and not the others? To encourage energy conservation, for example, the government could pay auto companies a subsidy if they install more energy-efficient machinery. This will, all other aspects being equal, reduce their energy cost. The total cost of the products they produce will drop.

Why energy and not the cost of money? The government could just as well subsidize the cost of General Motors' borrowing. If the market rate for a GM bond was 7 percent, the government could offer to write a check to reduce this to 6 percent. GM would reduce their costs by this method just as well as the conservation route.

About the same argument could be made for any of the other input factors going into the cost of a car. The government could subsidize the cost of land, health care, wages, and a host of other costs.

There is no inherent reason why, if the government decides to subsidize the auto companies in some way—to preserve jobs or for other reasons—it should concentrate on energy as opposed to other factor costs. If the government subsidizes one factor cost to the exclusion of others, the total result will be "sub-optimal," to use economics jargon.

Suppose we as a society have decided to save our car industry from foreign competition at all costs. It would be better to reduce most, if not all, of the factor costs, rather than focus on one, regardless of how desirable it appears at first glance.

The example of the auto industry could be applied to all the goods and services we as a nation produce. Having the government subsidize, directly or indirectly, just the cost of energy by requiring conservation will almost certainly not yield the desired result of reducing total costs.

NOTES

1. Friedrich A. Hayek, *The Constitution of Liberty* (Chicago: University of Chicago Press, 1960), 369–370.

2. Kenneth E. Train, "Discount Rates in Consumers' Energy-Related Decisions: A Review of the Literature," *Energy* 10 (Dec. 1985): 1243–1253.

3. Nathan Rosenberg, "Energy Efficient Technologies: Past and Future Perspectives," paper presented at the conference, "How Far Can the World Get on Energy Efficiency Alone?" Oak Ridge National Laboratory, Oak Ridge, Tenn., Aug. 1989.

4. Michael J. Walsh, "Energy Tax Credits and Housing Improvement," *Energy Economics* 11, no. 4 (Oct. 1989): 275–284.

5. Discussed in such articles as William J. Baumol, "On Recycling as a Moot Environmental Issue," *Journal of Environmental Economics and Management* 4 (1977): 83; William J. Baumol and Edward N. Wolff, "Subsidies to New Energy Sources: Do They Add to Energy Stocks?" *Journal of Political Economy* 89, no. 5 (1981): 891.

6. Matthew Wald, "Oil Imports Are Up. Fretting about It Is Down," *New York Times*, 26 Jan. 1997, sec. 4, p. 3.

7. Q_B minus Q_A will depend on the size of the tariff (going from supply curve S to S′), the proportion of imported oil (distance OO″ divided by distance OO′), and the elasticities of supply and demand in the economic region under consideration.

8. Baumol, "On Recycling."

9. D. J. Miller, "Alternative Energy Sources," in *Nuclear or Not? Choices for Our Energy Future*, ed. Gerald Foley and Ariane van Buren (London: Heinemann Educational Books, 1978), 101–106.

16

Selling Energy Conservation

Appliances that supposedly conserve energy, such as fluorescent lightbulbs designed to replace the familiar incandescent ones, are in stores. In addition, there are now whole catalogs of these allegedly energy-saving devices and equipment. It is worthwhile to take a brief tour through one of them.[1]

• • •

First, the bad news. Not one of the contraptions pictured can save energy overall or globally. What one citizen saves, another, somewhere in the world, squanders. The situation, as far as the globe is concerned, is the same as before. However, there are some items in the catalog (*Real Goods*) that may save energy, water, or other resources for their owners, if not for the nation or the world. In some cases, the cost to do so is reasonable. In others, the price for conserving a kilowatt hour or two is astronomical.

The analogy is wearing sweaters to save heating costs. If you just reach for a sweater that you already have in a drawer or closet, you are paying close to nothing for the chance to lower the thermostat a bit. (Of course, sweaters eventually wear out, but we will assume that this may take years.) But you may rush out to buy sweaters made of wool from Angora rabbits, fed on nothing but organically grown carrots, and created by a famous French designer. Those sweaters may cost hundreds of dollars. Chances are you will never recover your investment. You may be the smartest-looking person on your block, but that has nothing to do with conservation.

In the following, there is no attempt to deter anyone from buying from the *Real Goods* catalog, or any other catalog for that matter. People have the right to make up their own minds. If catalog publishers could not rely on flights of fancy, they would go out of business. However, in the long run, we are all better off for having more knowledge, not less.

Let us start with the basics—recycled toilet paper. It is obvious that the more paper is reused, the fewer trees will be cut down. The catalog advertises twelve rolls using recycled paper at $8, and ninety-six rolls for $55. This is between 55 and 70¢ a roll. At the supermarket, you can buy a roll for as little as 25¢ for a house brand. National brands cost more, but still less than the recycled variety. For most people, at those prices, the trees will still be crashing down.

Page 21 of the catalog has a variety of water-saving showerheads. Each of them would save water, but to what end? Many water bills in this country are calculated by tax assessors counting the number of bathtubs and showers in the house, not the actual amount of water use. There is no meter. So if those without meters save water by installing these special showerheads—or taking fewer showers—they have saved exactly nothing.

Of course, those people who have their water metered may save money in the long run. New showerheads do not cost that much. But a new water-saving toilet—between $190 and $215 on page 22 of the catalog—might take decades to pay back its cost for metered water customers. A brick in the tank, costing perhaps a quarter, would do almost the same job for close to nothing. It seems as if conservationists have succumbed to the same consumerism that afflicts the rest of us.

For those who are wondering what to do with all the water they have saved, there is an answer on page 13—an automatic water sprinkler. Press a button, and you can water your lawn for up to twenty-four hours, according to the blurb. Few would be so wasteful as to water the grass for a whole day, but presumably the water saved from those efficient showerheads has to go someplace.

The above descriptions may have suggested that everything in the catalog is nonsensical or too expensive. Not true. One of the ways it makes sense is with tankless water heaters. As the catalog states, "Keeping 40 gallons of water hot at all times in case you might need it is the same as leaving your car running in the garage 24 hours per day, seven days a week, just in case you might decide to go for a drive."

In much of Europe and Japan, citizens heat water on the spot, with a gas heater under a small tank of water. Many Americans have used them on foreign trips and never ran out of hot water in the middle of a shower.

Again, the world as a whole cannot profit from this device. But the homeowner can. Just how much he or she will save will depend on the cost of the device. Some can be expensive, ranging up to $900 for a large model. Some are cheaper, going down to as low as $245 in the catalog. Many users will come out ahead financially, but those who use massive amounts of hot water every day probably will not.

The catalog also lists a number of solar energy collectors. In principle, this has little if anything to do with conservation. We can be just as wasteful or thrifty using solar or wind energy as the more conventional kind. It is just another type of energy production.

Some proponents of solar and other nonconventional energy say that since it uses "free" energy from the sun, the amount of resources used will be less. These statements are not quite true, since the solar collectors themselves use materials such as steel, copper, and glass.[2]

Page 24 of the catalog shows some used solar collectors, formerly employed in a California power plant. Depending on the number ordered, the price varies from $450 to $500 a panel. What do you get for this? The panel is rated at 100 watts. When the sun is beating down, that is the maximum obtainable. The sun does not shine all the time. A typical *capacity factor*—the ratio of actual output to the theoretical maximum—might be about 20 percent, or 0.2. On average, about 480 watt-hours might be produced each day (0.2 × 24 × 100; the number 24 refers to the hours in a day).

The average price per kilowatt hour of electricity in recent years has been about 8¢. 480 watt-hours is 0.48 kilowatt hours, so the money saved daily is about 4¢ (8¢ × 0.48). It would take a week to save a quarter's worth of electricity, hardly a bargain for something that cost about $500. Somehow the notion of conservation—saving, not spending—seems to be lost here.

The solar panel described is just that, a bare panel. It produces electricity at a voltage of 18 volts. Everything in ordinary houses works at 110 volts, with the exception of the dryer and the electric range. Converting the voltage would cost extra, as would batteries for the times when the sun does not shine.

Not to worry. All these problems are taken into account in photovoltaic systems created for whole houses, described on page 25. The biggest, constructed for larger homes, costs $10,500. In principle, you could plug in all your present appliances without worrying about voltage and other electrical mysteries.

Would you be coming out ahead in terms of energy conservation? The catalog says that the system produces 3.6 kilowatt hours on average each day. Again at 8¢, this is 29¢ of electricity every day (8¢ × 3.6).

Is it worth over $10,000 to produce this? Without getting into complicated equations and mathematics, I will use a rule of thumb from real estate agents. On average, depending on the interest rate, a mortgage amortized over thirty years requires about 1 percent of the original amount to be paid every month. In other words, if you take out a $100,000 mortgage at rates on the order of 8 to 9 percent (prevailing over much of the mid-1990s), you would have to pay about $1,000 monthly to retire it over three decades.

Suppose that the photovoltaic system lasted thirty years, quite an accomplishment. It is doubtful that a complete system has ever lasted that long. This means that the $10,000 invested is the equivalent of $100 monthly, again depending on interest rates. The rates on an add-on system such as this might be higher than mortgage rates.

If we save 29¢ a day, we reduce our electric bill by about $9 a month. But we are paying $100 a month, every month, for the privilege of sticking it to the electric company. Conservation still has a long way to go.

One of the biggest users of electricity in the average house is undoubtedly the refrigerator. Of course, some of that usage is because teenagers spend too much time contemplating its contents. There is no question that the standard refrigerator could become more energy efficient by making the insulation in its walls thicker.

How much is this greater efficiency worth? The catalog shows what they call the "Sun Frost," allegedly the world's most efficient refrigerator. As expected, it does have thicker walls and doors. Because of that, the interior space is small. The model shown has only twelve cubic feet, which makes it close to the smallest on the market, not counting office-style small refrigerators. While prices vary for these appliances, you could probably get a twelve-cubic-foot model for about $600 without extensive shopping around.

The Sun Frost costs $2,400, or four times as much. We can forego the arithmetic, but it seems likely that it would be a long time, if ever, before the large investment is paid off by the energy savings. Conservation loses again.

Some advocate fluorescent lightbulbs as replacements for incandescent ones. Are they worth it? While prices vary from brand to brand, one listed on page 42 of the catalog costs $25. It requires 18 watts of power, and is stated to produce the same amount of light as a 75-watt incandescent bulb. In deciding if we come out ahead by buying this bulb, recall that most people do not like the light from fluorescent bulbs. If they did, most houses would now be lit by them. Almost everyone knows that a fluorescent uses less electricity than incandescents for the same light output, and still they are confined primarily to offices and factories.

Let us suppose that we have all been psychologically transformed, and fluorescent is the same as incandescent to us. How much do we save? Suppose the bulb is on for two hours a day. In those two hours, we have saved

$$(75 - 18) \times 2 = 114 \text{ watt-hours}$$

where the numbers in the brackets are the wattage ratings of the two types of lightbulbs. Over a year, we would save

$$114 \times 365/1,000 = 42 \text{ kilowatt hours}$$

where the 1,000 reflects the change from watt-hours to kilowatt hours. Again using the rate of 8¢ per kilowatt hour, this is $3.32 saved annually (8¢ × 42). It would take about seven years to pay off the initial cost, not counting the money that would have been saved by investing the $25 in a bank. Few lightbulbs last seven years. It is doubtful that the fluorescent bulbs would last that long either. While estimated lifetimes are sometimes listed on packages, not many have much faith in these numbers. They always seem to burn out a lot faster than expected. The fluorescent ones probably will suffer the same fate. Again, conservation comes out a loser.

On one of the pages advertising the fluorescent bulbs is a message from Pacific Gas and Electric (PG&E), a California utility. All their customers can buy up to ten of these $25 fluorescent bulbs. They pay a reduced price of $15. Their maximum saving is then $100. Where does the money for this magnificent gesture come from? The other customers of PG&E, of course. The poverty-stricken residents of crime-ridden housing projects and slums of California, who never will read this catalog pitched at the affluents, are helping to pay for the well-to-do to indulge their tastes. Quite a commentary on how society is organized.

On the face of it, most of the proposed conservation measures from this catalog are money-losers. They may save a small amount of energy here and there, but the cost to do so far outweighs the savings in many cases.

There are, admittedly, a few devices, like the instantaneous hot water system, that probably will enable the average homeowner to come out ahead in both money and energy savings. But even the most efficient conservation device in this or any other catalog cannot save a bit of energy globally. What the readers of this catalog save—if they do save at all—will be used up by those who have never read it.

NOTES

1. Real Goods, *Catalog* (Ukiah, Calif.: Christmas, 1991), 48 pages.
2. See, for example, Herbert Inhaber, *Energy Risk Assessment* (New York: Gordon and Breach, 1982) for a detailed listing.

17

Resource Depletion

Perhaps the fundamental rationale behind conservation measures, other than the psychological one of waste, is that we are somehow running out of oil, gas, and other energy sources. The economists call this *resource depletion*.

About ten years ago, two academics made a bet. Ordinarily, this would not have attracted much attention. In this case, the prominence of the two professors assured that one day it would be reported in the pages of the *New York Times Magazine*.[1] One was Paul Ehrlich, a biology professor at Stanford University and the author of *The Population Bomb*. The other was Julian Simon, a professor of business at the University of Maryland. He has pioneered in applying economics to many fields, including the auction for overbooked aircraft.

The bet dealt with the change in prices of metals and commodities like aluminum. If we are running out of iron ore, bauxite, copper, and other materials, their prices should gradually rise over time. From year to year, that might not hold, as new ore bodies are discovered. However, over a long enough period, the materials should cost more and more. That is, if we are truly using them up.

Ehrlich, being a prominent environmentalist and believer in the "fixed amount of anything" theory, clearly thought that prices should rise. Simon was convinced that we cannot run out of anything in the ordinary sense. In his estimation, prices would fall or at most be about level.

Ordinarily, differences of opinion of this type are confined to cocktail party chitchat, and forgotten as quickly as the identity of the last hors d'oeuvre. In the case of Ehrlich and Simon, their differences were strong enough to inspire a bet, and a public one at that.

A decade later, the time of reckoning had come. Who won? Simon, of course. The price of all ten materials on the list the two professors had agreed on had either fallen or stayed about the same. The "Chicken Little" theory of history, in which we are rapidly running out of everything and anything, had again been disproved. We still hear trumpeting about running out of oil, wood, natural gas, iron ore, and a host of other commodities. At least those like Professor Simon, who thought that Chicken Little was a fraud and a windbag, got some satisfaction and a few dollars.

Jerry Taylor, in a speech to a conference in Washington, dredged up long-forgotten headlines that told of imminent oil and gas shortages.[2] None came true. One reason why this happened is because of the headlines themselves. They suggested to the industry that piles of money could be made. The oilmen (few women in those days) rushed out from enjoying a big cigar at the Petroleum Club, explored vigorously, and found new reserves. These prevented the very shortages predicted in the headlines.

We often confuse the annual listing of oil reserves with what is actually in the ground. Nobody on earth, even the greatest geologist, knows exactly how much oil, gas, coal, and uranium is beneath our feet. How much reserves the world has in a given year is a function of how much we are willing to pay for energy at that time. If the price is high, it can impel geologists to leave their offices for the field; if it is low, they may give up the profession entirely.

The following are a few of the hundreds of dire predictions that have been made in the last few decades. None of the authors of the predictions were punished for being wrong. They all went on to bigger and better things. But society as a whole would have suffered considerably if their gloomy advice had been followed. We would have had to install a gigantic government bureaucracy, the like of which the world had never seen, to ensure that not a bit of energy was being "wasted." It is a good thing those headlines are just yellowing newspaper clippings.

1. In 1939, just before World War II, the U.S. Department of the Interior said there was only a thirteen-year supply of oil left. Over five decades later U.S. reserves are far higher than in Roosevelt's time.

2. The State Department concluded in 1947 that no new oil reserves would be found in the United States. The very next year, 1948, marked the discovery of 4.8 billion barrels, the best yearly record until the discovery of the Prudhoe Bay fields in Alaska.

3. The Secretary of the Interior shortly afterward said that the end of U.S. oil supplies was around the corner. Yet production kept rising for the next five years.

4. The State Department said in 1950 that the world oil reserves would be gone in fourteen years.[3] These reserves multiplied by ten times in the interval.

5. In 1979, after the second oil shock, the International Energy Agency (IEA) in Paris said that the world's 645 billion barrels of oil reserves would be mostly gone in six years.[4] By 1990, only half of these original reserves had been used. New oil had been found in abundance, and total reserves now totaled about 1 trillion barrels, or 50 percent more than the 1979 levels.

These predictions, made by the experts of the time, fell flat on their face. Their authors were not stupid, but did not quite understand the link between geology and economics.

Some predictions about oil reserves can be true. Valid estimates can be made if their authors know that oil reserves are not inherently a fixed quantity, but as flexible as a baby's skin. Otherwise, predictions will be consigned to the scrap heap of forgotten studies.

• • •

While we can never know exactly how much of a specific mineral is still mineable, as Julian Simon noted in the famous bet, we can use a surrogate measure—its price. If the price rises inexorably, it is a good indication that we are, at least temporarily, depleting supplies. When the price of watermelons rises in the fall, we know that there are not too many left in the fields. We can determine this even without a drive in the country to investigate.

Take copper, for which we have long-term data. The economist Herfindel found that its price, allowing for inflation, had not risen significantly between 1870 and 1957.[5] In the more than thirty years since, this lack of trend has continued. Yet in those three decades the world used more copper than in all previous recorded history.

Hendrik Houthakker, an economist at Harvard, divides attitudes toward resources into two groups: the pessimists and the optimists,[6] The first considers it obvious that low-cost minerals will be exhausted within decades, if not sooner. This will ruin society, in their estimation.

The optimists, among whom most economists fall, think that we will always find substitutes. They point to the example of whale oil.

In the time of Herman Melville's *Moby Dick*, it was becoming clear that excessive hunting was reducing the stock of whales. No calculations were made at the time, but they would have shown that before long, all the whales would be dead. Then the lack of their oil for lighting lamps would have left everyone in the dark. As the price of whale oil skyrocketed, substitutes, such as coal oil, kerosene, and others were found. After a while, the price of whale oil meant nothing in particular.

The optimists find that copper is not the exception to the rule. The prices of minerals relative to all the other commodities in society has remained about constant for many years, allowing for blips from time to time. Yet these minerals were being depleted at historically unprecedented rates.

Houthakker describes mineral exhaustion in terms of a "backstop technology." When all the rich deposits of a particular mineral have been depleted, we can make do with ordinary rocks. As Houthakker writes, "One day, conceivably, copper would have to be extracted from common rock, where it occurs only in relatively minute amounts."[7] Of course, processing rocks would be more expensive than using mineral deposits, but it could be done. No mineral has had to use common rocks as a source. The progression of most minerals has been in just the opposite direction, from geochemically scarce to geochemically abundant.

For centuries, petroleum was found only in natural outcrops and leaks from the earth. Because it was so scarce, its uses were very limited. Geologists believed that there was little of it around. Along came Colonel Drake of Pennsylvania. In Titusville he showed that there was far more petroleum than anyone had ever dreamed of. Later, when it seemed that what he had found would be exhausted, the huge oil fields of the American Southwest and Saudi Arabia were discovered. What had seemed scarce became abundant.

None of this suggests that we should waste mineral resources, whatever that may mean. As well, recycling of some minerals will always occur. Almost all the gold that has ever been produced has been recycled. A few atoms of the gold chains around the neck of Cleopatra may be producing the same glittery effect on the finger of a young lady in the next office. But, the shouts that we are running out of this or that mineral and we must recycle or die are surely wrong. There is a lot more gold, copper, bauxite, iron ore, and other minerals in "them thar hills."

NOTES

1. John Tourney, "Betting on the Planet," *New York Times Magazine*, 2 Dec. 1990, 52.

2. Jerry Taylor, "Energy Conservation: The Case Against Coercion," Paper presented at the National Energy Policy: Central Planning Reconsidered conference, Cato Institute, Washington, D.C., 16 Jan. 1992.

3. "Fear Is Expressed of U.S. Oil Scarcity," *New York Times*, 11 June 1950.

4. Richard McKenzie, *The Sense and Nonsense of Energy Conservation* (Washington, D.C.: American Petroleum Institute, 1991).

5. Hendrik Houthakker, review of *Toward a New Iron Age? Quantitative Modeling of Resource Exhaustion*, by Robert B. Gordon, Tjalling C. Koopmans, William D. Nordhaus, and Brian J. Skinner, *Journal of Political Economy* 98 (April 1990): 440–445.

6. Ibid.

7. Ibid.

18

Workers and Energy Conservation

One of the major contentions of energy conservation proponents is that it creates more jobs than supplying new energy. More workers will be required to install insulation, per unit energy saved, than to drill oil wells, per unit energy produced. Since every economy is in continual need of new jobs, this makes conservation a "good thing." This chapter explores this contention.

• • •

The key question in determining whether conservation creates or destroys jobs is whether the conservation actions are subsidized, either by governments or electric utilities. If they are, the total number of jobs will decrease. If they are not, then the economy will select the appropriate number of jobs in both the conservation and the energy production industries.

Consider a specific example. For simplicity, assume all conservation is based on insulation manufacture, and all energy generation on oil production. Every year, a certain amount of insulation goes into attics, and so many barrels of petroleum are shipped to refineries. Both conservation and energy production, in this scenario, have a certain number of jobs associated with each.

These activities, and the number of jobs tied to them, go up and down depending on price and other factors. Before 1973, the date of the first oil shock, insulation production was weak. Now it is stronger.

Then the government steps in. It decides that conservation is more important than energy production, and subsidizes the former. This subsidy can be in the form of straight cash payments for those who conserve, or financial penalties on the energy production industries.

The number of jobs in conservation industries goes up, and those in oil production drop. If the number of jobs created in the former is greater than the number of jobs lost in the latter, then conservation is a clear winner. Or so it seems.

But these calculations ignore the effect on the rest of the economy, outside the conservation and energy production industries. All other businesses—and consumers—pay higher taxes for the extra subsidies to conservation. Because of these taxes, they will tend to employ fewer and fewer workers.

When we subtract the job losses in the rest of industry from the jobs created in the now-booming conservation field, we may well find that the total number of jobs has gone down, not up. Doing a wonderful thing for one segment of the economy often produces a drag—and resultant loss of jobs—on the economy as a whole.

• • •

Consider the fallacy of composition.[1] One economic or conservation proposal is applied to a small area of life. If it works, we start a second scheme. This also works, but not quite as well as the first one. Undaunted, we go on to a third, and we start to see failure looming. The extension of what seemed to be a good idea in one town or region flops when we extend it to the entire nation. Putting it in economics jargon, the sum of positive microeconomic effects can yield a negative macroeconomic effect when added together.

Take an example. The government wants to relieve unemployment, a noble goal. It spends so many millions of dollars in state A on a make-work scheme—perhaps shoveling dirt from one hole into another—and some previously unemployed people collect checks. The welfare rolls drop. The Works Project Administration under Franklin Roosevelt was accused of doing precisely this during the Great Depression, but it was never proved.

The scheme to relieve unemployment is microeconomics in the correct direction. The effect in state A is favorable. People there drop out of unemployment lines. Now the government, seeing a great success ahead, decides to set up the scheme in all states. It carefully tabulates the figures as the money is dispensed—so many thousands are put to work.

At the same time, something peculiar is happening to the rest of the economy. Factories are closing throughout the land. The overall unemployment rate, taking these new shut-downs into account, has gone up, not down.

Why has this happened? More and more taxes are levied on the working population to pay for uneconomic job-creation schemes. The goods and services the rest of us produce are gradually priced out of the international market. Imports flood in, and domestic factories shutter their doors. This happened to the U.S. steel industry in the 1970s and 1980s.

None of this implies that government schemes to relieve unemployment are inherently unworkable. Rather, they have to be designed so they do not suffer from the fallacy of composition, that is, producing an overall effect opposite to that of the successful small scale effect.

A government subsidy for one energy-saving measure may indeed conserve a resource. When the system is extended across many types of conservation, the total effect is likely to be the opposite of what was intended. The fallacy of composition takes over.

• • •

In many nations, labor unions are the prime intermediary between workers and capital. Put yourself in the position of a union official. The company president drops by your office. (This analogy comes from Len Brookes, an energy economist in Bournemouth, England).[2]

He says, "I want to tell you something before I announce it publicly. I plan to put in a rotatilt machine in building A. As you know, it takes seven workers to do the job there now. The new machine will let us do it with three workers."

Your first impulse is to say, "What a minute. That's going to put four brothers and sisters out of work. We just won't tolerate this."

If you are a union official who has taken a course or two in labor economics, you might not react that way. You might say to yourself, out of earshot of the company president, "It's true that four workers will be laid off when that new machine is installed. But the company has been putting in new machinery since I can remember. The workforce has gone up in size, not down, in spite of these changes. Maybe I shouldn't react too fast to this new machine."

At the same time you are mulling over employment effects, you have also indirectly addressed the issue of energy conservation. Most new machinery in the factory will tend to cause unemployment the day it is turned on. Yet if the industry as a whole improves its productivity with these machines, its overall employment will tend to rise, depending to some extent on what happens in the economy as a whole. The macro effect is then precisely the opposite from the micro effect.

In the same way, we buy a more energy-efficient car than our old one. Our micro effect is that we use less energy to get from point A to point B. But overall energy use will tend to rise, as Jevons predicted in the nineteenth century. People will drive more as they use less gasoline in their spiffy new models. More cars will be bought, as gasoline becomes a smaller and smaller fraction of a household's budget. Overall, the gasoline pumps will be busier than ever.

The computer was first introduced commercially in the 1950s. At that time, hundreds of thousands, if not millions, of people worked in the data industry, transferring numbers painfully from ledger book to ledger book—by hand. It was obvious to almost everyone that, as computers became more common, most of those people would be spending their time in the unemployment lines. A few computers would handle all the nation's data needs.

Precisely the opposite happened. We now have millions of computers, large and small. The manuscript for this book was typed on one. Yet the demand for labor in the data handling and processing field has grown tremendously. More people work in it than ever before.

Each time a new piece of equipment is plugged in, unions could obstruct it with slowdowns and wildcat strikes. While these happen from time to time, union officials, and presumably most of the workers they represent, know that in the long run labor demand will go up, not down. If unions in the data handling industry had protested the installation of computers, their workers would have spent the rest of their days on welfare.

In the same way, we install an energy-saving device in our home or business. We do save energy this way. But if the device is effective, eventually energy use by all of us will rise, not fall.

NOTES

1. L. G. Brookes, review of *A Low Energy Strategy for the United Kingdom*, by G. Leach, *Atom* (March 1979): 3–8.

2. L. G. Brookes, "Nuclear Energy = More Jobs?" *Energy Manager* 2 (July/Aug. 1979): 21–23.

19

Examples Conservation Advocates Do Not Want You to Hear

We tend to read only what are called the success stories of conservation, although the articles often mention only potential and not confirmed examples. However, there have been many failures of conservation. Of course, these flops do not prove by themselves that conservation does not exist. Nonetheless, they are a useful antidote to the almost uniform euphoria that greets the word conservation.

Saving transportation energy can involve going from a Cadillac to a Chevrolet to a Geo. But why stop there? Travelers who use the least energy and yet travel at highway speeds do not even own a car. They are hitchhikers.

Dave Reichel and Scott Geller, professors in Virginia, describe an experiment in energy conservation in Eugene, Oregon.[1] The test started in 1972, before the first energy shock of 1973. The idea was simple enough. If we look down a highway from a bridge, almost all the cars roaring by contain only the driver. Presumably some of the vehicles could be taken off the road and energy saved if their drivers knew that they could get a ride in someone else's car to wherever they were going. The simplest way is to hitchhike.

Hitchhiking probably arose shortly after the first car took to the cow paths they called roads at the turn of the century. I have engaged in it myself, although the thought of energy conservation did not enter my mind at the time. I simply could not afford a car.

In the Eugene program, designated spots were chosen. Anyone who wanted a ride would wait at those points. They did not even have to stick out a thumb. Because of the danger of accidents when motorists pull over to the side of the road to pick up hitchhikers, the Eugene authorities went to some lengths to avoid this. The spots were away from intersections and had lots of room. The chances of accidents were greatly reduced.

What happened? Energy planners are good at measuring inputs to programs, but can fail miserably when they try to estimate the outputs. They could probably say with some certainty how much money was spent on building the hitchhiking corners and erecting the signs. They could probably even guess how many people were picked up. But how many gallons of gasoline were saved as a result of all this; that is another matter.

The Eugene experiment ended not because an official peered at a computer printout one day and found that only three gallons of gasoline had been conserved. The managers of the experiment had no way of telling how much had been saved. But they got more than they bargained for with the carefully planned hitchhiking stops. According to a member of the Eugene police department, the stops quickly became the haunts of muggers and rapists, especially at night. A lonely hitchhiker under a dim street lamp—what could be better prey? After a year, the hitchhiking scheme was shut down for this reason. The fanfare greeting the shutdown was much less than accompanied its opening. Curiously, the need to save energy at the end of the hitchhiking experiment was greater than at the beginning, with the oil crisis of 1973 underway. Energy conservation, it seemed, was not as simple as some people had imagined.

• • •

Over the past two decades, there have been hundreds, if not thousands, of energy conservation projects, both on the state and federal level. With few exceptions, they have been pronounced a success. Have they really accomplished much? Clive Seligman, a professor of psychology at the Canadian University of Western Ontario, investigated this question.[2] He found that while many words are written about the wonderful achievements of these programs, it is difficult to pin them down on concrete achievements. Seligman studied the Massachusetts "Project Conserve," administered on the state level, asking this fundamental question: Did the program work?

Its purpose was to "assist homeowners to save energy and money by providing them with individualized, unbiased information on energy conservation techniques and materials." Homeowners (tenants were apparently not included) were to fill out a twenty-nine-item questionnaire about their home, appliance, and other energy use. Within six weeks of mailing the form in, they would get a computerized analysis of their homes. This information recommended attic insulation, reduced thermostat settings, storm doors and windows, and other conservation measures, as needed. The information told the recipient how much he or she would save annually.

The administrators of Project Conserve claimed that it was a success. One reason was that 135,000 households sent in questionnaires, a large number. But, as Seligman notes, "A cynic could point out that 135,000 households are still less than 15% of the households [in Massachusetts] who were sent questionnaires."

We know the number of pieces of mail, but we still do not know how much energy, if any, was saved. The administrators of Project Conserve came to four conclusions, according to Seligman:

(1) Homeowners are interested in energy conservation and there is a need for programs like Project Conserve.

(2) Such programs can be run at the state level.

(3) The media are concerned and give generously of their resources.

(4) There is a place in the elementary and secondary schools for coursework related to energy conservation.

But, as Seligman observed, "Notice, in these conclusions, that no mention is made of the amount of energy actually conserved, the ability of people to accurately report their energy habits and house characteristics, the adequacy of the computer model, or follow-ups on whether homeowners acted on the advice they received."

Professor Seligman is an expert on program evaluation, that is, determining if highly publicized government programs do what they are supposed to. While the administrators thought they had adequately evaluated their program, he does not think so. It is all too easy to add up the pieces of mail popped in a mail box and conclude that a program is a roaring success.

About the same is encountered by breakfast food manufacturers, who from time to time make offers on the sides of their packages to little children. "Send in a box top and $1, get a giant code breaker ring that glows in the dark." The mailbags at the cereal companies fill with envelopes. But unless the sales of the cereal increases, the campaign is a flop. Kellogg knows that it is in the business of selling cereal, not magic rings.

The evaluation of the vast majority of energy conservation programs concentrates on the side shows of the project—the radio and television spots mentioning it favorably, the postcards sent in, and the like. Unless we can tell how much energy was truly saved, we have not evaluated these programs at all.

• • •

We may imagine that the more we tell consumers about energy use and waste, the less energy they will use. There is strong evidence that this is not so.

Lou McClelland and Rachelle Canter, in a book on the psychology of energy conservation, give the reason.[3] Many consumers think that energy-consuming activities cost more than they actually do. When they get information on the costs, they often use more energy than previously.

For example, suppose that a household is told that lighting their house costs $10 a month, and they should cut down. But they may have imagined that it cost $20 or $30. When given the true information, they may decide to light even more bulbs than they had in the past.

In the same way, proposed rate hikes by public utilities are often greeted by howls of outrage by the public, even though in many instances the rate increase amounts to only a few extra quarters a month for the average homeowner. Citizens obviously imagine that what they think is their already sky-high electricity bill will skyrocket to the heavens. They have misjudged on both counts. The simple device of giving consumers more information on energy, in the hopes they will conserve, may not work. The message will be effective only if people have not already overestimated their energy bill.

• • •

All that is required to conserve energy is to hand out some pamphlets, or for some personality to tell us on television not to waste. Just follow these steps, and watch the consumption levels plunge. That is the way the text-books tell it. The truth is different.

This was evident in what could only be described as a comedy of errors in San Francisco. After considerable effort, including financial incentives to consumers, energy use went up, not down.

The scenario began simply, as described by Edward L. Vine and his colleagues from nearby Lawrence Berkeley Laboratory, part of the University of California, in the scientific journal *Energy*.[4] Elderly tenants in public housing projects in San Francisco were the target. However, the organizers skipped over a simple fact that eventually sunk their efforts—the tenants did not pay a penny toward their personal electricity and gas bills. The most wasteful of the lot paid the same energy bill as the most penurious; that is, nothing.

A series of public workshops told the tenants why they were to save: to reduce the Housing Authority's energy bills. The originators of the project obviously did not know the lay of the land. The life of most tenants in public housing is a continuous battle against the mysterious authority. Asking tenants to help the landlord in this context is like asking the homeless to contribute to a fund for Donald Trump.

If the apartment buildings had had reasonable temperature controls, energy could possibly have been saved. They did not. The radiators had shut-off valves that could have been used to reduce heating when the rooms got too warm. However, the advanced age and weak physical condition of many of the tenants prevented them from bending down to adjust the often-stuck valves. Some of them had come from other countries, like China, where they were not familiar with mechanical devices. As a result, regulating the valves was, as Dr. Vine notes, "incomprehensible" to them. Even when the elderly tenants had the strength to turn the valves, they were often afraid to rotate them for fear they would accidentally turn the heat completely off, or make the room too hot. Consequently, most of the settings on the valves were "as the [maintenance] man set it," sometimes months or years previously.

Tenants sometimes got too hot or too cold. How did they get comfortable again? In the same way that people did in the Middle Ages—by opening and closing windows.

About one tenant in eight had a radiator valve that was broken, missing, or otherwise inoperable. For them no heating adjustments could be made no matter how sincere they were about conservation.

If conservation propaganda is ever to work, it has to trade on the guilt that some of us feel when we "waste" energy. This did not happen in the San Francisco experiment. Almost all tenants thought they were already using the minimal amount of energy necessary to keep life and limb together. Any less, in their estimation, would reduce their already low standard of living.

Most energy researchers, confronted with these attitudes, would have given up then and there, but the dogged scientists pushed on. While most of the project could be part of a textbook on how not to conserve, there was one good feature: a control group. In most conservation experiments, a system to reduce energy use is tried on a number of people. Energy is duly saved. But if a control group, not subject to exhortations and pamphlets slipped under their door, had been used for comparison, we might find that their energy use also went down. Using a control group is a standard scientific procedure, one that is rarely used in conservation studies.

How did the two groups differ? Both got tenant education, pamphlets on why they should save, public meetings, thermometers so they could find out how warm or cold a room was, and so on. One group got incentives to save energy, and the other did not. In principle, the first group should have saved more. Since the energy use of both groups went up, it is difficult to say how much extra savings were created by the incentives.

How much were the incentives? Originally, the payments were to be $10 a month for three months. Afterward, variable amounts were to be paid, depending on how much the building as a whole saved in energy. There was no way to measure how much a specific tenant reduced energy use, if at all.

Because of bureaucratic delays, a lump sum of $30, the total incentives for the three-month trial period, was mailed to tenants over a year after the program began. By that time, many of the tenants had forgotten what the conservation program was all about. The brief explanation was given in English only, but many of the tenants were Chinese–American. The latter were unable to understand why they had received the money.

Only two-thirds remembered receiving a check at all. Of that fraction, half thought that it was for energy conservation in general, not specifically connected to their own efforts.

The incentives were supposed to be for future conservation, not what had happened in the past. Many tenants misunderstood this. They viewed the money as a reward for what had already taken place.

The results of all this confusion? Gas use went up in both buildings. Electricity use did go down, but not sufficiently to offset the increase in gas use. The experiments produced results opposite to what was anticipated.

There were tremendous energy savings in one building during one four-day period. When this was tracked down, it was because of the main gas furnace breaking down and not being repaired. The lack of responsiveness that the Housing Authority demonstrated during this emergency was one of the reasons why the tenants were not enthusiastic about helping their landlord.

• • •

About the same thing happened in the Midwest. Traer, Iowa is not a town that makes the national news too often. Given its experience in energy conservation, which was contrary to commonly accepted expectations, it is likely to remain in obscurity. The events there took place in 1987 and 1988, and were described in the magazine *Home Energy* in 1990.[5] The concept was the Great Light Bulb Exchange. Supposedly inefficient incandescent bulbs were to be exchanged for efficient fluorescent ones.

Most energy conservation measures seem to work in the laboratory, but meet with a yawn when they are tried out on the public. Not so in Traer, possibly because of the well-known civic-mindedness of Iowans. About 60 percent of the population took part. On average, each home exchanged thirty-eight lightbulbs, an enormous quantity. The fluorescent bulbs handed out in exchange were designed to screw into incandescent sockets, and were not the four-foot-long snap-in versions on kitchen ceilings. Thus, citizens just had to spend a few seconds changing the bulbs.

The results of the great experiment disappointed conservation mavens. Instead of the great savings expected, residential energy use increased 8 percent afterward. This is more or less what could be predicted. Clearly, the good citizens of Traer thought that their bills would drop close to zero after the exchange. So why not let the lights burn all night, and have the Christmas lights glow from Thanksgiving to St. Valentine's Day? Why not let them burn all year, to provide good cheer all the time? Exactly what went through the minds of Traerians is not known, but some of their thoughts must have been along these lines. The energy conservationists had to crawl back home, their tails tucked between their legs. Energy conservation seemed like such a good idea on paper, but just did not work when all too fallible humans were involved.

• • •

Many of the studies of energy conservation have been performed by technical types: engineers, physicists, and the like. It is no surprise that they often miss what goes on in people's heads, as opposed to their electricity meters. Not so with the previously mentioned Scott Geller. He wanted to know how water can be conserved, taking psychological attitudes into account.[6]

Water conservation is not exactly the same thing as energy conservation, although there are similarities. In principle, we all can use less water. In practice, most of us linger in the shower a little longer than we have to, and postpone repairing a leaky faucet.

In Geller's experiments, the average water use per day for each of the residences he considered was about 200 gallons. To reduce this, he used a variety of what academics call "interventions." Some were educational—handbooks describing why water should be conserved and how to do it. Others were attempts to change behavior. For example, people in the experiment were told every day how much water they had used the previous day. Presumably, if they had used a lot they would feel guilty and use less. The final intervention was physical devices, such as toilet dams (the equivalent of a brick in the tank), flow restrictors for showers, and the like. People who participated in the experiments were subject to one or more of the three approaches.

The results were disappointing. Those who were given the physical devices saved about seventeen gallons per day, or about 8 percent. Those who got education or similar attempts to alter their behavior were even more lackadaisical in their conservation behavior. They saved four gallons a day, or about 2 percent.

Geller did not say how much his work cost, but the experiment must have been far from cost-effective. The cost per gallon of water saved may have been comparable to that of champagne.

Geller was mystified by the poor results, especially in those households that had water-saving devices installed. He notes the following:

The 17-gallon average water savings was less than expected from manufacturers' estimates and laboratory data. For example, a toilet dam is expected to save 2 to 3 gallons of water per toilet flush, and thus 17 gallons of water should have been saved after 6 to 8 flushes, or less than 3 daily flushes per individual in the study. Furthermore, the shower flow restrictors limited the flow of water to 3 gallons per minute, which should save more than 17 gallons of water in a single shower. . . . Thus, with no change in daily water consumption behaviors, the installation of toilet dams, shower flow restrictors and faucet aerators should have resulted in much larger water savings than found in the present study.

I conclude that the people in the experiment should have been saving thirty, forty, or even sixty gallons per day without any effort on their part. The devices that were installed should have done the job automatically. Why did this not happen?

The answer is clear: the bounce-back effect. People with the devices installed knew they were about to save huge amounts of water. So why not let the lawn sprinkler run just a little longer? There was also enough saved for a long soak in the tub instead of a quick shower. And what about those hot tubs that just went on sale?

About the same factors apply in energy use. When we are told about how much we are saving, the natural human tendency is to loosen up a little—or maybe a lot—in our energy use. The energy planners, staring intently at the array of numbers on their computer screens, never realize this.

• • •

Many stories can be told about bulbs, which to many people symbolize energy use. The following is a series of three.

In early June 1992, the E-lamp caused a sensation across the country. Even *USA Today*, not noted for its scientific coverage, featured the invention in a major story.[7] Simply put, it is a bulb that uses a different principle to generate light. Instead of heating a tungsten wire as in an ordinary bulb, radio waves bombard gas under glass, exciting a phosphor that produces light. The exact way that it works is not that important here. After all, over the centuries many ways of making light have been tried. Incandescent and fluorescent have been the cheapest for half a century, but there is no guarantee that they will not be abandoned someday.

The new bulb could play a part in conservation. The news story stated that 25 watts going into an E-bulb produces as much light as 100 watts in an ordinary bulb. We then would save 75 watt-hours per hour the light was on, or 0.075 kilowatt hours. At a national rate of about 8¢ per kilowatt hour, this is 0.6¢ per hour. This does not sound like much, but there are billions of lightbulbs in the nation.

So the new bulb has great conservation potential if—if. The following is based on claims made by the developer, Interscience Technologies. As we all know, claims for new technology are sometimes a trifle optimistic. That is why we have a Securities and Exchange Commission. Certainly the E-lamp is much more complicated than the ordinary bulb, which in turn is not too different from what Edison invented a century ago. Perhaps not all the claims will turn out to be true.

The second major claim for the E-lamp, besides its efficiency, is long life. It supposedly has a lifetime of 15,000 to 20,000 hours, in contrast to a regular bulb's 750 to 1,500 hours.

For simplicity, let us assume that the E-lamp has a lifetime of 15,000 hours and an ordinary one has 1,000 hours. The E-lamp's developers say that their product never does burn out, but merely decreases in light output, that is, gets dimmer. At some point it makes sense to replace the E-lamp to increase its light output. In that way, it is more like a car that never wears out completely, but gradually needs more and more gasoline and oil to travel the same distance as before. Eventually it gets traded for a newer model.

How many years will the new bulb last? That depends on how long it burns each day. The editors of *USA Today*, in their description, assumed that it would be on four hours a day. Doing the mathematics, that translates to a lifetime of ten to fourteen years. But most bulbs are not on that long. If there are five hours between the time most people get home from work (around 6 P.M.) and the time they retire for the night (around 11 P.M.), the *USA Today* assumption implies that a typical lightbulb is on 80 percent of the available hours. This cannot be true. On average a lightbulb is on two hours or less per day.

This makes the lifetime of the E-lamp twenty to twenty-eight years. On one hand, this seems like a cause for celebration. A whole generation can go by without the need for re-lamping.

On the other, buying a lightbulb lasting a quarter-century implies that most of its use will be by people other than the buyer. On average, Americans move about every five years. So the cost of the E-lamp will be incurred by its owner, but most of its benefits will go to someone else. That fact alone will tend to decrease its sales, regardless of its other merits.

The E-lamp is to cost $10 to $20. Let us assume a typical cost of $15. It is possible that its price will decrease in coming years because of mass production. However, it is inherently more complicated than an ordinary bulb, and so will always cost more.

If the E-lamp were an ordinary industrial product, we would want to amortize its cost, that is, write it off over its lifetime. The average householder would not do this, of course. He or she would either buy it or pass it by. From society's viewpoint, we want to know the total cost. This is the sum of the annual amortization plus the running cost.

Assume a typical amortization rate of 10 percent. This is higher than typical interest rates, but is often used by industry to determine if a proposed investment will pay for itself. If we use this value, the annual amortization cost is about $0.1 \times \$15$, or \$1.50. Assume the E-lamp uses 25 watts and burns two hours per day. If the electricity rate is 8¢ per kilowatt hour, its running cost per year is

$$25 \text{ (watts used)} \times 2 \text{ (hours used per day)} \times 365 \text{ (days in year)}$$
$$\times 8 \text{ (cents per kilowatt hour)}/1{,}000 = \$1.46$$

where the factor of 1,000 converts watt-hours to kilowatt hours. Its total annual cost is the sum of the amortization cost plus the running cost, $\$1.50 + \$1.46$ or \$2.96.

Now consider the ordinary 100-watt bulb. *USA Today* says its cost is \$2, but they obviously have not been in a hardware store for some time. Not long ago, I bought a four pack, admittedly on sale, at a national hardware chain for \$1. Let us assume, to give the E-lamp a financial break, that a typical price for an ordinary bulb is 70¢. This is then one-twentieth that of the E-lamp at \$15.

The amortization cost of the ordinary bulb, again at an amortization rate of 10 percent, is then 0.1×70, or 7¢. Its running cost, using the same assumptions as above, is

$$100 \text{ (watts used)} \times 2 \text{ (hours used per day)} \times 365 \text{ (days in year)}$$
$$\times 8 \text{ (cents per kilowatt hour)}/1{,}000 = \$5.84.$$

The total cost of the ordinary bulb is then $\$0.07 + \$5.84$, or \$5.91. By this calculation, the E-lamp comes out ahead, by a margin of $\$5.91 - \$2.84$, or about \$3.

But the amortization rate is not necessarily the same as the discount rate. The amortization rate is used by industry for investments, such as a factory, about which much is known. The discount rate for energy-saving devices, used by consumers as they calculate whether to buy, tends to be much higher. If it were 30 percent, a value that is often implicitly used by consumers, the annual amortization cost for the E-lamp would be $0.3 \times \$15$, or \$4.50. Its total annual cost would be $\$4.50 + \$1.46$, or \$5.96. Using the same assumption for an ordinary bulb, its annual amortization would be $0.3 \times \$0.70$, or 21¢, for a total annual cost of $\$0.21 + \$5.84$, or \$6.05. So if a discount rate of 30 percent were used by consumers, the E-lamp would cost, on an annual basis, only slightly less—$\$6.05 - \$5.96$, or 9¢—than an ordinary bulb.

We may indeed see the E-lamp around in coming years (although a quick search of a large hardware store in early 1997 did not turn it up), if it can overcome a panoply of "ifs":

1. If the claims for long life are valid
2. If it really uses one-fourth the electricity of an ordinary bulb
3. If people do not say to themselves, "Why should I buy an expensive bulb for the next tenant (or owner) of this house or apartment?"

• • •

Sometimes the efforts to conserve go too far. This was evident in a recent Christmas season, when a proposal to reduce lighting at the fabled Rockefeller Center tree met with widespread derision.

The suggestion, reported in the journal *Science*, was by Carolyn DeCusatis.[8] She noted that the big New York tree had about 20,000 7-watt bulbs. At an average rate of 10¢ per kilowatt hour (electricity, as most other goods and services, is more expensive in New York than the rest of the country), this works out to about $14 per hour.

She proposed replacing the bulbs with light-emitting diodes (LEDs), which use much less electricity. DeCusatis said that 20,000 four-bulb clusters of LEDs would cost only 90¢ an hour, so each hour's savings would be about $13. Over the course of the Christmas season, this would amount to $2,000 to $3,000, depending on how long the lights were on.

Who would object to saving that money? But that is only part of the total picture. First, LEDs are fine for car dashboards, where the amount of light needed is small. On a Christmas tree, they would appear dim. We would have to increase the number of bulbs greatly to produce the equivalent brightness. Much of the savings would disappear as the number of LEDs doubled and redoubled.

Second, LEDs are highly directional by nature. They send their light out in a narrow cone. This again is fine for the displays on a videocassette recorder, where the user needs only a small angle of light. On a Christmas tree, the effect of LEDs would be odd. From where you stood, you would see only a few of the many on the tree. The others would be at the wrong angle, and you could not see them from where you stood. You could view them all by walking around the tree, but not at one time. On even the smallest Christmas tree you can see almost all the lights simultaneously. This is what gives the glowing effect.

Third, LEDs cost more. The article did not give the exact cost, but they are substantially more expensive than ordinary Christmas bulbs, which often cost only a few cents. In 1996, I bought a string of about thirty bulbs for $1, or about 3¢ each. If LEDs were to replace ordinary bulbs, the operators of Rockefeller Center would have to lay out thousands of dollars in up-front costs. It might be many years, if ever, before they recoup their capital cost from the electricity savings.

Fourth, the proposal to substitute LEDs as used in car dashboards for Christmas tree lights overlooks why cars use them. They may save a little energy in a vehicle, but this is of no consideration to a car designer. They may cost more than an ordinary light, but again the car designer does not worry much about this. The main consideration is that LEDs last much longer than regular lights. A car owner might have to spend $20 or $40 for labor to replace a dashboard light worth a quarter. If he could be assured that his dashboard lights will almost never burn out, he would have more faith in the reliability of the vehicle. LED use is then based on their prime advantage, extremely long life. That does not play a part in Christmas tree lights.

Fifth and finally, the giant Rockefeller Center tree plays a part in attracting thousands of shoppers to midtown Manhattan during the holiday season. The extra business generated must be in the millions or tens of millions of dollars. Even if Rockefeller Center operators pleaded poverty and said they did not have the money for the tree's electrical bills, surrounding merchants would raise the funds in a few minutes. A few thousand dollars in light bills pales in comparison to the millions that would be lost if the plug on the tree were pulled or inadequate LEDs were used.

There is no question that LEDs might save some energy if they substituted for Christmas tree lights. Yet their drawbacks far outweigh the advantages of a few dollars saved. We can use a pile driver to crack a walnut, but why bother?

• • •

Not long ago, I went into a store to buy an outdoor floodlight to replace one above the garage that had burned out. I saw two on sale, both claiming to put out the lighting equivalent of 150 watts.

The first was said to use 120 watts and was priced at $5.97. The package on the second asserted it used just 90 watts and cost $8.97. If I was interested in conservation at any cost, I obviously would have bought the second one with little thought. It would have saved 30 watt-hours each hour that it burned.

Let us leave aside the mystery of why these bulbs were not simply labeled as 90 and 120 watts. Given that few of us have testing labs in the basement, their avowal that they both illuminate at the rate of 150 watts can be accepted. The question was, what is the better buy and why?

Each of the two bulbs had a stated life of 2,000 hours. We can assume that this is not too far from the truth. So over 2,000 hours the more expensive bulb will use $30 \times 2,000$ or 60,000 watt-hours less than the cheaper one. This is then 60 kilowatt hours. If the average national rate per kilowatt hour has been about 8¢ in recent years, this is 8×60 or $4.80 saved by buying the more expensive bulb. The true cost of the conservation bulb is then $8.97 − $4.80, or $4.17. In this sense, then, the initially expensive bulb is cheaper than the ordinary $5.97 one. Conservation has paid off.

But the calculation is based on all the electricity in the two cases being used in one year. Suppose the bulbs are used with an automatic switch that turns them on at dusk and off at dawn. If there are about 4,000 hours of darkness or semidarkness per year, the bulb would burn out in about half a year. Conservation would still win in this case.

Most people probably use outdoor floodlights on average a few hours a week to light the house for guests or during a party. In that case, the bulb could last many years before the 2,000 hours were used up. For these people, conservation may not pay off. The difference in the two prices is $3. Suppose the people who use their floodlights rarely buy the cheaper version and put the $3 difference between the two in savings, either in a bank or mutual funds. This may seem like a trivial amount to invest, but remember that hundreds of thousands of people may be involved in buying floodlights. If a million people save (or do not save) $3 each, that is a total of $3 million in question.

A typical investment return might be on the order of 8 percent, averaged between bank long-term interest and the stock market. Those who buy the cheaper bulb will get a return of 0.08 × $3, or 24¢ each year. Best of all, from their viewpoint, that 24¢ comes in every year. At the end of five years, they have received a return of 5 × 24¢, or $1.20. They still have the original $3 they saved. This makes a total of $4.20. They will have spent an extra $4.80 on electricity, so they have lost only about 60¢, almost even. Anyone who uses a floodlight for less than about 400 hours a year—the 2,000 hour lifetime divided by five—will be about indifferent between using the regular bulb or the conserving one. The 400 hours annually is about eight hours a week.

This point about indifference is perhaps the reason both bulbs were on the shelf and the conserving bulb had not driven the regular one from the market. While most people cannot do the above calculations in their heads, they do know that a premium of $3 over a regular cost of $5.97—or about 50 percent—is steep for doing a supposedly good deed. Many people would buy the cheaper bulb.

• • •

The *Real Goods* mail-order catalog, described in Chapter 16, offered a refrigerator that supposedly was the world's most efficient, along with a variety of other claimed energy-saving devices.

Ordinarily, a device of this type would remain on the back page of seldom-read catalogs and make little impression on the national consciousness. However, the Sun Frost refrigerator was featured in a full-page discussion in the February 1994 issue of *Consumer Reports* (*CR*). This magazine is the most widely read consumers' magazine, and has a high reputation for detailed analysis of most products. Make a false claim about what you sell, and you will probably find yourself skewered in *CR* eventually.

The editors bought one of the Sun Frost refrigerators at a cost of about $3,000. At that price, it was more expensive than any other machine on the market. A refrigerator of the same interior capacity—19 cubic feet—could probably be bought for as low as $800. Note that this model is larger than the 12-cubic-foot model mentioned in Chapter 16.[9]

CR is usually quite sympathetic to energy efficiency and the devices that produce it. In this case, however, the Sun Frost was thoroughly panned, based on its enormous price. At three to four times the cost of an ordinary large-capacity refrigerator, it imposed on buyers a hefty premium for the privilege of saving energy.

The device was pictured on *CR's* pages, and it looked approximately the way we would expect. It had much wider walls than ordinary refrigerators, along with a thicker door. The result was a much smaller cooling volume. *CR's* editors said that its outside dimensions were larger than ordinary refrigerators, making it impossible to fit into many of the standard kitchen niches. *CR's* editors warned those contemplating ordering the Sun Frost to measure first.

The device clearly looks as if it should be more efficient. The editors took it to their lab, and found that indeed it was. However, exactly how much more depended on the measurements. The manufacturer based its efficiency on a freezer compartment temperature of about 23 degrees. Ordinary freezers have a recommendation of 0 degrees, to preserve foods longer. The higher the freezer temperature, the less energy any refrigerator, Sun Frost or otherwise, will use.

CR said that keeping frozen food at 23 degrees was dangerous, leading to quick spoilage and potential contamination. They set the Sun Frost's freezer temperature back to 0 degrees, and remeasured energy use.

The Sun Frost was still more efficient than competitors, but now the margin had narrowed significantly. The savings per year over the best competitor was on the order of 100 kilowatt hours. At an average cost of about 8¢ per kilowatt hour, this works out to an $8 savings per year. For the privilege of saving this amount, buyers will pay an extra $2,500. They may conserve energy, but they are not conserving money.

Devices like the Sun Frost refrigerator come and go, and there is no reason to be excessively hard on it. Its designers might claim that it is the first of its kind, and therefore some bugs need to be worked out. But some fundamental points are raised by the entire affair.

The Sun Frost, as depicted on the pages of *CR*, is massive, almost like a styrofoam cave. Its engineers have clearly packed in as much insulation as they felt they could get away with and still have a food-storage device. Yet in spite of this, the saving was still small. This implies that some ultimate limit of energy efficiency has been reached, unless the engineers of the Sun Frost were utterly incompetent. There is no reason to believe that they were. So while we are told to save ever more energy, at least in the refrigerator field, we seem to have gone about as far as we can go. The alternative is to spend $2,500 to save $8 a year, something not too many people will do.

For most of human history, we got along without refrigerators. Some of us can remember the iceman coming down the street, and the water from his melting ice blocks dripping behind him as he hauled his wares up the steps. But as soon as refrigerators came down in price, the iceman and his wonderful chips, delightful to suck on, disappeared.

Few would voluntarily return to those days. We will continue to use our refrigerators, sometimes using a little more energy than the conservationists would like. We can improve their energy efficiency slightly, but we will never give them up.

• • •

The arrival of the compact car saved millions of barrels of gasoline over the years, or so it seemed. This is trumpeted by advocates of ever more stringent mileage standards.

There is at least one counterexample to the claims. Consider where I worked, a large defense site in South Carolina. In the 1950s and 1960s, according to the old-timers with whom I talked, people would arrive at work in carpools. The site is isolated from large population centers and has various checkpoints for entrance. As a result, nobody could use public transportation—everyone had to drive.

All this was long before the days of government-mandated mileage standards and energy conservation programs. It just made sense to travel the twenty or thirty miles in a group.

I asked one of the old-timers when things had changed to the present, almost-universal one person per car. "In my estimation," he said, "it was when smaller cars came in. They couldn't fit four or five people in the new Japanese models. People just started driving by themselves."

In a corridor, I once saw an aerial view of the site, taken some years back. It showed few of the many parking lots that now crowd around each of the facilities. Things have certainly changed.

When I went to work (I took a carpool myself), I saw a steady stream of cars, mostly small and carrying only the driver, heading to work as well. The old-timers say it was never like this long ago, when cars were massive by today's standards.

The small car may have benefits, but in one particular area in South Carolina it inadvertently led to the demise of hundreds or thousands of carpools. The total amount of gasoline used to commute, even taking the lower consumption of smaller cars into account, probably went up substantially.

• • •

Conservation is usually treated as a very serious matter. After all, if the fate of the planet hangs in the balance, jokes are not permitted. Occasionally, however, a bit of humor slips in to a discussion of saving energy. People get tired of grim warnings to "save or else!"

So it was with a columnist for the *Augusta* (Ga.) *Chronicle*, Glynn Moore.[10] He started off by recalling a pamphlet that had been issued by the U.S. Department of Energy on how to economize on gasoline. Moore could save 12 percent by keeping his car tuned, 15 percent by buying radial tires and keeping them properly inflated, 20 percent by not using the air conditioner, and 20 percent by driving carefully. He added them up and came up with a total saving of 67 percent if he followed all these steps. Using one gallon where he had previously used three just did not seem to make any sense.

The advice to tune the engine overlooked a far bigger potential savings, in his estimation. A mere 12 percent savings shrinks in comparison to 100 percent. When the engine is badly out of tune, it will not start. If it does not start, it cannot use any gas. Those savings really do pile up.

The air conditioning advice also did not ring true with Moore. First, anyone trying to drive any distance on a muggy day in the South without air conditioning has more endurance than most of us. Second, just to save that extra buck at the pump, Moore followed the pamphlet's advice. He soon found that the open windows needed to prevent occupants from ending up as a damp smudge on the front seats increased the car's wind resistance. This slows the car and requires more fuel to keep rolling. Savings turn into waste.

The columnist noted other useful suggestions from the government: Buy a subcompact to get good gas mileage. Moore wondered if he should spend $12,000 just to save a few hundred dollars. Try to maintain a smooth, steady speed. Anyone who advocates this has not been out in city or suburban traffic recently.

Pump your own gas at self-service stations. It is not clear how this can save gasoline. Moore notes that there might be an unintended financial drawback. He notices drivers unwittingly put high-priced premium gas into cars that need only unleaded.

Take public transit instead of driving. Moore observes that the subway does not go anywhere near his home.

After going through the government pamphlet, the columnist realized that it did not bear much resemblance to reality. He then came up with a list of his own suggestions.

First, remove excess weight. This goes beyond getting rid of the junk and toys from the back seat and trunk. Reduce the amount of gas in your tank. Each gallon weighs about eight pounds, so toting fifteen gallons around is an extra 120 pounds of unnecessary weight.

Moore proposes that we buy just $1 of gas at a time and drive around with the tank nearly empty. This will be the equivalent in savings of having one less person in the car all the time. Of course, he notes that you will have to drive as if there was an egg under the accelerator to keep from running dry. Think of the gallons you will save.

Another suggestion is to drive no more than fifty-five on the highway. Chances are frustrated eighteen-wheel truck drivers will nudge you ahead to meet their deadlines. So many nudges, so many gallons of gasoline you will not have to buy.

Everyone knows you can save energy by coasting downhill. The spoilsports tell us we should not put the car in neutral when we are doing this. Why listen to them?

Suppose you live in Kansas, where an ant mound is regarded as a hill. What to do to take account of this savings source? Moore suggests that you put thirteen-inch wheels on the front of your car, and sixteen-inch wheels on the back. That way, you will always be driving downhill. You might have to stop at gas stations only rarely.

Teenage drivers are notorious for burning both rubber and gas. Moore suggests packing them off to live with relatives until they can afford to buy their own vehicles. Savings will be sky high.

Whenever you step on the brake, you waste the energy you used to get up to speed. The obvious thing to do is to go through stop signs and red lights. Some people have already adopted this practice. The savings in gas alone, Moore estimates, will more than pay for the extra traffic fines and hospital bills you rack up. As Roy Rogers and Dale Evans would croon, "Happy trails to you."

NOTES

1. David A. Reichel and E. Scott Geller, "Application of Behavioral Analysis for Conserving Transportation Energy," in *Advances in Environmental Psychology*, vol. 3, *Energy Conservation: Psychological Perspectives*, ed. A. Baum and J. E. Singer (Hillsdale, N.J.: Lawrence Erlbaum Associates, 1981), 53–91.

2. Clive Seligman, Larry S. Becker, and John M. Darley, "Encouraging Residential Energy Conservation through Feedback," in *Advances in Environmental Psychology*, vol. 3, *Energy Conservation: Psychological Perspectives*, ed. A. Baum and J. E. Singer (Hillsdale, N.J.: Lawrence Erlbaum Associates, 1981).

3. Lou McClelland and Rachelle J. Canter, "Psychological Research on Energy Conservation: Context, Approaches, Methods," in *Advances in Environmental Psychology*, vol. 3, *Energy Conservation: Psychological Perspectives*, ed. A. Baum and J. Singer (Hillsdale, N.J.: Lawrence Erlbaum Associates, 1981) 1–25.

4. Edward L. Vine, B. K. Barnes, Evan Mills, and Ronald R. Ritschard, "The Response of Low-Income Elderly to Tenant Incentive Programs," *Energy* 14, no. 11 (1989): 677–685.

5. "Mixed Results from Traer's Light Bulb Retrofit," *Home Energy* 7 (Nov./Dec. 1990): 6–7.

6. E. Scott Geller, Jeff B. Erickson, and Brenda A. Buttram, "Attempts to Promote Residential Water Conservation with Educational, Behavioral and Engineering Strategies," *Population and Environment* 6 (Summer 1983): 96.

7. Kevin Maney, "Technology Helps Build a Better Bulb," *USA Today*, 3 June 1992, B–1.

8. "Twinkle Twinkle Little LED," *Science,* 3 Jan. 1992, 27.

9. "The World's Most Efficient Refrigerator," *Consumer Reports* 59 (Feb. 1994): 74.

10. Glynn Moore, "Driving Downhill and Other Guaranteed Gas-Saving Tips," *Augusta* [Ga.] *Chronicle*, 12 June 1994, 2.

20

The International Scene

Conservation is not merely a matter of one country's saving or wasting of energy. The effects extend beyond borders. In this chapter we will look first at some of the broader issues, such as the Third World and national security, and then at specific countries like Japan and Canada. We will demonstrate that even if one country is an exemplar of saving, the effect does not and cannot extend worldwide.

When one considers energy consumption in Third World countries such as Nigeria and Haiti compared to the industrialized nations such as the United States and Canada, the results are obvious. The former nations use much less energy *per capita*, perhaps a factor of ten less, than industrialized nations.

According to conventional wisdom, this proves that people in the Third World are somehow better or more moral than their industrialized counterparts, since they use less of the world's resources. This is not quite the truth.

People in the Third World are not that different from people elsewhere. They use energy to suit their circumstances. A villager in Sierra Leone will not have a refrigerator, so the energy he devotes to that end is zero. Chances are he has a motor scooter at best, so his transportation energy will be much less than that in the West. Even if he won a car in a lottery, he would not have the money to buy the gasoline. He has never been on a plane, so he rings up a big zero in that area as well.

None of this makes him more virtuous than anybody else. Consider an example. In China, for centuries commercial energy use was very low. This should have made hundreds of millions of Chinese peasants more moral than the degenerates in the United States. In the 1980s, a new set of economic policies, deviating strongly from the failed Marxism of Mao Tse-Tung, was instituted. Economic growth and energy use skyrocketed. By the early 1990s, China had one of the highest economic and energy growth rates in the world.

Did the Chinese suddenly become a fallen people? Hardly. Circumstances changed, and a Chinese peasant who once trudged to the fields now may use a motorcycle instead. Rather than his wife pulling the plow, he may rent a small tractor. Ask him to go back to the old ways, and you are liable to get a punch in the nose.

A news article discussed complaints from U.S. environmental groups, such as the Environmental Defense Fund and the Natural Resources Defense Council, to the World Bank.[1] The groups said that the international lending agency was not following its own guidelines to promote conservation in Third World nations.

The bank rejected the arguments. They noted, "Two billion people in developing countries have no access to electricity whatsoever. How many of these people can use, let alone afford, the $25 lightbulbs or the high-efficiency air conditioners that rich-country lobby groups say are so essential for energy efficiency?" Ultimately, there is no morality attached to the use or nonuse of energy. Someone whose electric bill is half that of his neighbor is not twice as virtuous. If this were true, the billions of people in the Third World would tower above the Western world in terms of energy morality. This is nonsense. When they suddenly use more energy, as the Chinese are doing, we find that people from the Third World have feet made of clay kilowatt hours.

• • •

Consider relative energy use in terms of industrialized countries. "Look at Sweden," we may be told, "The Swedes use much less energy per unit of gross domestic product (GDP) than we do. If we were as efficient as them, we'd save enormous amounts of oil, gas, and coal. We wouldn't have to drill for oil or build nuclear plants."

Many European countries use energy in a different way from the United States. This is not because they are in any way morally superior or inherently more efficient than us, but because the structure of their society and industry is different. For example, we think nothing of shipping something 3,000 miles across the continent. There is no way that a Swede could send a package even half that distance and have it stay within his country.

Consider Canada. Americans have a soft spot in their hearts for their northern neighbors, but using the standards that energy conservationists apply to the Swedes, those Canadians are nasty indeed.

In 1973, before the first oil shock, Canada used 38.3 megajoules per 1980 dollar of GNP. A megajoule is the amount of energy used to burn a 100-watt lightbulb for about three hours. The use of 1980 dollars indicates that the effects of inflation have been removed from the calculations. (In the following, in the interests of simplicity, only the number of megajoules, not the full unit, is used.)

In the same year, the United States used only 35.6, so American and Canadian energy efficiencies were not too far apart. Americans could not claim that they were righteous compared to Canadians, or that the latter were a group of gas-guzzling wasters.

By 1985, the United States was using only 27.5 units, a decrease of about 23 percent. Canada also improved, but dropped only to 36.0. The gap had widened. Americans used about one-fourth less energy per unit of output than Canadians.

Did Canadians become ogres in the interval? Did all the old Belchfire 8s discarded by Americans get shipped north? Of course not. Canadian industries tended to be the ones that were heavy energy users, whereas Americans shifted to less energy-intensive fields, like computer manufacture. Many American steel mills closed in the 1980s, but most Canadian ones remained open. If a nation produces steel it has not necessarily fallen into moral degeneracy.

Conversely, if a nation shuts down steel mills, it is not entitled to pin a gold conservation medal on its chest. Merely dividing a nation's energy use by its output of goods and services does not tell us much about anything.

• • •

One of the matters that conservationists agree on, regardless of their other differences, is the peaceful nature of what they advocate. The argument goes as follows: If we all conserve more, then the world will not get into wars over oil and natural resources. These sources of conflict, which have been the basis of most of the world's armed clashes, will gradually fade away. The world will finally become a truly peaceful place.

It seems logical on its face. Battles over natural resources, although sometimes hidden under other guises, have led to the slaughter of millions. Many historians have said that the two World Wars were propelled by claims by Germany, the former Austro–Hungarian empire, and Japan that they were not getting their share of the world's resources.

Will energy conservation solve that problem conclusively? One of the goals of government mileage standards for cars is to cut down on foreign oil imports. The economists call this "autarky," the ability of a country to supply all of its needs for a commodity or service by itself. For example, suppose that the United States decided that orange juice was a strategic import. The cry might go up that we should no longer rely on unstable Brazil. In recent years, about one-third of American juice came from that nation.

If we carried out such a policy, we might decide to produce all orange juice by ourselves. Suburbs of Miami, once used to grow oranges, would be reconverted into groves. The cost would be a lot higher than importing the juice, but no matter. We would not be dependent any longer, as the song goes, on the planters down in Santos.

There is no economic or moral reason why a country should not engage in autarky, if it is ready to pay the price. For example, it was revealed in the mid-1980s that the integrated circuits and other electronic components of some American nuclear weapons were made in Japan. They were used because they were apparently cheaper than U.S.-made versions. If the generals thought that reliance on foreign parts for their weapons would endanger our security, they could press Congress to specify only U.S.-made parts be used. This would cost the taxpayers more, but Congress could well decide that this was a bill worth paying.

Consider how autarky relates to energy. After the oil shock of 1973, President Nixon commissioned Project Independence. This was the only full-fledged attempt by the Federal government to determine what would be required for energy autarky. The analysis, in many volumes, envisioned the United States as completely free of all oil imports, not merely reducing their level. We would not merely cut off imports from Iran, Iraq, Libya, and all the other disreputable countries, but from friends like Canada, Mexico, and Venezuela.

Unfortunately for those who like quick fixes, the authors of Project Independence estimated that eliminating oil imports forever would cost tens, if not hundreds, of billions of dollars. A large array of nuclear power plants—many more than the approximately 110 working now—would supply energy for the millions of electric vehicles that would be needed. Oil drilling would be extended into areas that had never before had a drill penetrate them, like national parks and forests.

Congress took one look at the costs associated with Project Independence and promptly shelved it. The cost of complete energy autarky was just too great. In the two decades since, Congress has never again opened that can of worms.

No conservationists ever endorsed Project Independence with its message of complete autarky. Rather, conservation proposals since then have stressed partial autarky. That is, if we can raise the mileage standards high enough, or make enough people buy refrigerators with thicker styrofoam walls, we would not have to import oil from certified nasties like Muammar Khaddafi, the late Ayatollah Khomeini of Iran, and other assorted dictators. (To avoid using the names of changing dictators, we will collectively call them the "despots" here.)

On the face of it, this seems to make sense. If, by taking a few apparently simple and nonpainful steps, we can avoid dealing with these suspicious characters, why not? Life is not quite that simple. If the United States demands the right to partial or complete autarky, it could well have unpleasant consequences in other countries. In the long run, those consequences could hurt the United States much more than the benefits we would derive from stopping oil imports from the despots.

There are two major problems resulting from this move toward energy conservation. First, we would cut off many of our international friends at the knees, not a wise thing to do in diplomacy.

Contrary to public opinion, most of our oil imports do not come from anti-Western nations. A large proportion, year in and year out, is derived from democracies like Canada and Venezuela. Even in OPEC, sometimes held up as an organization hostile to the United States and the West, most of our oil from that group of nations has come to us from reasonably benign countries like Saudi Arabia, Kuwait, and Nigeria. We thought enough of Kuwait to risk American soldiers in its liberation in early 1991.

Suppose, for the sake of argument, that 5 percent of our oil imports in a given year derived from the despots. We might hear, "If we just raised our mileage requirements for cars by one, two, or three miles per gallon, we would not have to import oil from these unreliable countries. They could impose an embargo on us at ten minutes' notice. It's just a lot easier to conserve than to deal with those countries." Petroleum does not work that way. Oil is oil is oil, and its origin can easily be concealed when the price is right.

Suppose that we follow this conservation advice, and our oil imports go down by 5 percent. Suppose that this is the exact proportion brought in from the despots. We might like to think that the amounts brought in from these countries would drop to zero under this action. We would finally be rid of that group of dictators.

What is much more likely to happen is that the imports of all our suppliers would drop by about 5 percent. Imports from friends like Canada and Mexico would fall by about the same proportion as that of our quasi-enemies. Since the imports from our friends are much greater in magnitude, they would be hurt much more than enemies of the United States.

Envision the conversation the Canadian Ambassador has with the Secretary of State: "You call us your closest friend, but your conservation measures have cut our oil exports to you. Our industry is suffering. Thousands of oil workers have been laid off. If that's what you do to a friend, what do you do to your enemies?" The Mexican Ambassador is even more incensed: "People in Mexico are very poor, Señor Secretary. They are relying on income from oil exports to the Colossus of the North to help raise their living standards. The Canadians already live well, so a drop in their income won't hurt them so much. But what about the millions of impoverished Mexican peons? Your actions have harmed them, through no fault of their own."

If the United States is to retain world influence, it has to treat its friends in a hospitable manner. The hypothetical conversation sketched out above suggests that what seems like an innocuous conservation measure, applying solely to this country, can have substantial and unpleasant side effects.

If we merely wanted to cut out hostile countries from the U.S. petroleum market, a much simpler way would be to just ban their imports. This was precisely what was done with imports from China (known at the time as Red China) from 1949, the year that Mao took over, to about the mid-1970s. The United States said that everything from that country was contraband and subject to seizure. We still do the same for Cuban goods. It is a harsh measure, but at least it gets the point across to the offending country.

Most important, it is simple. The analogy to the complication of cutting off unfriendly countries with conservation measures is that of cigars. The Cubans supposedly produce the world's best cigars, and millions in the United States would smoke them if they had the chance. Suppose now that there had never been an embargo against Cuban goods, but we still wanted to keep imports from that island to a minimum.

We could have elaborate and expensive campaigns against cigar smoking, telling of all the dangers. Billboards, newspapers, television, and radio programs would all carry the story: Cigars can be harmful to your health. But inevitably someone would say, "If we really want to punish Fidel Castro, wouldn't it be a lot simpler and cheaper just to ban imports from Cuba?"

That is precisely what Dwight Eisenhower decided in 1960, and seven presidents have continued to carry out that policy. If we really want to get back at Middle East dictators, there are much less complicated measures we can take than imposing elaborate conservation rules.

• • •

The partial energy autarky described might fail because the United States is not alone in the world. In turn, this relates to the conservationist claim that the steps they advocate would, at the very minimum, promote peace.

Put yourself in the position of the Prime Minister of another nation. You tell your advisor, "I see in the newspaper that the United States has imposed all these conservation laws to cut down on oil imports. What did my chief economist call it, 'autarky' or 'anarchy?' Whatever. If the United States does this, maybe the rest of the world isn't too reliable. Perhaps our country shouldn't depend on others, either. Secretary! Call my Energy Minister."

After some time, the energy minister of this country, whom we will call Mr. Suliman, arrives. Our fictional conversation continues.

"Mr. Prime Minister, here I am. I came as quickly as I could."

"Sit down, Mr. Suliman. I have a few questions to ask you. You have been in charge of our nuclear program, have you not?"

"That's correct, Mr. Prime Minister."

"And what was the purpose of that program, may I ask? It was started decades before I took office."

"Well, it was determined in 1957 that we were importing too much energy. This made us dependent on other countries. When we built our nuclear plants we became more self-reliant. Every government since then has endorsed that goal."

"And I myself have supported that aim. Imports of coal and oil have clearly gone down. I have these reports right here in this file. But what about imports of uranium to power those nuclear reactors?"

"Prime Minister, geologists have scoured the nation, looking for uranium. They have found none. As a result, all the uranium we use in those reactors has to be imported."

"So in a sense, you could say that we've gone from one form of dependence to another."

"Well, yes, that would be one way of putting it."

"As you can see from my desk, I have been reading the paper. The United States is adopting stringent measures to cut down on their energy imports. This may be a lesson for our nation. How can we cut down on importing uranium? We cannot stop those reactors, they are too important to us."

"One way would be to reprocess the fuel after it is used. We can separate the plutonium, and then use it in breeder reactors. It would take time, Prime Minister, but eventually we would not have to import any uranium at all. The scientists in our ministry are confident they can build these breeder reactors."

"Mr. Suliman, that settles it. If we are going to live in a world where energy imports are reduced on five minutes' notice, we cannot let our country suffer. Bring me the papers to authorize the breeder program this afternoon, and I will sign them on the spot."

Alert readers will have noted a key word in the above hypothetical conversation—plutonium. Plutonium is the ingredient in modern atomic weapons. Yet breeder reactors can be operated without using their plutonium to make bombs. The French have demonstrated that.

Other countries may not be that meticulous. For example, Pakistan has been suspected for years of using plutonium from its reprocessing plant to develop its own nuclear weapons. Japan is believed by some of its neighbors of having no valid reason for a reprocessing plant to extract plutonium from spent nuclear fuel rods.

What does all this have to do with conservation measures that the United States might undertake? We clearly have it within our power to promote energy autarky, by conservation or other rules.

But other countries can do this too. For many of them, a major import is uranium for their nuclear reactors. One way of eliminating these imports is by means of reprocessing spent fuel rods. Arguments about conservation do not have much meaning for many Third World countries, since they already conserve much more vigorously than we do.

The more hands that plutonium gets into, the greater the chances of some of it finding its way into weapons. So what seems like an innocuous conservation program in the United States may lead, in the long run, to greater chances of war worldwide. One rolling rock can start an avalanche, and this well may happen here.

• • •

National security is related to autarky. We often hear, "If we as a nation only conserved more, we would not have to import so much oil. When we have enough energy efficiency, we can dispense with other nations and use our home-grown resources. Our national security will be improved."

The oil industry replies, "All this is true. But improving energy efficiency can take many years. In the meantime, we need gasoline at the pump today. We can get it if we drill in such places as the Arctic National Wildlife Refuge."

Advocates of nuclear power say, "We do not know what the fuss over drilling versus not drilling is all about. We have a perfectly good energy source here, all set to go. It does not need oil or other fossil fuels. Build more reactors, and we can forget about the despots and whoever takes their place in the future."

All these arguments miss the point to some degree. Even if we were the most energy efficient nation in the world, in the long run we would have to import oil in increasing quantities.

The reason is simple. The United States has been explored for oil more than any other country in the world. Geologists agree that it is highly unlikely that any major new fields will be developed in the future. As noted in Chapter 15, the

United States is a declining petroleum province. Over the next few decades, more and more of the world's petroleum resources will be concentrated in the Middle East and other Third World countries, regardless of how strict we are about conservation.

The argument of the "drill at any cost" group also fails for this reason. Even if we find enormous amounts of oil in the Arctic and off the shores of the East Coast, eventually it will all be used up. This argument has been made by environmentalists opposed to drilling in these previously untapped areas. This does not mean we should not drill, just that it will not solve our import problems for all time.

About three-fourths of our electricity derives from fossil fuels. Most of this is coal. Until the early 1970s, a substantial part of electricity was fueled by oil. Because of its higher cost since then, oil now generates only a small percentage of total electricity production. Nuclear power, at more than 20 percent of electricity production, now fills the role that oil once had. But if the remaining tiny fraction of oil-fired electricity were replaced by nuclear tomorrow, the effects on oil imports would be minimal.

So regardless of what system is used—strict conservation, drilling in new areas, or building more reactors—in the long run the United States will import more and more oil. Is this a bad thing?

Not really. Other countries that have done quite well economically in the past few decades, like Germany and Japan, have essentially no oil. They are at the mercy of the Middle Eastern oil barons, yet they seem to have escaped that sword dangling over their heads.

As well, as I have said, most of the oil that the United States does import today does not come from the most unstable countries. There once was a television advertisement stressing the need to reduce imports and produce more energy at home. To increase the sense of alarm over these imports, they showed clips of Saddam Hussein of Iraq, Muammar Khaddafi of Libya, and the late Ayatollah Khomeini of Iran, all at the top of unpopularity charts. If most of the oil we imported came from these three countries, then there would be cause for enormous concern. In reality, only a tiny fraction of present imports derives from these admittedly hostile nations. Most of it comes from countries with whom we have traditionally been friends, like Canada, Mexico, and Venezuela.

• • •

In future oil embargoes, national security will not decrease as much as some expect because oil is what the economists call *fungible*, that is, transferable without too much trouble. Consider the worst imaginable oil import scenario. The King of Saudi Arabia is driven from office by a group of radicals who proclaim their undying hatred of the United States in frightening terms. "We will never trade with the cloven-hoofed ones as long as we're in office!" they shout, "All exports to the United States are hereby canceled."

This sounds bad, since we have been importing from the Saudis for decades. What to do? There is one fact we know about each regime—monarchist, socialist, capitalist, Islamic fundamentalist—that has controlled part of the Mideast oil wealth since petroleum was discovered in what is now Iraq before World War I. They sell oil. Regardless of their feelings toward outside countries, Middle Eastern regimes will market their petroleum to someone. Their need for cash is so great that they cannot afford to let the petroleum sit in the ground forever.

Returning to the Saudi scenario, the radicals may strike the United States off their list of countries eligible for sales, but they will market their oil to France, Germany, Japan, and a host of other nations. And France, Germany, and Japan, having many oil brokers who want to make a quick profit, will sell some of what they import to the United States. It will cost us a little more than it would if it were imported directly from Saudi Arabia, but the important fact is that the oil cannot be cut off for long.

Now the radicals may say to the French (if the French are the ones selling Saudi oil to the United States), "We know you're cheating on the American embargo. So now we're cutting *you* off." So the French are now in the same boat as the United States. In a little while, the Germans start sending oil surreptitiously to the United States, as the price that Americans are willing to pay rises. If the new Saudi government cuts off one country after another, they will soon end up with no oil customers. That is something that no Middle Eastern country with oil to sell, regardless of their political views, has ever done.

The Dutch fell under a strict oil embargo at the time of the first oil shock in 1973. This is almost forgotten in the United States, where it is believed that the only nation suffering the embargo was right here. The Dutch, for some reason, were regarded by OPEC as supporting Israel too much, and were therefore an enemy. Newsreels of the time showed Dutchmen pedaling away on their bicycles as gasoline shortages developed. But after a few days, hardly any Dutchmen rode bicycles more than they had previously. (Bicycles are a common sight in that country even when the oil flows freely.) They were able to get supplies of oil from other European countries who had not been cut off. They probably had to pay a bit more. Nonetheless, the nation did not stop running.

What does all this have to do with conservation? The argument that conserving enough will ensure national security just does not wash. We can always get enough oil from foreign countries if we are willing to pay for it. If we want to generate all our energy in this country, we do not necessarily have to conserve: We can drill much more for oil and build more nuclear reactors. Conservation and energy efficiency, by themselves, cannot guarantee national security.

• • •

National security was most under threat from the Russian bear, and we spent trillions to combat it. In 1989, the world watched as the Berlin Wall was breached. It marked the beginning of the end of the Cold War, which was dissolved without the hot war that many had feared.

The end of four decades of hostility between the Soviets, their satellites, and the West also affected arguments for conservation. For years, we had been told we had to become energy independent. Otherwise, the Soviets would be able to put a stranglehold on us, a lock that they could not achieve by military means. This inspired, for example, the vast and complicated system of oil quotas that existed from the 1950s until the first oil crisis in 1973. It is often forgotten now, when the United States buys petroleum from just about anywhere, that nations who for decades wanted to sell oil could send only so much. We did not want to become too dependent on outside sources of supply.

Of course, some ascribed baser reasons to this policy. The oil patch barons of Texas profited mightily from having their wells pumping, rather than rigs in Canada or Venezuela.

Now the same old Cold War arguments are being trotted out. We do not want to become too dependent on Saudi Arabia or ever buy oil from the despots. The argument makes no more sense than in the long-forgotten quota days, or when we thought that Russian tanks would someday rumble down Unter den Linden in Berlin. Oil crises will arise from time to time as governments and oil companies try to manipulate the price and supply of petroleum. But oil can be easily transported and smuggled into nations that need it. The Soviet Union was for years the world's largest oil producer. Its government crumbled and fell, but the oil continued to flow. If Saudi Arabia's government changed, about the same statement could be made.

The Cold War is over, but the arguments made for energy independence, spawned over those four decades, continue to be made. They should have been knocked down with the Berlin Wall.

• • •

We think of U.S. laws as applying only to this country. Other nations, while they may think that some of our regulations are peculiar, do not have much right to object.

Or do they? In March 1994, news reports circulated that the General Agreement on Tariffs and Trade (GATT) might take action against the United States about American automobile gas mileage laws.[2]

GATT was the foremost international trade agreement, and the organization based on it was a subsidiary of the United Nations. Set up during World War II to reduce the trade wars that had marked the 1930s, it was continually on the outlook for practises that could hinder free trade. In the mid-1990s, it was succeeded by the World Trade Organization (WTO), with similar goals.

Of these restrictive practices there is no end. The Japanese are past masters in the art. They allow most goods into their country—provided some samples are "inspected" by taking them apart and putting them together. This introduces endless delays and extra costs, making industrial imports into Japan much rarer than in other advanced countries.

How does this relate to conservation? According to the news report, some foreign manufacturers find U.S. fuel-economy standards harder to meet than American manufacturers. The standards are then a "nontariff barrier," in the WTO jargon.

It might seem strange that American car companies, traditionally accused of making big gas-guzzlers, could use the fuel-economy laws against foreign manufacturers. The latter were not identified in the report, so we do not know if they are Japanese, European, or from elsewhere.

The claim of discrimination against foreign products may not be so outlandish. American regulators and lawmakers are much more amenable to U.S. interests than foreign ones. If Toyota wants to change American fuel-economy laws to accord with the way they design vehicles, they will get a much less sympathetic hearing on Capitol Hill than General Motors. This is in the nature of things.

As the news report states, "Environmental laws that restrict trade usually have been found out of compliance with GATT's [WTO's] free-trading rules." Long ago, countries would try to keep out imports just by jacking up tariffs. Later on, it became fake inspections and other nontariff barriers. In the past two decades, countries that want to build a trade wall around themselves have sometimes used environmental issues to do so.

For example, members of Congress have suggested that the United States restrict products from countries that do not use special fishing nets that keep dolphins from drowning. This is a commendable environmental goal. But is it beyond the realm of possibility that some members of Congress who endorsed this proposal might represent American fishing interests that now use these special nets?

The same reasoning applies to the fuel-economy laws. When they first became law in the late 1970s, U.S. manufacturers opposed them adamantly. They believed the rules would give advantage to Japanese small-car manufacturers, and the laws certainly did.

Now the shoe is on the other foot. U.S. carmakers apparently have mastered the art of building cars using less gasoline. At least some foreign carmakers have not.

WTO takes no stand on whether cars should have fuel-economy rules. It is only concerned whether these and a host of other supposedly environmental laws are being surreptitiously used to reduce imports. This does not apply only to the United States, of course. Many countries have joined the environmental bandwagon and used these sentiments to keep out foreign goods.

If the United States is found guilty of using fuel-economy rules to reduce foreign competition, it could face sanctions from WTO. Those sanctions could hurt severely. In that case, the United States would have to decide if the fuel-economy rules are worth it. The average fuel economy of U.S. vehicles would probably have increased substantially even without those laws. If we take away those rules, we will not find Geos transformed overnight into tail-finned Cadillacs.

• • •

In the early winter of 1993, a strange spectacle unfolded in Japan. The Uruguay Round of GATT was approaching its climax. It was a time when

countries had to sign on to reduction of trade barriers or the vastly complicated multinational agreement would be canceled.

Japan already had the most restrictions on imports of any industrialized
country. As part of the new GATT agreements, Japan had said it would lower
at least some of its trade barriers. But there was one point on which the Japanese were adamant—rice.

Ever since World War II, Japan had forbidden the importation of rice. The
claim was that rice is a national symbol as well as a staple of their diet. The
Japanese said the national psyche would be irrevocably damaged if foreign
rice were permitted.

The Japanese were serious about the restrictions. Perhaps the best example
occurred at an agricultural trade show there. An American exhibitor thought
he would demonstrate that rice from the United States was of good quality.
He gave away small bags of American rice, containing a few ounces each.
When Japanese authorities got wind of this, they demanded that the exhibitor
leave the country at once and threatened to shut down the American part of
the trade show. It is not recorded if the Japanese tried to round up all the
American rice grains and burn them, but the thought probably occurred to a
few bureaucrats.

All this took place under the Liberal Democratic regime which ruled Japan
for most of the post-war period until 1993. In that year, a coalition of small
parties took over. They examined the rice policy and found that its major
effect was to make rice farmers very rich. Since rice could be sold in Japan
for perhaps five times the world price, anyone growing rice could become
wealthy in short order. As for the national psyche, Japan had changed tremendously since the defeat of 1945. Whatever the national psyche was, it had
been altered irrevocably through unprecedented prosperity.

So the new Japanese government lowered the barrier—but only an inch.
They promised to allow foreign rice up to a few percent of the Japanese crop,
phased in over a six-year period. Japanese rice farmers could continue to
drive Mercedes and take their vacations in Europe and the United States.

What does this have to do with conservation? One of its main arguments is
that importing foreign oil, electricity, or other forms of energy would produce
a dangerous reliance on foreign sources. We must conserve, ever more strictly,
to keep this from ever happening. If we imported considerable foreign energy, disaster would stalk the nation. At an opportune moment, those das-
tardly foreigners would pull the plug, block the pipeline, and stop the ships.
Then we would be left to freeze in the dark, a victim of our trust in inherently
shady aliens. Precisely the same arguments were used by the Japanese to
justify keeping foreign rice out. At some unspecified moment, foreigners would
cut off the white stuff, leaving Japanese to starve. In this scenario, it is not
specified exactly what foreign rice producers would do with their product.
Presumably they would heave it into the sea to spite the Japanese.

Both sets of arguments are nonsense. The Japanese would suffer no ill
effects to their national psyche if most of their rice came from California and

Arkansas. A few farmers might have millions in their bank accounts, instead of tens of millions.

In this country, we may want to conserve for various reasons, but keeping the foreign energy wolf from the door should not be one of them. The Japanese import almost all their energy, and it does not seem to have damaged either their national psyche or economy. It is likely that we would also suffer few ill effects.

• • •

One of the great fallacies in the way we talk about conservation is that of multiplication. That is, someone saves so many kilowatt hours by installing an energy-saving lightbulb. We then hear, "If we could get a million people to do exactly the same thing, the amount of energy saved would be a million times that number of kilowatt hours."

The multiplication does not work. The people who install the special lightbulbs do save energy, but society as a whole does not. Even if the nation as a whole somehow does save, the world does not. You cannot multiply the two numbers—the amount saved per lightbulb and the number of people who install them—and get a total saving to the nation.

An analogy to this is the price of Tokyo real estate. In the late 1980s, stories circulated in the West about the enormous amounts being paid for Japanese land in their big cities. The prices were often in the millions, or even tens of millions, per acre.

From these numbers, it was all too easy for some Westerners to multiply the prices by the total area of Tokyo, Yokohama, and other Japanese cities. The product of these numbers was what they claimed was the total value of Japanese urban land. When the calculations were performed, the Japanese had more value in their urban real estate than the total worth of the United States—all our land, factories, houses, vehicles, mines, and everything else in the country. From this calculation, it was all too easy to mourn the decline and fall of the United States.

The real estate multiplication fallacy, as with conservation, was false. There is no reason to doubt the cost of some Tokyo land described in breathless prose in the financial pages. However, we cannot determine the total value of all the land in Tokyo by multiplying its acreage by yen paid per acre for land on the Ginza.

There are two reasons for this. The first is that little Japanese real estate comes on the market per year compared to American urban land. As a result, the prices paid are higher than they would be if the American pattern of frequently buying and selling were followed.

The second reason is more substantial. Suppose you owned 1,000 acres in downtown Tokyo, and had to sell it off within a month or two. Suppose further that the first acre you sell goes for $5 million, probably not too far from what has happened from time to time. You are pleased by this and pocket the huge check. If each of your 1,000 acres sells for this amount, you will make $5 billion. You might even get on the list of the Japanese *Forbes 400* at this rate.

Flushed with success, you put your second acre on the market. The bids are disappointing. You can only get $4 million. Every day you put more land on the block, and the price keeps on dropping, with some fluctuations depending on specific locations. By the end, you are lucky if you get $5,000 per acre, in contrast to the $1 million you got initially. You have much less than the $5 billion that danced before your eyes.

You do not have to have an economics Ph.D. to figure it out. The glut on the market, created by acre after acre being offered, depressed the prices. Have a five-year-old open a lemonade stand down the block, and he or she might get 10¢ a glass. Then all the neighboring kids get the idea of making a small fortune just as the first tyke did. They open up their stands nearby, with predictable results. There will be too much supply on the market, and not enough customers. If the children want to sell their beverages, they will have to lower their prices. Down it will come—10¢, 8¢, 5¢, or even 3¢.

Merely multiplying the amount of energy saved by a particular energy-efficient device by the number of potential users—or going without the service in the first place—ignores the laws of economics. These laws apply not only to Japanese land tycoons and urchins selling lemonade, but to the use and nonuse of energy.

NOTES

1. "World Bank Charged with Ignoring Own Energy Policies," *Chemical & Engineering News* 72 (28 March 1994): 72.

2. John Maggs, "GATT May Force Change in Environmental Law," *Augusta* [Ga.] *Chronicle*, 20 March 1994, 16A.

21

Morality, Politics, and Energy Conservation

Whether conservation exists or should exist is more than a matter of numbers on a chart or electricity bills. For millions, it is a matter of morality. It is a sin, or something close to it, to waste energy.

All of us are aware of the "sin taxes" that the government imposes on commodities like tobacco and alcohol. At the end of Prohibition in 1933, stiff imposts were placed on beer and liquor as a concession to those who wanted the ban to continue.

While tobacco is legal, millions of people would like to see it disappear. Since this is unlikely to happen soon, most states and the Federal government levy heavy taxes on the weed.

Besides the moral question of whether using tobacco and alcohol is a bad thing, we also have the fiscal aspect. If governments need new sources of revenue, they have often found it politically difficult to raise income taxes. The simplest solution usually is to hike the sin taxes, adding 5¢ a pack or 25¢ a bottle. The reasoning is straightforward: "Most people would not notice it."

As a result of decades of tax increases on these presumably sinful products, most of what you pay for a carton of cigarettes or a bottle of liquor goes to the government. Some have estimated that the cost of a cigarette might be one-third or one-fourth of its present level if it were taxed at the same rate as other commodities.

Leaving aside the morality of these taxes, there is a certain health justification. Thousands die every year from lung cancer and other diseases induced by the coffin nails. Millions of families have been destroyed by alcoholism.

What does all this have to do with energy conservation? From time to time, politicians have proposed sin taxes on gasoline. For example, John Anderson, running as an independent republican for president in 1980, suggested a tax of 50¢ per gallon. Paul Tsongas, also running unsuccessfully for the Democratic presidential nomination in 1992, advocated the same thing.

This was put forth as a type of sin tax on petroleum products. We were told, "You're naughty folks for using so much gasoline. You must be punished, and punished severely. We have to hit your pocketbook the next time you pull up to the pump."

Were these sin taxes, and not just ordinary measures to raise revenues? They were proposed on just one of the many energy products we use—gasoline. There was no suggestion to tax coal, nuclear power, natural gas, or solar collectors, although President Clinton in 1993 proposed taxes on many of these energy forms. In these high-visibility proposals by presidential candidates, gasoline stood alone in the spotlight.

• • •

In terms of morality and conservation, does Christianity enter into the equation? A preacher once said that some Christians feel that if they deny themselves the goods of the world, they are somehow doing God's work. He said that this was not so. Merely refraining from consuming does not necessarily mean that poor people will have more goods and services at their disposal.

He was, of course, in favor of charity toward the poverty stricken. However, just doing with less does not accomplish anything. All it gives, in his opinion, was an unjustified sense of self-righteousness.

Merely denying oneself energy or other goods does not do much for our fellow man. It may make us feel good for a moment or two, but that does not help the unemployed family down the block.

• • •

We put our moral judgments into action when we vote for candidate A over candidate B. Yet we all know that each of our votes is a tiny proportion of the total. In a presidential election, it might be one out of a hundred million. Obviously, one vote cannot sway the outcome. Yet if everyone took that attitude and did not vote, representative democracy would cease to exist.

In an election, we encourage everyone to vote. Conservation advocates say that in the same way we must encourage all to conserve.

On the face of it, the analogy seems to be valid, but when we look at it more closely, it falls apart. First, everyone uses energy to some degree. There is no question of voting or not voting, as in elections. We are all in the energy boat together.

Second, a winner is declared in an election, regardless of how many people have taken part. Even if only one person votes, someone is certified as the victor. In the United States, we generally have about a 60 percent turnout for presidential elections, in contrast to the 80 percent or so common in Europe. But on January 20, every four years, someone appears on the Capitol steps to take the oath. He is as much the president as if 99 percent of the electorate had voted.

So the analogy between voting and conservation is weak. There is always someone to fill the office after the votes are counted. Whether conservation works will always depend on more than one person taking part or abstaining.

• • •

From voting, we can go on to the concept of nonvoting, that is, when a dictator rules. It might appear there is no connection with dictatorship and conservation, but at least one well-respected environmentalist thought there might be.

Dr. Patrick Moore, who was President of the Greenpeace Foundation in Canada at the time he spoke, was the man. Moore, a burly biologist, was almost the epitome of a raging environmentalist.

His observation is a long one but deserves quoting here. It reveals another side of conservation:

The Scandinavian countries use 50% of the per capita energy that we use in North America. If we were able to conserve energy to that extent, it would be dangerous for us to do it quickly because the economy would fall apart. If we were to shut down half the oil refineries, half the coal mines and half the nuclear power plants, then half the energy sector of North America would be eliminated. Just think of the economic implications there are to conserving energy. Energy conservation is not a motherhood issue; it could bring down the whole economy, and we're liable to wake up in a military dictatorship. These are tough decisions and it's going to be difficult to conserve 50% of the energy we're using now without putting everyone out of work in the process. These are the kinds of problems we have to face up to.[1]

There is some truth in what Moore says, leaving aside the hyperbole. There has been a trend toward a lower ratio of energy to gross domestic product for about a century now. We produce ever more goods and services for the same amount of energy used. This ever-decreasing ratio is an improvement in energy efficiency. The ratio drops slowly, at perhaps 1 to 2 percent a year.

What Moore is talking about are Draconian measures, in which conservation is the major goal of society. If that were true, we might drive down the ratio by 5 percent or more per year.

The result will be more than a brief year-end press release from energy officials heralding a new low for the energy per unit of GDP. Whole industries may be put out of business, and millions laid off in pursuit of the goal.

In the midst of this social chaos, some type of dictator may arise. Dictators have followed major disorders throughout human history, and conservation-based disruptions may not be different.

Moore put his finger on a major drawback of conservation, one that is rarely mentioned in print. In pursuing a goal of reducing energy use at virtually any cost, we may wipe out precisely that which we are trying to preserve. In the words of an American soldier during the Vietnamese conflict, "We had to destroy the village to save it."

NOTE

1. E. P. Hincks, ed., *Nuclear Issues in the Canadian Context* (Ottawa: Royal Society of Canada, 1979), 187.

22

Food and Energy Conservation

Dieting and energy conservation are more similar than they first appear. They work, or can work, for one person, but often are not effective for all society.

• • •

Consider an individual who decides he is overweight. He may want to reduce after looking in the mirror or finding difficulty getting into his clothes. He goes on some sort of diet and loses weight. In that sense, dieting has been effective.

In the same way, someone may decide that he or she is using too much electricity. They may come to this conclusion for moral or economic reasons. They cut down on their energy use.

To this point, the food and energy situations are about equal, but the long-term consequences for energy use are different. If one person cuts down on energy, he or she makes the remaining energy cheaper for the rest of us. We will tend to use a bit more, taking advantage of its slightly lower price. Overall, the total energy use remains about equal. This is a form of conservation of energy not envisioned by the physicists.

It is not the same for weight loss. If overweight Joe reduces, he does not affect the weight of anyone else. In that sense, there is no conservation of mass, as the physicists call it.

We have been swamped by endless diet plans over the last few decades. There is scarcely a week that goes by when a diet book of some type does not appear on the *New York Times* list of best sellers, or a guest on a talk show does not tell of his wondrous new plan. Beef, pork, and fish producers tell us of the weight-loss potential of their foods in expensive ad campaigns. In the grocery store, items fortunate enough not to contain cholesterol trumpet this fact from their labels, while other foods without this virtue blare out other weight-loss advantages they possess.

What is the result of all this? Official statistics compiled by the Department of Health and Human Services show that we are getting heavier, not lighter. A researcher in the spring of 1994 found that although young Americans supposedly eat fewer fatty foods than they did a decade previously, they weigh about ten pounds more. All the advertisements, videos, talk show appearances, books, and personal recommendations have flopped in this broad (no pun intended) sense. Our average weight is climbing, not falling.

Those who hawk these books and videos might respond, "True enough. But if it hadn't been for my patented grapefruit-and-liver dieting plan, Americans would have weighed even more. We might be confronted with citizens the size of smaller dinosaurs if my book had not been published."

We now enter a part of Disney World known as Fantasy Land. Suppose the average American male weighs 175 pounds today. According to these diet books and plans, they saved him from weighing 250.

There is an analogy here to energy conservation. Conservationists might say, "Yes, energy use in autos, or households, or industry went up by 3 percent last year. If it hadn't been for government regulations that were imposed, it would have risen by 5 percent, or even 10 percent."

Claims of this type, for both weight loss and energy conservation, are unprovable. What might have been is a good basis for a novel, but not for public policy.

• • •

Diets and energy conservation have another factor in common. They do work, but usually for just one person at a time.

Joe, noticing the bulge around his middle, decides on some action. He cuts out visits to McDonald's, goes for long walks, and eats fish until he imagines he is developing gills. Lo and behold, he gets some good news from his bathroom scales in a few weeks.

Martha has read her seventeenth article in the last few weeks on why we are running out of energy. She decides to do something about it personally, as all the articles advocate. She takes the bus instead of her car to work, turns out lights when they are not needed, fills the dishwasher before running it instead of using it to wash one dish, and in general cuts down on all her energy use. She does not have an immediate signal on her accomplishments as does Joe, but over the next few months she notices her electricity bill has gone down somewhat.

Now what happens to Joe? He may be one of the fortunate ones who have the willpower to stick with his diet and continue it on a lifetime basis. If that happens, he will never again emit a groan when he steps on the scales.

But if he is like most dieters—about 90 to 95 percent by some estimates—there will be a relapse. After a while, the smells wafting out of McDonald's and Kentucky Fried Chicken will prove irresistible, and he will be lining up at the counter. The cycle will start all over.

If the diet books of last year, five years ago, or even a generation back had been effective in keeping weight off permanently, there would be little need for this year's crop of new-and-improved books and plans.

None of this means that dieters who slide back to the land of butterfat and gravy are "bad" people. They are simply subject to normal human reactions and feelings. If we were constructing a policy to get the entire nation to lose ten pounds, we simply could not build it on the mountain of advice dispensed by diet gurus. These writers have done quite well for themselves financially— advances of $100,000 or more are not unknown in the diet-book field—but really have not kept the weight off.

About the same applies to individual energy conservers. Martha may indeed cut back on her energy use for a month, two months, or even longer. Then she sees an advertisement in the paper for a cut-rate vacation to Florida, and off she goes. She may even say to herself, "Well, I've saved all this money on the utility bill and the gasoline pump. I deserve a present to myself for this wonderful accomplishment. Besides, I'm not really spending the money on energy. It's just a vacation."

Of course it is. But energy will be used in flying her there. Staying at home, no matter how boring, is much more energy efficient than flying. There will be fuel for the car she rents, and energy for heating and cooling the hotel she stays in. Hotels use far more energy per day per guest than we do at home. Energy will creep into the vacation in a hundred different ways. She will not see a bill at the end of her trip subdivided into energy and nonenergy costs. She will rationalize, "The trip didn't use all that much energy. I'm still saving as much as I can."

Although millions of Americans say that they conserve energy in one way or another, overall energy use remains constant or even rises. While the conservers do indeed take specific actions to save energy, in other ways there is backsliding.

The dieter may reach for a bowl of ice cream after a meal of rabbit food as a celebration. The energy conserver, who has valiantly taken a crowded bus downtown instead of an automobile, may start thinking about installing a hot tub with all the energy savings.

Overall, the result for society is about a wash or even a retreat. Americans weigh more than ever, on average, in spite of an unprecedented barrage of messages telling us how we can lose weight. On the energy front, since 1973 we have been told, as never before, why and how we can save energy. Yet we use more than we did then.

• • •

All the food that both dieters and nondieters eat comes from the farm. Consider how the concepts of energy conservation could be applied to calculating the maximum amount of food that could be raised on this planet. This is analogous to estimating the most energy that could be saved.

Somewhere on earth there is the world's best farmer. Call him X. He has the world's most efficient farm equipment, fertilizers, and technology. He may be in the American Midwest, with its enormous bounty of corn and other crops. He may be in Japan. Farms there are tiny by American standards, but the output per acre is among the highest in the world.

If we wanted to know the maximum amount of food production on earth, we would multiply the food per acre that farmer X grew by the total number of arable acres. This would be an interesting number, and probably would be quoted in all the media, but ultimately it would tell us nothing about which specific programs we should employ to raise world food production. Farmer X may have access to unlimited financial credit and hold a Ph.D. in agricultural science and an MBA. What does he have in common with an illiterate farmer in India, with a broken-down bullock and a few acres, except that they both work the land?

In the same way, conservation advocates point to the most energy-efficient refrigerators, cars, houses, and other users of energy. They say, in effect, "If everyone had the most energy-efficient refrigerator, we could save so many billions of kilowatt hours."

Whatever that number is, it bears about the same relation to reality as a maximum food production number. It certainly cannot be achieved. For example, this marvelous refrigerator, while using little electricity, may be expensive, so few people could afford it. Its potential for saving energy will not be fulfilled.

As Fereidoon Sioshansi writes, "The answer to this hypothetical question [about the maximum amount of food the world can produce] is very different from what can reasonably be expected given what we know about the limitation of introducing new farming equipment and technology to under-capitalized and less-developed countries."[1]

Farmer X exists, just as the most efficient refrigerator sits somewhere in a laboratory. We cannot make much policy about food production or conservation using them as examples.

• • •

Someone once phoned in to Dr. Dean Edell's medical radio talk show with a question about liposuction, a procedure for removing fat from thighs and other overloaded body parts. The operation is usually performed on the severely overweight. Dr. Edell noted that while the operation seems to work on the part that is being vacuumed out, some of the excess fat seems to migrate to other parts of the body. That is, someone's thighs may look closer to normal after liposuction, but his or her upper arms or backside may receive an unwanted infusion of fat cells. The person may look about as fat as ever after the operation, although the fat may be distributed differently.

What does all of this have to do with energy conservation? The parallels are striking. We conserve in one area, but find, through mysterious means, that we are using more energy in another. We buy an energy-conserving fluorescent lightbulb to put a few more pennies in our pocket, but we proceed to let it burn as a safety light, day and night. Then we wonder why the utility bill is not much lower than in the past.

Energy is like the fat that many of us wish we could get rid of. Reducing it in one area seem to make it appear in another.

• • •

Popcorn might seem to have no connection at all to conservation, but consider the advertisements for so-called premium popcorn, such as Orville Redenbacher's or Paul Newman's. Their advertisements make two pitches. First, it tastes better. Second, there is less waste. All or virtually all of the kernels pop.

There is no accounting for taste, and this dictum applies to lowly popcorn. To many, there is not all that much distinction between the premium brands and those less favored by nature, but undoubtedly there are those who can detect the difference. The second claim relates to conservation. Not long ago, I performed an experiment. It is true, as the advertisements state, that there is almost no wastage with the premium brands. When I popped ordinary corn, some kernels did not make it. I did not count the number of kernels that missed their chance of glory, but I would estimate they were on the order of 5 percent.

You have to pay a steep premium to eliminate that 5 percent wastage. Premium popcorns are often twice the price of the ordinary kind. Half the ordinary kernels would have to be failures before you would come out ahead.

The little parable relates to conservation. Many conservation devices require a steep price to save a tiny amount of energy. If the cost per unit of energy saved were calculated and sent as a bill by the electric company, consumers would go ballistic. Yet some of us cheerfully pay a lot more for popcorn, in the hope of saving the wastage of perhaps 2¢ worth of kernels.

• • •

Food is also part of what used to be called the "free lunch." Long ago, bars would advertise this. Come in around noon, and you could eat all the sandwiches you want. Of course, bars were not in the habit of feeding the hungry without recompense. Unless their patrons quaffed enough beverages, the bars would either go out of business or abandon their offer of free lunch. The source of the gratis food was obvious to all except the most inebriated patrons.

There is a modern-day counterpart to all this. Conservation, we are told, solves all energy problems. It is cost-free and there are only winners. Nobody can possibly lose.

Although we are rightly suspicious of free lunches supplied by saloons, we tend to be gullible when it comes to conservation. It all seems so easy—we just drive smaller cars, or turn off the lights more frequently. Surely this is the free lunch promised—but not really delivered—in the old drinking holes.

There is no free lunch for conservation, either. Society as a whole cannot really conserve, no matter how hard it tries. Individuals can conserve, but those who do not will tend to use a bit more energy than they would have otherwise, and conservation measures usually involve some type of costs, either financial or otherwise. In Chapter 16, the high prices of energy-saving lightbulbs are described. In many cases, the bulbs would burn out long before they had saved enough money to pay for themselves.

But surely driving a small car to save gasoline is a free lunch? Not true. It is correct that small cars tend to cost less than large ones, although the margin has significantly narrowed in a generation.[2] There is another cost, not immediately apparent in the pocketbook. All other factors being equal, a large car is safer to drive than a small one. This relates to the laws of physics, and has nothing to do with conservation. So when a conservation-conscious person opts for a smaller vehicle, he or she may pay a high price if unlucky—being injured more severely than if a large car had been chosen. The free lunch was not there.

About the same applies to other forms of conservation, such as switching off lightbulbs. This again seems cost-free. But tens of thousands of people are injured every year by falls in the home. How many of those falls were because of inadequate lighting, people saying to themselves, "I don't really need to flick on the light, I can see where I'm going"? Turning off ever more lights would inevitably increase the injury rate.

Nobody would mindlessly inflict a greater rate of injuries because of falls, especially on our fragile senior citizens. Yet this is what is indirectly proposed in making our nation gloomier through conservation. What appears like a free lunch again disappears.

To summarize, although food and its eating, growing, and dispensing do not appear to have a relationship to conservation, they do. We usually deal with food in a more sensible manner than with conservation proposals.

NOTES

1. Fereidoon P. Sioshansi, "The Myths and Facts of Energy Efficiency," *Energy Policy* 19 (April 1991): 231–243.

2. Long ago, a Cadillac was substantially larger than a Chevrolet. Nowadays, a small car may cost more than a large one. Although the Lexus and the Infiniti are considerably more expensive than the Chevrolet Caprice or Ford Crown Victoria, their dimensions are smaller.

23

Where Do We Go from Here?

Most books on energy conservation conclude with a long list of suggestions for both the public and governments. Drive a smaller car, or better yet use a bicycle or walk. Governments should ban waste and mount a crash program of energy-conserving regulations and research. The United Nations should ensure that the Third World uses the minimum amount of energy necessary to industrialize.

Readers looking for this set of prescriptions here will be disappointed. My argument is that what we generally call conservation can exist in small areas, such as a household; however, when we try to extrapolate our personal savings to a city, state, nation, or the world, our vast hoped-for energy savings vanish like the morning dew on a sun-drenched meadow. If this is true, all the research and all the regulations that human brains can devise will not help much.

• • •

We cannot run out of energy. Stanley Jevons said as much last century, and his message is being revived today. We may well have to pay more for some forms of energy, and some, such as nuclear, may eventually supplant the fossil fuels we mostly use today.

None of this transformation should be a surprise. In the nineteenth century, wood was the most common fuel in the United States. It still is number one in some remote regions of the world today. Gradually, as much of the forest was chopped down, society shifted to coal. It was around this time of change that Jevons wrote that coal could not, in the ordinary sense, be exhausted.

Problems with coal became evident at the close of the last century. The new-fangled horseless carriages could not use the fuel, so petroleum products— still based on ancient fossils—were developed.

Now we are in the midst of yet another transformation. Concerns are once more raised about running out of energy. This latest transformation is different in that a vast array of government regulations in many countries is designed to prevent this exhaustion. In Jevons' day, the concern about running out of coal was expressed primarily in letters to the London *Times* and dinner party conversation in the stately homes of England. No government thought of imposing regulations on the "waste" of coal.

The French have a saying for it: *La plus ça change, la plus c'est la même chose.* The more things change, the more they stay the same. The main difference between the present transformation of energy sources and previous ones is that now we have a giant government apparatus accompanying it.

What specifically could and should be done about conservation? We can divide the response into two parts: government and private actions (or inactions). I am skeptical about many government actions that have as their noble objective the reduction of energy waste. President Jimmy Carter, at the height of the late 1970s so-called energy crisis, said that all Federal buildings had to be heated and cooled only slightly. However, his rule was honored primarily in the breach. A few years later, there was almost no trace of his rule, except in some dusty copies of the *Federal Register*.

From time to time, I visit government buildings. I have been in many that are blastingly hot in winter and chilling frigid in summer. While some bureaucrats may have followed the president's dictums to the letter, those who did not more than made up in "waste" for those who did.

Even if some government conservation regulations worked exactly the way they were supposed to, the overall effect on society will be zero or close to zero. If the government saves energy somehow, the rest of us will obtain energy a bit more cheaply and thus "waste" about the same amount that has been "saved."

• • •

Is there any purpose for government actions in conservation? A reasonable role is to fund research in those energy production and efficiency areas that are too long-term for private industry. This sounds so vague as to be unworkable, but a trio of examples can demonstrate my reasoning.

Much house insulation is made of strands of fiberglass. Suppose that by twisting the fiberglass in a new way the material could resist the flow of heat better than now. That is, the so-called R-value for the same piece of insulation would rise, making it more valuable. I see no reason why government should undertake this kind of research. Fiberglass companies have research departments, and they could determine whether they could make money by introducing this innovation.

A second example would be nonconventional sources of natural gas. Thomas Gold, a professor at Cornell University, has proposed that we should look for natural gas in places that oil companies usually avoid. He feels that natural gas arises from geological sources as well as the fossils of ancient creatures. I am summarizing a complex theory here, and I apologize to Professor Gold if I have compressed his ideas a bit too much.[1]

I am not in a position to judge the validity of Professor Gold's thinking. Certainly many in the oil and gas industry are highly skeptical. But if he is like many other professors in the sciences, some of the funding for his research came through the Federal government, via the National Science Foundation and other agencies. The funding of such possible left-field energy-generating activities is well within the ambit of government energy efforts, even though many of them will prove will-o'-the-wisps. Professor Gold's concepts are clearly long-range and most oil and gas companies are interested primarily in the next gusher.

As the third and final example, consider nuclear energy. At the conclusion of World War II, when its possibilities for both tremendous destruction and benefit had been revealed, there were no private companies with the resources to investigate the power possibilities. As a result, in every country of the world where nuclear power was developed, governments did all the initial funding. The United States, under the Eisenhower administration, was the first to gradually wean nuclear power away from government funding, and most other countries have followed the American lead.

What can we conclude about the proper role of government in energy production and conservation research? From these simple examples, government-sponsored research can provide benefit if it concentrates on the long-term waters where few if any private companies have the temerity to dip their toes. In the nature of research, most efforts will be futile. But as soon as some benefits appear, the government should gradually reduce its role.

• • •

Private research in energy conservation will go on, no matter what public opinion is about how much energy is left in the ground. Profits will often, though not always, be made when greater energy efficiency is developed.

For example, when regulations to increase fuel efficiency were put in force in the late 1970s, many manufacturers had to switch immediately from V-8s to small four-cylinder engines to meet the rules. Regardless of their merits in fuel efficiency, the acceleration of these smaller engines was certainly different from what American motorists had come to expect.

The automobile manufacturers poured enormous amounts of money into developing engines that could provide better acceleration and at the same time meet the fuel-efficiency standards. Anyone who walks into an automobile showroom in the mid-1990s will notice a vast array of V-6 engines in such formerly "small" cars as the Honda Accord and Toyota Camry, engines that often rival in horsepower the block-long versions of the 1950s. The research of the auto manufacturers has paid off.

In the same way, half a century ago off-shore oil drilling was confined to Lake Maracaibo in Venezuela. Now huge off-shore rigs spring up from the North Sea to Alaska. None of this was required by government regulation. Oil companies realized that there was a vast amount of oil under the seas. While it would always be more expensive than that found on land, at least it was there.

So while there is a dollar, yen, or peso to be made from research on either providing more energy efficiency or more energy, private enterprise will usually find a way to do it. Many, but not all, decisions are too difficult and complex to be left to government.

This disparagement of the role of government in terms of conservation should not be taken as a rewriting of Voltaire's dictum that "all is well in the best of all possible worlds." There is a considerable role for government in many phases of life, something that is often forgotten in the United States especially.

James Michener, the distinguished novelist, wrote an article for an October 1995 issue of *Parade* magazine, the Sunday insert for certain newspapers. He discussed the rise and fall of civilizations, and predicted that American civilization would crumble by the middle of the twenty-first century. In part, he predicated his dire forecast on the reluctance of many Americans to harness government to serve national needs such as education. He contrasted this with the civilizations of Asia, just now coming into their own in an industrialized world. There, how big government should be is not a matter of ideology as it is in the United States. It is merely a matter of what has to be done.

Regardless of who sits in the White House and who rules Congress, there is much unfinished business for the Federal government in health care, environment, education, and generally taking care of those who have fallen behind in the race for the twenty-first century. But energy conservation is an area where I do not think there is much to be gained by a major federal role.

• • •

Published around the turn of the century, *Looking Backward*, by Edward Bellamy was one of the most influential of the so-called "utopia" genre.[2] It peered in the rearview mirror from the twentieth century to the nineteenth, showing all the improvements that had been made in the interval. The book cast a spell on many American reformers.

One of its most amazing (for the time) predictions was about information fed into homes. Although radio had not been invented when he wrote, telephones had been. Bellamy said that music would one day be transmitted from concert halls into homes by phones. The mechanism turned out to be different, but the principle was accurate.

What does all this have to do with conservation? Like many utopians, Bellamy wanted to clean up what he regarded as the complications, noises, and confusions of modern life. One of his most vivid passages is when the time traveler, who had been to an uncluttered future where everything proceeded in a predictable and orderly fashion, returns to his home in Boston in the nineteenth century. The streets are a jumble of signs, people hawking their wares, and utter chaos—at least by the calm and clean standards that Bellamy envisioned. His future was orderly. Everything had been decided in advance by intelligent men—actually retired workers. (Curiously enough, none of Bellamy's women of the twentieth century made major decisions.)

So it is with conservation advocates. They are tired of the claims and confusion spread by different oil companies, gas firms, nuclear power proponents, and the tremendous "waste" they see on all sides. If only the government or some such wise agency could stop all this. This agency would arrange everything so waste and commotion could be forever eliminated.

It is not that simple. As long as people inhabit the planet, things will always be messier than some would like. This applies to energy as well as other aspects of life. No agency can get rid of waste any more than it can enforce joy.

NOTES

1. Thomas Gold, *Power from the Earth* (London: Dent, 1987).
2. Edward Bellamy, *Looking Backward, 2000–1987* (1888; reprint, Cambridge, Mass.: Harvard University Press, 1967).

Annotated Bibliography

Adams, R. C., and A. D. Rockwood. "Impact of Improved Building Thermal Efficiency on Residential Energy Demand," Battelle Pacific Northwest Laboratories, Richland, Wash., May 1981. Lab report shows that residents use more energy following techniques to improve energy efficiency.

Adelman, Morris. "Oil Fallacies." *Foreign Policy* 10 (Spring 1991). "The great oil shortage is like the horizon, always receding as one moves toward it."

Alchian, Armen A. and R. Allen. *University Economics*. Belmont, Calif.: Wadsworth, 1965. Conservationists fail to understand that "using goods can mean converting them into even more valuable sources of wealth."

American Petroleum Institute. *Energy Security White Paper: U.S. Decisions and Global Trends*. Washington, D.C.: The Institute, 1988. Higher energy prices accounted for 80 percent of total U.S. energy efficiency gains since 1973.

Anderson, Kent P., ed. "Key Issues in Least-Cost Planning." Working Paper No. 10, National Economic Research Associates, Los Angeles, Aug. 1991. Found that claimed benefits of demand-side management programs were grossly overestimated. "Since accurate measurement is costly and difficult, and since casual measurement is likely to suggest success, it will be tempting to employ casual measures, declare victory, and claim rewards."

Andersson, Ronald, and Lewis Taylor. "The Social Costs of Unsupplied Energy: A Critical Review." *Energy Economics* 8, no. 3 (July 1986): 139–146. If energy is not supplied, the effect is much greater than just so much money saved.

Barkovich, Barbara R. *Regulatory Interventionism in the Utility Industry: Fairness, Efficiency and the Pursuit of Energy Conservation*. Westport, Conn.: Quorum Books, 1989. Analysis of the California Energy Commission, 1975 to 1984.

Baron, Seymour. "Energy Cycles: Their Cost Inter-relationship for Power Generation." *Mechanical Engineering* 98 (June 1976).

Basken, Paul. "GOP Attacks Energy Budget, Priorities." United Press, 9 Feb. 1995. Senator Frank Murkowski of Alaska, chair of Senate Energy Committee, said, "It is dangerously unrealistic to believe that our dependence on foreign oil will be alleviated through these [conservation] measures."

Baum, Andrew, and Jerome E. Singer, eds. *Advances in Environmental Psychology.* Vol. 3, *Energy Psychological Perspectives.* Hillsdale, N.J.: Lawrence Erlbaum Associates, 1981. Many papers on psychology of conservation; see McClelland and Canter, Reichel and Geller.

Baumol, William J. "On Recycling as a Moot Environmental Issue." *Journal of Environmental Economics and Management* 4, no. 1 (1977): 83. Increased recycling will always decrease the amount of oil available to society; that is opposite to what most people think.

Baumol, William J. "On the Possibility of Continuing Expansion of Resources." *Kyklos* 39, no. 2 (1986): 167. The quantity of exhaustible and unreproducible energy sources may rise unceasingly, year by year.

Baumol, William J., and Sue Anne Batey Blackman. "Unprofitable Energy Is Squandered Energy." *Challenge* 23 (July/Aug. 1980). This article by the former head of the American Economic Association is influential; it demonstrates that energy subsidies, of whatever ilk, waste energy.

Baumol, William J., and Edward N. Wolff. "Subsidies to New Energy Sources: Do They Add to Energy Stocks?" *Journal of Political Economy* 89, no. 5 (1981): 891. A tariff on oil is preferable to government subsidies to innovative energy sources.

Beck, B. *Proceedings of the 24th Annual Conference of Western Regional Family Economics—Home Management Educators*, ed. C. A. Dickinson. Corvallis, Ore.: Dept. of Family Resource Management, Oregon State University, 1984. Some consumers reduce energy conservation efforts after installing energy-saving devices; this is an example of the "bounce-back" effect.

Beckman, Petr. "Belongs to All of Us." *Access to Energy* 1 (April 1991). "Can you imagine the shoe industry preaching that it is less profitable to renew their machinery than to force people to resole their shoes and if possible to go barefoot?"

Bernstam, Mikhail. "The Wealth of Nations and the Environment." Paper no. 45, Institute for Economic Affairs, London, January 1991. The United States used 55 percent less energy per unit GNP in 1990 than in 1929, illustrating greater long-term energy efficiency without Draconian measures.

Berry, Linda G. "The Market Penetration of Energy Efficient Programs." Report CON-299, Oak Ridge National Laboratory, Oak Ridge, Tenn., 1990. A discussion of difficulties in getting ratepayers to volunteer for audits and follow-up improvements after energy-saving devices are installed.

Blackmon, Glenn. "Conservation Incentives: Evaluating the Washington State Experience." *Public Utilities Fortnightly* 127 (15 Jan. 1991): 24–27. Background to the 1990 law which greatly reduced financial incentives for conservation measures.

Bohi, Douglas R., and Mary Beth Zimmerman. "An Update on Econometric Studies of Energy Demand Behavior." *Annual Review of Energy* 9 (1984): 105. Gives elasticity for residential demand for electricity: −0.2 in short run, −0.7 in long run. Long review article with many references.

Bourgeois, Bernard, Patrick Criqui, and Jacques Perrebois. "Energy Conservation versus Supply Strategies: Implications for Industrial Policy." *Energy Journal* 9 (July 1988): 99–111.

Bradley, Robert L., Jr. "Should the United States Prepare for Another Oil Crisis?" Roswell, Ga.: Southern Regulatory Policy Institute, Issue paper no. 2, Dec. 1989. "There will be volatility in the world [oil] market, and any quest for 'energy security' and 'energy independence' through activist policy is illusory."

Brandis, Pamela, and M. Hosein Haeri. "The Persistence of Energy Savings Over Time: Two and Three Years after Participation in an Energy Retrofit Program." Paper presented at the 1989 Energy Program Evaluation Conference, Chicago, 1989. Over a three-year period, there was a 33 percent decrease in net electricity savings compared to the first year.

Brookes, Leonard G. "Confusing the Issue on Energy Efficiency." *Energy Policy* 19 (March 1991): 184–186. Criticizes Tokes' comments and denounces "energy efficiency aficionados"; a polemical article.

Brookes, Leonard G. "Energy Efficiency and Economic Fallacies: A Reply." *Energy Policy* 19 (March, 1991): 783–785. Greater energy efficiency increases energy use; reiteration of Jevons' arguments.

Brookes, Leonard G. "Energy Efficiency and the Greenhouse Effect." *Energy & Environment* 1, no. 4 (1990): 318–330.

Brookes, Leonard G. "Energy Intensities: Myths and Realities." *Oxford Energy Forum* 21 (May 1995): 2–4. Argues against energy conservation for its own sake; quotes Gordon Solow in short article.

Brookes, Leonard G. "The 'Fifth Fuel' and the Greenhouse Effect." *Energy World* 18 (Feb. 1990): 2. There is no "fifth fuel" (other than coal, oil, gas, and nuclear) from conservation.

Brookes, Leonard G. "The Greenhouse Effect: The Fallacy in the Energy Efficiency Solution." *Energy Policy* 18 (March 1990): 199. Energy savings from increased efficiency will not substitute for new energy supplies.

Brookes, Leonard G. "Nuclear Energy = More Jobs?" *Energy Manager* 2 (July/Aug. 1979): 21–23. Mentions fallacy of composition in terms of unemployment.

Brookes, Leonard G. Review of *A Low Energy Strategy for the United Kingdom*, by G. Leach. *Atom* (March 1979): 3–8. Decries use of physical as opposed to economic conservation models; mentions fallacy of composition in terms of wages.

Brooks, Ronna. "Idling Trucks Negate the Savings from Recycling." *Buffalo News*, 21 Dec. 1991, C2. Conservationist tries to get motorist idling car to stop.

Brown, M. A., and D. L. White. "Evaluation of Bonneville's 1988 and 1989 Residential Weatherization Program: A Northwest Study of Program Dynamics." Report CON-323, Oak Ridge National Laboratory, Oak Ridge, Tenn., Dec. 1992. Free riders are not accounted for. Costs per kWhr saved ranged from 6.9¢ to 11.4¢, as computed by Joskow and Marron in July 1993.

Brown, Stephen P. A. "Reducing U.S. Vulnerability to World Oil Supply Disruptions." *Economic Review* (Federal Reserve Bank of Dallas) (May 1982): 1–13. Past attempts to legislate specific conservation technologies were inefficient. Legislation ignored many low-cost methods of conservation.

Brown, Stephen P. A., and Keith R. Phillips. "U.S. Oil Demand and Conservation." *Contemporary Policy Issues* 9 (Jan. 1991): 67–72. The relationship between prices and consumption.

California Energy Commission. *Energy Report 1990*. Report P106-90-002(A), Sacramento, Calif., Oct. 1990. "The additional conservation deferred the construction of newer, less polluting units and caused the system to rely upon the existing, more polluting plants."

Caner, Phoebe. "The Drive to Verify Energy Savings." *Electricity Journal* 43 (May 1992). Finds that twenty-seven out of thirty-two "negawatt" programs run by electric utilities produced savings below the engineering estimates on which they were based. Fifteen of the thirty-two produced savings of less than half of the engineering estimates.

Canes, Michael. "Oil's Tenacious Lock on Health of Economy." *Forum for Applied Research and Public Policy* 7 (Spring 1992): 18. Known oil reserves are greater today than at any other time in recorded history.

Carlsmith, Roger, W. V. Chandler, J. E. McMahon, and D. J. Santini. "Energy Efficiency: How Far Can We Go." Report ORNL/TM-11441, Oak Ridge National Laboratory, Oak Ridge, Tenn., 1990. "Information regarding the technical viability of such [efficient energy] technologies under full-scale, actual usage conditions are often scarce."

Cavanaugh, R. "Responsible Power Marketing in an Increasingly Competitive Era." *Yale Journal on Regulation* 5 (1988): 331–358. Payback for energy efficiency changes has to be less than six months to three years or it will not be instituted.

"CFC Group Changes Name, Shifts Focus to Global Warming." *Chemical & Engineering News* 71 (25 Oct. 1993): 19. New freon-replacing chemicals have small global-warming potential but save energy.

Cherfas, Jeremy. "Skeptics and Visionaries Examine Energy Saving." *Science* 251 (11 Jan. 1991): 154. Dahlem, Germany conference on "Limiting the Greenhouse Effect"; News report; "Nobody doubts that vast energy savings are possible; everyone doubts that the energy will actually be saved . . . energy costs too little and efficiency apparently costs too much."

Cicchetti, Charles J., and Suellen Curkendall. "Conservation Subsidies: The Economist's Perspective." *Electric Potential* 2 (May/June 1986): 3–12.

Cicchetti, Charles J., and William Hogan. "Including Unbundled Demand-Side Options in Electric Utility Bidding Programs." *Public Utilities Fortnightly* 123 (8 June 1989): 9–20. Suggests ways to include conservation bids in supply auctions.

Clarkson, James A. "Industrial Energy Efficiency via Centralized Planning is a Bad Idea." *Strategic Planning for Energy and the Environment* 12, no. 2 (1992): 44–53. Criticizes demand-side management by public utility commissions; based on testimony before Georgia Public Utility Commission.

Coates, Brian. "Energy Savings and Cost-Effectiveness in the Commercial Incentives Pilot Program." Paper presented at the 1991 Energy Program Evaluation Conference, Chicago, 1991. Commercial rebate customers only obtained 30 percent of projected savings.

Cohen, Sam. "Fifty Million Retrofits Later." *Home Energy* 7 (May/June 1990): 11–16. "LBL's [Lawrence Berkeley Laboratory] experience suggests that engineering estimates of energy savings are notoriously unreliable, often overstating savings."

Condelli, Larry, Dane Archer, Elliott Aronson, Barbara Curbow, Beverley McLeod, Thomas F. Pettigrew, Lawrence T. White, and Suzanne Yates. "Improving Utility Conservation Programs: Outcomes, Interventions and Evaluations." *Energy* 9, no. 6 (1984): 485. Enormous literature survey on difference between what consumers say they do about conservation and what actually happens; contains many good examples.

Congressional Budget Office. *President Carter's Proposals: A Perspective*. Washington, D.C.: U.S. Government Printing Office, June 1977. "A large share of any tax credits [for energy conservation] would be a windfall payment to people who have already decided to add insulation."

"Conservation Power." *Business Week*, 16 Sept. 1991, 86. On Cape Cod, Massachusetts, residential utility customers saw rates rise by 5 to 15 percent to help pay for conservation programs that mainly help business.

"Consumers Not Yet Tilting toward Fuel-Efficient Cars." *Buffalo News*, 23 Aug. 1990, C9. War in Mideast has not swung consumers toward small cars; difference in annual fuel costs between Lincoln Town Car and Ford Escort, large and small cars respectively, is only about $108 annually, a pittance.

Costello, Kenneth W. "Ten Myths of Energy Conservation." *Public Utilities Fortnightly* 119 (19 March 1987). Energy conservation potential is vastly overestimated; this article gives ten reasons why this is so.

"Dim Bulbs." *USA Today*, 10 Nov. 1992, B1. The Federal Trade Commission found that General Electric forgot to tell customers that its "energy-efficient" bulbs produced less light than regular ones. The FTC had accused GE of misleading customers by false claims.

Divan, T. M., and D. T. Trumble. "Temperature Takeback in the Hood River Conservation Project." *Energy and Buildings* 13 no. 1 (1989): 39–50. Consumers set their thermostats higher in the winter and lower in the summer after conservation measures were installed.

Dubin, Jeffrey A. "Will Mandatory Conservation Promote Energy Efficiency in the Selection of Household Appliance Stocks?" *Energy Journal* 7 (Jan. 1986): 99–118.

Ecowatts: The Clean Switch. Bethesda, Md.: Science Concepts Inc., 1991. Since 1973, U.S. electricity generation increased by 50 percent while national energy efficiency improved by 40 percent.

Edwardsen, Elizabeth. "New Rules Help Utilities Sell Conservation." *Buffalo News*, 9 Dec. 1990. New York State Public Utility Commission requires utilities to spend millions on conservation pamphlets, tax breaks, and the like.

Einhorn, Michael. "The Effects of Energy Prices upon Appliance Efficiencies and Building Insulation." *Energy Journal* 7 (July 1986): 115–122.

"Energy and the Environment: A Power for Good, a Power for Ill." *The Economist*, 31 Aug. 1991. The world has ten times the amount of proven oil reserves that it had in 1950, and twice the known reserves of 1970. Proven reserves of coal and natural gas have also increased dramatically. This is in spite of ever-increasing use.

"Energy Edge Impact Evaluation." Report LBL-3077, Lawrence Berkeley Laboratory, Berkeley, Calif., Dec. 1990. A review of "Energy Edge" commercial buildings found that 23 percent had greater savings than predicted, and 46 percent had less.

"Energy Policy: What Now?" *Nuclear Industry* (first quarter 1991): 39–40. Japan appears more energy efficient than the United States, but only when standards of living, population density, industrial structure, and other factors are ignored.

"Energy Rebates Dropped." *Augusta* [Ga.] *Chronicle*, 9 Aug. 1995, 9A. Georgia Power will stop rewarding customers for making homes more energy efficient; it cost other customers $1.00 to $1.50 per month.

Engles, D., and H. D. Peach. "Energy Conservation Program Evaluation: Practical Methods." Useful results proceedings, Argonne National Laboratory, Argonne, Ill., 1985. "House doctoring" (intensive conservation measures) produced much fewer results than expected.

"EPA Ranks Geo Metro Most Fuel-Efficient Car." Reuters, 30 Sept. 1996. While the 1997 Metro averages about forty-six miles per gallon, Diane Steed, president of Coalition for Vehicle Choice, notes that in 1995, the top ten most fuel-efficient cars represented less than 1 percent of passenger car sales and only 0.6 percent of overall car and light truck sales.

"Fear Is Expressed of U.S. Oil Scarcity." *New York Times*, 11 June 1950. State Department predicted that global oil reserves would run dry by 1964. They grew ten times by 1990.

Flanigan, Ted, and June Weintraub. "The Most Successful DSM Programs in North America." *Electricity Journal* 16 (May 1993): 53–65. Excluded unsuccessful DSM programs: "Just when you think you've got significant levels of savings, you unfortunately may not!"

Flesher, John. "Fuel Ratings Skid Again for 1992 Autos." *Buffalo News*, 5 Oct. 1991, A–8. Average is 27.5 mpg, down slightly from 27.8 in 1991; six cars get 50 mpg or better; Lamborghini Diablo is worst, at 9 mpg city, 14 mpg highway; bill to increase ratings opposed by auto industry.

Frey, Cynthia J. "An Examination of Energy Take-Back." *Energy Systems and Policy* 12, no. 3 (1988): 205–218. After installing energy-saving devices, consumers often open previously closed-off rooms to heat, increase thermostat settings, and the like, reducing conservation effects.

Fri, Robert W. "Energy and Environment: A Coming Collision?" *Resources* 98 (Winter 1990): 1–4. Questions raised by cutting energy consumption in the interest of environmental protection.

Gattuso, James L., and Kent Jeffreys. "The Mounting Dangers of the 'CAFE' Mileage Standards." Report 676, Heritage Foundation, Washington, D.C., 13 Oct. 1988. CAFE (Corporate Average Fuel Economy) standards for autos save little or no fuel.

Geller, E. Scott. "Evaluating Energy Conservation Programs: Is Verbal Report Enough?" *Journal of Consumer Research* 8, no. 3 (1981): 331–334. Workshops demonstrating energy conservation techniques were ineffective.

Geller, E. Scott. "The Energy Crisis and Behavioral Science: A Conceptual Framework for Large Scale Intervention." In *Rural Psychology*, ed. A. W. Childs and G. B. Melton. New York: Plenum, 1983. Workshops demonstrating energy conservation techniques were ineffective.

Geller, E. Scott, Jeff B. Erickson, and Brenda A. Buttram. "Attempts to Promote Residential Water Conservation with Educational, Behavioral and Engineering Strategies." *Population and Environment* 6 (Summer 1983): 96. Those aware of the installation of water-saving devices conserved much less than those oblivious to the installation; example of bounce-back effect.

Gilmer, Robert W. "Energy Labels and Economic Search." *Energy Economics* (July 1989): 213–218. Claims small benefits ($20 to $45) from energy labeling of houses; shows very high discount rates for conservation in many household appliances.

Good Housekeeping. Dec. 1990, 78. "Tight home insulation" provides ideal conditions for common house-dust mites to thrive. They are a major cause of early childhood asthma.

Greenhalgh, Geoffrey. "Energy Conservation Policies." *Energy Policy* 18 (April 1990): 293–299. Useful, good philosophical basis; one of few to note ambiguity of the word "conservation"; quotes Jevons; useful data from Denmark.

Griffin, Waylon D. "The Limits of Conservation." In *Alternative Energy Sources II*, Vol. 9, *Conservation, Economics and Policy*, ed. T. N. Veziroglu. Washington, D.C.: Hemispheric Publishing, 1981. Good quotes and philosophy; notes that all conservation measures have a downside.

Gustaffson, Stig Inge, and Bjorn G. Karlsson. "Production or Conservation in CHP Networks?" *Heat Recovery Systems and CHP* 10, no. 2 (1990): 151–160. Energy conservation in district-heated buildings cannot be justified economically, nor can conservation in the electric power grid.

Gwartney, James D. *Economics—Private and Public Choice*. New York: Academic Press, 1976. Quotes Mitchell on lack of significance of proved oil reserves.

Hamilton, Martha, and Warren Brown. "Conservation Complacency in the U.S." *Washington Post*, 12 Aug. 1990, A26. The United States was 52 percent more efficient in its use of oil in 1990 than it was in 1973.

Hannon, Bruce. "Energy and the Consumer." *Science* 189 (July 1975): 95. Energy is needed to supply the added consumption arising from the spending of dollars saved as a result of more effective investment; that is, second-order effects.

Hannon, Bruce. "Energy Discounting." *Technological Forecasting and Social Change* 21, no. 4 (1982): 281–300. Claims conservation projects have high rate of return, but uses primarily theoretical data; good literature review.

Harris, Anthony. "A Head-in-the-Sand Approach to Oil." *Financial Times*, 13 Aug. 1990. Increasing fuel efficiency of U.S. cars has led to greater auto ownership and gasoline use.

Hartman, Raymond S. "Measuring the Effects of Utility-Sponsored Conservation Programs: Do the Programs Work?" *Energy Systems and Policy* 8 (Jan. 1984): 213.

Hartman, Raymond S. "Self-Selection Bias in the Evaluation of Voluntary Energy Conservation Programs." *Review of Economic Statistics* 70 (August 1988): 448–458.

Hartman, Raymond S., and Michael J. Doane. "The Estimation of the Effects of Utility-Sponsored Conservation Programmes." *Applied Economics* 18 (1986): 1. Average consumer in Portland saved only 387 kWhr out of average use of 23,000 kWhr, about 2 percent, after audit and zero-interest loan. Suggests uselessness of audits.

Hausman, Jerry, and Paul L. Joskow. "Evaluating the Costs and Benefits of Appliance Efficiency Standards." *American Economic Review* 72 (May 1985): 220–225.

Hayek, Friedrich A. *The Constitution of Liberty*. Chicago: University of Chicago Press, 1960. "Industrial development would have been greatly retarded if 60 or 80 years ago the warning of the conservationists about the threatened exhaustion of the supply of coal had been heeded; and the internal combustion engine would never have revolutionized transport if its use had been limited to the [then] known supplies of oil."

Heberlein, Thomas A. "Conservation Information: The Energy Crisis and Electricity Consumption in an Apartment Complex." *Energy Systems and Policy* 1 (1975): 105–117. Pamphlets and handbooks on energy conservation were ineffective.

Hebert, H. Josef. "Murkowski—Energy." Associated Press, 12 Jan. 1995, no. 1422. Sen. Frank Murkowski (R–Alaska) proposes to lift the ban on Alaskan oil being exported outside the United States.

Heicke, G. A. "A Detailed Comparison of Energy Audits Carried Out by Four Separate Companies on the Same Set of Buildings." *Energy and Buildings* 14, no. 2 (1990): 153–165. Four separate audits carried out in the European Community all gave different results and all differed from benchmark; casts doubt on auditing concept.

Heilbroner, Robert, and Lester C. Thurow. *The Economic Problem*. New York: Prentice-Hall, 1978. The only elementary economics textbook I was able to find that explicitly showed the implications of conservation theories on a supply–demand curve.

Hileman, Bette. "Curbing Global Warming—Clinton Unveils Ambitious Action Plan." *Chemical & Engineering News* 71 (25 Oct. 1993): 4–5. Administration plan would reduce emissions "below what they would otherwise be"; spurious reasoning here.

Hirst, Eric. "Actual Energy Savings after Retrofit: Electrically Heated Homes in the Pacific Northwest." *Energy* 11, no. 3 (1986): 299–301. About 20 percent of residential retrofit participants experienced no savings or an increase in electricity consumption.

Hirst, Eric. "Electricity Use and Savings: Final Report, Hood River Conservation Project." Report DOE/BP-11287-16, Bonneville Power Administration, Portland, Ore., 1987. Three thousand homes were fitted with various weatherization measures; only 40 percent of predicted savings were achieved.

Hirst, Eric. "Evaluating Demand-Side Management Programs." *Electric Perspectives* 14, no. 6 (1990): 24–30. A Niagara Mohawk pilot program offered free water heater blankets, free pipe insulation, and free low-flow showerheads; they got a 12 percent response rate.

Hirst, Eric. "The Hood River Conservation Project: A Unique Research and Demonstration Effort." *Energy and Buildings* 13, no. 1 (1989): 3–10. In this project, an average of over $6,000 per household was spent, but only 85 percent of eligible homes decided to participate even with this enormous incentive.

Hogan, William W., and Dale W. Jorgenson. "Productivity Trends and the Cost of Reducing CO_2 Emissions." *Energy Journal* 12, no. 1 (1991): 67–85. Production factors in the United States mean that technical progress increases energy use.

Horn, John. "Some Celebrities Miscast in Environmentalist Role." *Buffalo News*, 22 April 1990, A14. Movie stars at Beverly Hills party idle limousines for hours, are criticized by environmentalists.

Hoshide, R. K., and W. F. Rock, Jr. "Where Are My Energy Savings?" In *Retrofit Opportunities for Energy Management and Cogeneration: Proceedings of the Eleventh World Energy Engineering Conference*, pp. 523–527. Fairmont Press, Lilburn, Ga.: 1989. Savings are not being realized in spite of conservation programs. The optimistic approach to energy conservation measures "is sometimes used because it may make the selling, approval and funding of the project much easier."

Hotelling, Harold. "The Economics of Exhaustible Resource." *Journal of Political Economy* 39 (April 1931): 137. One of the first articles, after Jevons, to discuss mathematically the exhaustion of natural resources.

House, Lon W., Jr. "DSM Evaluation Methodology and Verification Needs." Testimony before the California Energy Commission, 11 Oct. 1991, Docket 90-ER-92. Demand-side management (DSM) programs do not have adequate verification of claimed results: "If the DSM programs displace a new, no-emission resource that was to replace an existing utility fossil-fired generation source, emissions may increase in the DSM case."

House, Lon W., Jr. "Uncommitted Demand-Side Management Assumptions and Projections." Testimony before the California Energy Commission, 26 Nov. 1991, Docket 90-ER-92. Demand-side management projections of savings are grossly inflated.

Houston, Douglas A. Direct testimony on behalf of Southwire Company before the Public Service Commission, State of Georgia, 1992, Docket 4132-U. Devastating critique of demand-side management programs in Georgia. They accomplish little or nothing in the guise of saving energy.

Houston, Douglas A. *Demand-Side Management: Ratepayers Beware!* Houston, Tex.: Institute for Energy Research, 1992. Shows flaws in demand-side management by electric utilities. Long monograph with many references and examples.

Houthakker, Hendrik. Review of *Toward a New Iron Age? Quantitative Modeling of Resource Exhaustion*, by Robert B. Gordon, Tjalling C. Koopmans, William D. Nordhaus, and Brian J. Skinner. *Journal of Political Economy* 98 (April 1990): 440–445. Criticizes "pessimistic" attitude toward resource depletion and gives many examples of how resources are not used up. Much valuable insight in lengthy review.

Hudson Institute. *Energy, Economy and the Environment: A Balanced Policy for the 1990s*. Indianapolis, Ind.: Hudson Institute, 1991. If the proved oil reserves of 1950 had really been all the oil left in the ground, the world would have run out completely by 1970.

Hughes, John P. "The Anti-Competitive Effects of Industrial DSM Programs." Paper presented at the Fourth National Conference on Integrated Resource Planning, Burlington, Vt., September 1992. Criticizes demand-side management in a general way; disputes claims there are no losers.

Hughes, John P. "Will Power Be There When it is Needed?" *Forum for Applied Research and Public Policy* (Fall 1992): 48. Demand-side management is not working well. Costs per unit saved far exceed expectations.

Hughes, John P., and Barbara S. Brenner. "DSM: When Should Industrials Just Say No?" In *Proceedings of 6th National Demand-Side Management Conference.* Palo Alto, Calif.: Electric Power Research Institute, 1993. Criticizes demand-side management from a variety of viewpoints. Some shareholders get enormous incentives from DSM.

Iblher, P., and W. Brog. "Influence of Consumer Behavior on Energy Demand in Households." In *Beyond the Energy Crisis: Opportunity and Challenge*, ed. R. A. Fazzalore and C. B. Smith. Oxford: Pergamon, 1981.

Impact Analysis of the Energy Initiative Program Final Report. Boulder, Colo.: RCG Hagler, Bailly, 1992. Savings rate of 50 to 60 percent of engineering estimates documented for both residential and industrial demand-side management programs.

"Industrials Charge that DSM Budgets of New York Utilities Are Excessive." *Industrial Energy Bulletin* (12 Oct. 1990): 1–3. Costs per kW capacity of large-scale demand-side management are as high as $4,082; statewide average twenty-year avoided capacity cost was only $1,032.

Inhaber, Herbert. "Does Conservation Exist?" *Silver Kris* 21 (magazine of Singapore Airlines) (January 1994): 44–45. Short article explaining why conservation in the sense it is usually given does not exist.

Inhaber, Herbert, and Harry Saunders. "It Costs More to Save Energy." *New York Times*, 20 Nov. 1994, sec. 4, p. 15. Shortened version of *The Sciences* article.

Inhaber, Herbert, and Harry Saunders. "The Road to Nowhere." *The Sciences* 34 (Nov./Dec. 1994): 20–25. Gives many examples of why conservation does not exist, and shows historical analogies.

Jamieson, D., and R. L. Qualmann. "Computer Simulation/End-Use Metering or Can We Count on Energy Savings Estimates in Designing Demand-Side Programs?"

Paper presented at the American Council for an Energy-Efficient Economy, 1990 Summer Study on Energy Efficiency in Buildings, Performance Measurement and Analysis, pp. 10.105–10.114. Washington, D.C.: The Council, 1990. In a review of sixteen commercial buildings that installed conservation measures, significant discrepancies between predicted and actual savings were found.

Jevons, W. S[tanley]. *The Coal Question: Can Britain Survive?* 1865. Reprint, London: Macmillan, 1906. The father of quantitative economics was the first economist to note improving energy efficiency leads to greater energy use, not less; many examples are given.

Johnson, D. "Inflation and Incomes." Letter to *Financial Times*, Nov. 1978. If one company's wages rise by 5 percent, a similar increase nationwide will not produce the same effect.

Jones, P. M. S. "Greenhouse Warming—a Comment." *Energy Policy* 17 (Dec. 1989): 613–614.

Joskow, Paul L. "FERC Should Not Include Demand-Side Bidding in Its Rules." *Electricity Journal* 2 (Aug./Sept. 1988): 36–38. Denounces conservation auctions in testimony before Congress; uses examples of "negagallons" and "negafood"; suggests principles for demand-side programs.

Joskow, Paul L. Testimony before U.S. House Committee on Energy and Commerce, Subcommittee on Energy and Power, 31 March 1988. Evaluates demand-side management programs.

Joskow, Paul L., and Donald Marron. "What Does a Negawatt Really Cost?" MIT Economics Department discussion paper no. 596, Cambridge, Mass., Dec. 1991. Administrative costs of utility demand-side management systems ranged from 70 to 107 percent of direct measured costs.

Joskow, Paul L., and Donald B. Marron. "What Does a Negawatt Really Cost? Evidence from Utility Conservation Programs." *Energy Journal* 13, no. 4 (1992): 41–74. "The cost of a negawatt hour computed from utility reports significantly underestimates the true societal cost of conservation achieved this way."

Joskow, Paul L., and Donald Marron. "What Does a Negawatt Really Cost? Further Thoughts and Evidence." *Electricity Journal* 6 (July 1993): 14–26. Continuation of 1991 paper. "Everyone agreed that the Lovins . . . numbers, in particular, drastically understate the true costs of conservation programs. . . . The free banquet with caviar and champagne that the public is often promised is not likely to be achievable with current [DSM] practises."

Joskow, Paul L., and Donald B. Marron. "What Does Utility-Subsidized Energy Efficiency Really Cost?" *Science*, 16 April 1993, 260–261.

Kahn, Alfred E. "An Economically Rational Approach to Least-Cost Planning." *Electricity Journal* 4 (June 1991): 11–20. Denounces conservation for its own sake.

Kempton, Willett, and L. Montgomery. "Folk Quantification of Energy." *Energy* 7, no. 10 (1982): 817–827. How to measure rebound effect.

Khazzoom, J. Daniel. "Economic Implications of Mandated Efficiency Standards for Household Appliances." *Energy Journal* 11, no. 2 (1980): 21–40. Energy standards could increase, not decrease, energy use; one of the first to resurrect Jevons' nineteenth-century writings.

Khazzoom, J. Daniel. *An Economic Model Integrating Conservation Measures in the Estimation of the Residential Demand for Electricity*. Greenwich, Conn.: JAI Press, 1986. Two-thirds of initial savings disappear because of feedback effect.

Khazzoom, J. Daniel. "Energy Savings from More Efficient Appliances: A Rejoinder." *Energy Journal* 10 (Jan. 1989): 157–166.

Khazzoom, J. Daniel. "Energy Savings Resulting from the Adoption of More-Efficient Appliances." *Energy Journal* 8, no. 4 (1987): 85–89. Criticizes Lovins' inflated estimates of energy saving and shows his economic reasoning is wrong.

Khazzoom, J. Daniel. "Gasoline Conservation vs. Pollution Control: Unintended Consequences." *Journal of Policy Analysis and Management* 7 (Fall 1988): 710–714.

Khazzoom, J. Daniel, et al. "The Conflict between Energy Conservation and Environmental Policy in the U.S. Transportation Sector." *Energy Policy* 18 (June 1990): 456–458. Proposes changing from an emission standard of so many grams per mile driven to so many grams per gallon consumed, thus eliminating conflict between conservation and environment.

Knoll, Michael S. "The Crude Oil Windfall Profit Tax of 1980." *Resources and Energy* 9 (1987): 163. Gives one-page derivation of Hotelling's results and history of economists' view of resource depletion. Jevons was the first to consider it.

Kohlenberg, R. J., et al. "A Behavioral Analysis of Peaking in Residential Electricity Consumption." *Journal of Applied Behavioral Analysis* 9 (1976): 13–18. Posters advocating energy conservation were ineffective.

Kriz, Margaret E. "Low-Power Profits." *National Journal* 22 (22 Dec. 1990): 3075–3078. Some states are rewarding utilities that save energy.

Kreitler, Virginia. "On Customer Choice and Free Ridership in Utility Programs." Paper presented at the International Energy Program Evaluation Conference, Chicago, Aug. 1991. "Free riders" account for more than half of all participants in utility conservation programs.

Kushler, Martin G. "Use of Evaluation to Improve Energy Conservation Programs: A Review and Case Study." *Journal of Social Issues* 45 (Spring 1989): 153–168. Review of Michigan Residential Conservation Service home energy audit program.

Lehman, R. L., and H. E. Warren. "Residential Natural Gas Consumption: Evidence that Conservation Efforts to Date Have Failed." *Science* 199 (1978): 799–802.

Leonard-Barton, D. "Voluntary Simplicity Lifestyles and Energy Conservation." *Journal of Consumer Research* 8 (1981): 243.

Lerman, D. L., and J. Perich-Anderson. "Out of Control: An Alternative Approach to Outcomes Analysis of Commercial Sector Programs." Paper presented at the 1991 Energy Program Evaluation Conference, Chicago. A review of fifteen commercial utility conservation programs; about 50 percent of predicted savings materialized.

Liberatore, Robert G. "An Industry View: Market Incentives." *Forum for Applied Research & Public Policy* 5 (Spring 1990): 19–23. The cost per mile driven is cheaper in 1990 than at any other time in U.S. history.

Lindauer, John. *Economics, a Modern View*. Philadelphia: W. B. Saunders, 1977. In voluntary conservation, each person knows his or her efforts have no impact; one of the first suggestions of nonexistence of conservation in ordinary sense.

LoMonte, Frank. "Utility Appeals Surcharge Ban." *Augusta* [Ga.] *Chronicle*, 25 Nov. 1993, 19B. Georgia Power Co. has been adding conservation charge to bills; environmental groups want it to continue.

Longstreth, Molly, and Michael Topliff. "Determinants of Energy Savings and Increases after Installing Energy-Conserving Devices." *Energy* 15, no. 6 (1990): 523–537. Much evidence for bounce-back effect, in which conservation efforts produce greater energy use.

Macey, S. M. "A Causal Model of the Adoption of Home Heating Energy Conservation Measures." *Energy* 16, no. 3 (1991): 621–630.

Maggs, John. "GATT May Force Change in Environmental Law." *Augusta* [Ga.] *Chronicle*, 20 March 1994, 16A. Trade group is unhappy about U.S. auto mileage laws; views them as trade barriers.

Maney, Kevin. "Technology Helps Build a Better Bulb." *USA Today*, 3 June 1992, B-1. Claims for E-bulb include extremely long life, greater efficiency.

McClelland, Lou, and Rachelle J. Canter. "Psychological Research on Energy Conservation: Context, Approaches, Methods." In *Advances in Environmental Psychology*, Vol. 3, *Energy Psychological Perspectives*, ed. A. Baum and J. Singer. Hillsdale, N.J.: Lawrence Erlbaum Associates, 1981. Literature review on psychology of conservation; useful references to Milstein and others.

McDowell, A. A. "The Long-Term Persistence of Compact Fluorescent Lamp Usage in the Residential Market." Paper presented at the 1991 Energy Program Evaluation Conference, Chicago, 1991. Only 60 percent of compact fluorescents were still in use three years after they were installed.

McKenzie, Richard. *The Sense and Nonsense of Energy Conservation*. Washington, D.C.: American Petroleum Institute, 1991. The International Energy Agency in Paris predicted in 1979 that the world's oil reserves would be gone in six years; reserves increased by about 50 percent by 1990.

"Measured Energy Savings and Economics of Retrofitting Existing Single-Family Homes: An Update of the BECA-B Database." Report LBL-28147, Lawrence Livermore Laboratory, Berkeley, Calif., Feb. 1991. "With few exceptions, metered energy savings fell short of predictions in both the research studies and utility weatherization programs. . . . The annual reductions in electricity consumption of groups of participating homes were typically 67% of predicted estimates in eight weatherization programs sponsored by utilities."

"Measured Savings and Cost-Effectiveness of Conservation Retrofits in Commercial Buildings." Report LBL-27568, Lawrence Berkeley Laboratory, Berkeley, Calif., April 1990. Decreases in energy savings up to 20 percent one year after installation of devices.

Meier, Alan, B. Nordman, N. E. Miller, and D. Hadley. "The Data Behind the Hood River Analyses." *Energy and Buildings* 13, no. 1 (1989): 11. Conservation measures produce fewer results than anticipated. "Many houses . . . failed to show any significant savings from the retrofits."

Milstein, J. S. "How Consumers Feel about Energy: Attitudes and Behavior during the Winter and Spring of 1976–77." Report from Federal Energy Administration, Washington, D.C., June 1977. Homeowners accepted 66°F as a daytime thermostat setting when questioned, but actually had a setting of 70°F.

Mitchell, Edward J. *U.S. Energy Policy: A Primer*. Washington, D.C.: American Enterprise Institute, 1974. The amount of oil in the ground has no more significance than the inventory of shoes in a shoe store.

"Mixed Results from Traer's Light Bulb Retrofit." *Home Energy* 7 (Nov./Dec. 1990): 6–7. The "Great Light Bulb Exchange" proved to be a complete flop. About 60 percent of residences participated in a lightbulb exchange; thirty-eight bulbs per residence were traded for supposedly more efficient fluorescents. Average residential use increased an average of 8 percent.

Moore, Glynn. "Driving Downhill and Other Guaranteed Gas-Saving Tips." *Augusta* [Ga.] *Chronicle*, 12 June 1994, 2. Humorous column on inane suggestions to save energy.

Morell, Jonathan A. "Special Feature: Energy Conservation Program Evaluation." *Evaluation and Program Planning* 12, no. 2 (1989): 113–206. Contains seven articles; see Weinstein, Summers.

Morovic, Tihomir. *Energy Conservation Indicators*. New York: Springer-Verlag, 1987.

Morss, M. F. "Incidence of Welfare Losses Due to Appliance Efficiency Standards." *Energy Journal* 10 (Jan. 1989): 111–118.

Nadel, Steven. *Lessons Learned: A Review of Utility Experience with Conservation and Load Management Programs for Commercial and Industrial Customers.* Albany: New York State Energy Research and Development Authority, 1990. Administrative costs form 36 percent of total utility costs for utility demand-side management programs.

Nadel, Steven, and Kenneth Keating. "Engineering Estimates vs. Impact Evaluation Results: How Do They Compare and Why?" Paper presented at the 1991 Energy Program Evaluation Conference, Chicago, 1991. Actual results of forty-two conservation programs run by utilities were 59 percent of those projected; one showed only half the savings estimated.

National Economic Research Associates. *Assessment of U.S. Electricity Utility–Sponsored Conservation Programmes*. Washington, D.C.: The Associates, 18 Dec. 1987. Residential weatherization programs in the Pacific Northwest produced only 50 to 80 percent of savings estimated by engineering models.

"New Way of Looking at Energy Means Savings All Over State." *Buffalo News*, 25 Sept. 1991, B2. Editorial assumes that all will be winners under conservation regulations.

Nichols, Albert. "Estimating the Net Benefits of Demand-Side Management Programs Based on Limited Information." Report prepared by National Economic Research Associates, Inc., for the Office of Policy, Planning, & Evaluation, Environmental Protection Agency, 25 Jan. 1993. DSM for two Eastern utilities showed massive losses of $11 to $50 million to ratepayers. Society also lost.

Nietzel, M. T., and Richard A. Winett. "The Relationship of Demographics, Environmental Attitude and Time to Energy Conservation among Two Groups of People." *American Journal of Community Psychology* 5, no. 2 (1977): 195–206. Attitudes toward conservation are not the same as behavior; that is, people do not put their money where their mouth is.

Olsen, M. E. "Consumers Attitudes toward Energy Conservation." *Journal of Social Issues* 37, no. 2 (1981): 108–131. Author cannot find one study that shows the relationship between belief in the seriousness of the energy crisis and conservation behavior.

O'Neill, Maura. "DSM—It's a Contact Sport." *Electricity Journal* (May 1993): 88–89. First-year costs for DSM programs vary by a factor of five.

Page, T. *Conservation and Economic Efficiency*. Baltimore, Md.: Johns Hopkins University Press, 1977.

Parfit, Michael. "Sharing the Wealth of Water." In *Water—The Power, Promise and Turmoil of North America's Fresh Water*. National Geographic Special Edition, Nov. 1993, 20–37. Water demand in North America remained about constant from 1980 to 1993, in spite of dire predictions.

Percival, Robert V. "Conservation and Renewable Energy Sources as Supply Alternatives for New York's Electric Utilities." In *The Future of Electric Energy, a Regional Perspective*, ed. S. Saltzman and R. E. Schuler. Westport, Conn.: Greenwood Press, 1986.

Petersen, Frances. "Changes to IBP Buildings." Paper presented at the 1991 Energy Program Evaluation Conference, Chicago, 1991. A review of forty-six cases of institutional retrofits found 70 percent achieved less savings than predicted; average savings were 59 percent of that predicted.

Pickels, Steve J., and Philip Audet. "Second Generation Programs with an Increasing Utility Initiative." *Public Utilities Fortnightly* 120 (24 Dec. 1987): 9–13. Conservation costs underestimated; response rate to Residential Conservation Service audits has been 1.7 percent, one-fourth of what DOE expected.

Pierce, Richard J., Jr. "Electric Utility Regulation: The New Battleground in the Conflict between Markets and Central Planning." Paper presented to the 1992 American Bar Association convention, San Francisco, Calif., Aug. 1992. Skeptical of "negawatt" programs undertaken by utilities; most have achieved much less than was projected.

Pitts, Robert E., J. F. Willenborg, and D. L. Sherrell. "Consumer Adaptation to Gasoline Price Increases." *Journal of Consumer Research* 8, no. 3 (1981): 322. Many motorists increase miles driven after buying fuel-efficient cars; example of "bounce-back" effect.

Pitts, Robert E., and James L. Wittenbach. "Tax Credits as a Means of Influencing Consumer Behavior." *Journal of Consumer Research* 8 (Dec. 1981): 335–338. Tax credits are useless to influence consumer actions. Not one respondent considered the credit so important that the purchase would not have been made without it.

"Pre-Study Pacific Gas and Electric." Report issued by Division of Ratepayer Advocates, California Public Utility Commission, Sacramento, 15 Aug. 1991. Of Pacific Gas and Electric's projects, 43 percent experienced an increase in energy consumption after efficiency devices were installed.

Puin, Al, and G. Preda. "Energy Conservation Technologies: Economic and Social Aspects." *Economic Computation and Economic Cybernetic Studies* 21, no. 4 (1986): 5–12.

Ramain, Patricia. "Energy Demand Elasticity in Relation to Gross Domestic Product." *Energy Economics* 8 (Jan. 1986): 29–38.

Real Goods Catalog. Ukiah, Calif.: Christmas, 1991. Forty-eight pages of conservation equipment, such as screw-in fluorescent lightbulbs, solar-powered clocks, and the like. Most high-priced.

Reese, K. M. "Electric Cars in the News." *Chemical & Engineering News* 71 (25 Oct. 1993): 82. Waste from electric batteries, used in fossil fuel–conserving electric cars, is almost as difficult to dispose of as nuclear waste.

Reichel, David A., and E. Scott Geller. "Application of Behavioral Analysis for Conserving Transportation Energy." In *Advances in Environmental Psychology*, Vol. 3, *Energy Conservation: Psychological Perspectives*, ed. A. Baum and J. E. Singer. Hillsdale, N.J.: Lawrence Erlbaum Associates, 1981. Useful examples on application of psychology to reducing transport energy use.

Reifenberg, Anne, and Allanna Sullivan. "Rising Gasoline Prices: Everyone Else's Fault." *Wall Street Journal*, 1 May 1996, B1. Supplies real and nominal gas prices from 1960 to 1996, and average fuel economy from 1990 to 1996.

Reilly, Barry. "A Note on Demand Elasticities for Energy Imports." *Economic and Social Review* 17 (Jan. 1986): 117–158.

Rich, Daniel, and J. Roessner. "Tax Credits and U.S. Solar Commercialization Policy." *Energy Policy* 18 (March 1990): 186–198. Examines cost effectiveness of credits for solar energy in terms of energy savings since 1978.

Robine, Michel. "La Question Charbonniere de William Stanley Jevons." *Revue Economique* 41, no. 2 (1990): 369–394. Lengthy review, in French, of Jevons' *The Coal Question*; one of the few recent papers to discuss it in detail.

Rodgers, Paul, ed. *Proceedings of the 102nd National Association of Regulatory Utility Commissioners (NARUC) Annual Convention and Regulatory Symposium.* Washington, D.C.: NARUC, 1991. NARUC Conservation Committee admits that utilities lack information on most demand-side management.

Rogers, Eric. "Evaluating the Cost-Effectiveness of a Commercial and Industrial Conservation Program." Paper presented at the 1989 Energy Program Evaluation Conference, Chicago, 1989. Commercial and industrial lighting conservation programs realized only 45 percent of estimated savings.

Rogers, Eric. "Evaluation of a Residential Appliance Rebate Program Using Billing Record Analysis." In *Energy Conservation Program Evaluation: Conservation and Resource Management—Proceedings of the August 1989 Conference.* Argonne, Ill.: Argonne National Laboratory, 1990. Homes participating in the Wisconsin Electric Power Company's air conditioner rebate program actually increased their energy consumption.

Rose, David J. *Learning About Energy.* New York: Plenum, 1986.

Rosenberg, Nathan. "Energy Efficient Technologies: Past and Future Perspectives." Paper presented at "How Far Can the World Get on Energy Efficiency Alone?" Conference held at Oak Ridge National Laboratory, Oak Ridge, Tenn., Aug. 1989. Conservation will be a strong function of capital; a long, detailed paper with many historical examples and much data.

Rudin, Andrew. "Deficient Efficiency." *Public Power* (May/June 1995): 19. "Improve the perceived value of all rebate programs for efficient electricity end uses. If efficient consumption had dozens of benefits, as its promoters contend, then it does not require any subsidy."

Rudin, Andrew. "DSM Misses the Boat on the Fundamental Idea of Energy Conservation." *Energy User News*, Sept. 1992, 48. Demand-side programs will destroy themselves; they are not, and have not been, needed. "Efficiency and conservation aren't synonymous."

Ruff, Larry E. "Environmental Protection through Energy Conservation: A 'Free Lunch' At Last?" Paper presented at the MIT Conference on Energy and the Environment for the 21st Century, Cambridge, Mass., 26–27 March 1990. The free lunch is largely an illusion created by faulty economic reasoning.

Ruff, Larry E. "Equity vs. Efficiency: Getting DSM Pricing Right." *Electricity Journal* (Nov. 1992): 24. Mathematical models show that demand-side management is wrong. "There is a name for a utility with the knowledge and control necessary to implement a DSM give-away program efficiently: God."

Ruff, Larry E. "Least-Cost Energy Planning and Demand-Side Management: Six Common Fallacies and One Simple Truth." *Public Utilities Fortnightly* 5 (28 April 1988): 19–26. Useful, specific examples applicable to utilities but extendible to all energy users; philosophy is sound.

San Jose (Calif.) *Mercury*. 10 Dec. 1982, 6B. Electric utility's spending on conservation ads to promote insulation was greater than if it had given away the insulation for free.

Saunders, Harry D. "Does Energy Conservation Worsen Global Warming?" In *International Issues in Energy Policy, Development and Economics*, ed. Fereidun Fesharaki and James Dorian. Boulder, Colo.: Westview, 1992. Uses "diesel pill" example; agrees with Khazzoom and Brookes.

Saunders, Harry D. "The Khazzoom–Brookes Postulate and Neoclassical Growth." *Energy Journal* 13, no. 4 (1992): 131–148. Finds greater energy efficiency promotes greater energy growth, using econometric models.

Sav, G. Thomas. *The Dynamic Demand for Energy Stocks: An Analysis of Tax Policy Options for Solar Processes*. Greenwich, Conn.: JAI Press, 1984.

Sav, G. Thomas. "The Failure of Solar Tax Incentives: A Dynamic Analysis." *Energy Journal* 7 (July 1986): 51–66.

Sav, G. Thomas. "On Subsidies for Energy-Saving Durables." *American Economist* 30, no. 1 (1986): 56. Fuel input versus energy-saving stocks graphs; taxes placed on conventional fuels would reduce consumption.

Sazimi, H., R. P. Johnson, J. Carlyle, and E. Scott Geller. "Attempts to Encourage Water and Energy Conservation." Paper presented at the annual meeting of the American Psychological Association, New York, Sept. 1979. A wide variety of water conservation measures proved ineffective.

Schmalensee, Richard. "Appropriate Government Policy toward Commercialization of New Energy Supply Technologies." Working paper MIT-EL 79-052WP, Massachusetts Institute of Technology Energy Laboratory, Cambridge, Mass., Oct. 1979.

Schueler, Vincent. "Measuring the Impacts of Energy Efficiency Measures in Institutional Buildings with Billing Data: A Review of Methodological Issues." Report issued by the American Council for an Energy Efficient Economy, Washington, D.C.: Summer 1990. Energy Efficiency in Buildings Program Evaluation, p. 6.163. An average of between 59 and 80 percent of predicted energy savings materialized for five studies; "Engineering estimates tend to systematically over predict energy savings because they estimate technical potential—the savings assuming close to perfect installation and operation of the measures."

Scott, Anthony. *Natural Resources: The Economics of Conservation*. Toronto, Ont.: McClelland and Stewart, 1973. "It is ridiculous to say that conservation is a movement that has the welfare of the future particularly in mind; conservation will not necessarily increase the future inheritance [of later generations] but simply change its composition from capital goods to natural goods."

Searl, Milton, and Chauncey Starr. "Japan: Not an Energy Efficient Model." *Physics Today* 45 (Feb. 1992): 95, 97. Japan is twice as energy efficient as the United States, but there are underlying reasons for this. Appearances are deceiving; they do not have many of the energy-using facilities the United States takes for granted.

Sebold, Fredrick, and Eric Fox. "Realized Savings from Residential Conservation Activity." *Energy Journal* 6 (April 1985): 73–85. San Diego Electric found that electricity savings in a conservation program were 50 to 80 percent of estimates; gas savings were less than half of estimates.

Seligman, Clive, Larry S. Becker, and John M. Darley. "Encouraging Residential Energy Conservation through Feedback." In *Advances in Environmental Psychology*, Vol. 3, *Energy: Psychological Perspectives*, ed. A. Baum and J. E. Singer. Hillsdale, N.J.: Lawrence Erlbaum Associates, 1981.

Seligman, Clive, and R. Bruce Hutton. "Evaluating Energy Conservation Programs." *Journal of Social Issues* 37, no. 2 (1981): 51–71. Conservation programs do not measure accomplishments in terms of actual energy saved.

Shinnar, Reuel. "Net Energy or Energy Analysis." In *Economics of Resources*, ed. Robert D. Leiter and Stanley L. Friedlander. New York: Cyrco Press, 1976.

Shippee, G. "Energy Consumption and Conservation Psychology." *Environmental Management* 4, no. 4 (1980): 297–314.

Simon, Julian. "Why Conservation Is a Waste of Energy." *Orlando Sentinel*, 19 July 1992. Chasing after the rainbow of conservation is based on false assumptions.

Singer, S. Fred, ed. *Free Market Energy: The Way to Benefit Consumers*. New York: Universe Books, 1984.

Sioshansi, Fereidoon P. "The Myths and Facts of Energy Efficiency." *Energy Policy* 19 (April 1991): 231–243. Long review article; good literature compilation, but reasoning is shaky in part.

Skerrett, P. J. "The Real Cost of Saving Electricity." *Technology Review* (Feb./March 1993): 12–13. Paul Joskow and Donald Marron, at MIT, found that the cost of demand-side management programs at electric utilities is substantial, up to $1.81 per kWh of electricity saved.

Slesser, Malcolm. *Energy in the Economy*. New York: St. Martin's Press, 1978. "There are very few businesses that will conserve energy in the national interest. The motivation must be economic." Philosophy sound, but few examples.

Sohn, Ira. "U.S. Energy Security: Problems and Prospects." *Energy Policy* 18 (March 1990): 149–162. Long-term outlook for U.S. energy security is good; foreign oil dependence is not a problem.

Spare, P. H. "Fifth Fuel—the Debate Continues." *Energy World* 22 (April 1990). The wide-bodied jet brought more competition, not less.

Spenser, Milton. *Contemporary Economics*, 3d ed. New York: Worth, 1977. Conservation implies a balance between present and future consumption, nothing more.

"State Lawmakers Eye Plan to Ban Utilities from Servicing Appliances." *Electric Power Alert* 32 (15 April 1992). Demand-side management programs practiced by utilities in New Jersey have captured most of the market and are responsible for unemployment of 5,000 private contractors.

Suarez, Carlos E. "Long-Term Evolution of Oil Prices." *Energy Policy* 18 (March 1990): 170. Charts going back to 1860; very useful in historical studies.

Sumi, D. H., and B. Coates. "Persistence of Energy Savings in Seattle City Light's Residential Weatherization Program." Paper presented at the 1989 Energy Program Evaluation Program, Chicago, 1989. The Washington State program found a 27 percent erosion (decrease) in savings between 1982 and 1987.

Summers, Joe A., John G. Heilman, and Lawrence O'Toole. "Public Regardingness in Energy Conservation Attitudes." *Evaluation and Program Planning* 12, no. 2 (1989): 131–136. Feelings toward conservation.

Sutherland, Ronald J. "Market Barriers to Energy-Efficient Investments." *Energy Journal* 12, no. 3 (1991): 15–28. In the United States, consumers use a discount rate of about 20 percent in making energy investment decisions.

Sweeney, J. L. "The Demand for Gasoline in the United States: A Vintage Capital Model." *Workshops on Energy in Energy Demand and Supply.* Paris: International Energy Agency Organization for Economic Cooperation and Development, 1978. Resurrects Jevons' theory in context of auto gasoline use.

Taylor, Jerry. "Energy Conservation: The Case Against Coercion." Paper presented at the National Energy Policy: Central Planning Reconsidered conference, Cato Institute, Washington, D.C., 16 Jan. 1992. Long article points out futility of coercive measures to produce conservation; numerous examples and data.

Taylor, Jerry. "Energy Conservation and Coercion." *Policy Analysis* 189 (9 March 1993). Issued by Cato Institute, Washington, D.C. Update and revision of the earlier article.

Train, Kenneth E. "Discount Rates in Consumers' Energy-Related Decisions: A Review of the Literature." *Energy* 10 (Dec. 1985): 1243–1253. Finds very high discount rates for many appliances and cars.

Train, Kenneth E. "Incentives for Energy Conservation in the Commercial and Industrial Sectors." *Energy Journal* 9 (July 1988): 113–128.

U.S. House of Representatives. *Presidential Energy Program: Hearings before the House Subcommittee on Energy and Power.* 94th Cong., 1st sess., 1975. A listing of various incorrect predictions made by the U.S. Departments of Interior and State that oil reserves in the United States would run out.

Vine, Edward L., B. K. Barnes, Evan Mills, and Ronald R. Ritschard. "The Response of Low-Income Elderly to Tenant Incentive Programs." *Energy* 14, no. 11 (1989): 677–685. Gas consumption among the elderly rose after a conservation incentive program was started.

Vogel, Mike. "Energy Efficiency Called Better for Earth than Regulating Births." *Buffalo News*, 20 Feb. 1991. At a conference of the American Association for the Advancement of Science, Richard Rockwell says that conservation reduces pollution more than birth control.

Wald, Matthew. "Gulf Victory: An Energy Defeat." *New York Times*, 18 June 1991, D9. Producing $1 worth of goods and services in 1991 required 39 percent less oil and gas than in 1973.

Wald, Matthew. "Oil Imports Are Up. Fretting about It Is Down." *New York Times*, 26 Jan. 1997, sec. 4, p. 3. In 1980, oil sales in the United States were 8.5 to 9 percent of gross domestic product; in 1996, a little over 3 percent. Conservation over the past eleven years has not decreased oil imports.

Walsh, Michael J. "Energy Tax Credits and Housing Improvement." *Energy Economics* 11 (Oct. 1989): 275–284. Energy tax credits did not lead to more widespread or extensive energy conservation improvement activities.

Weinstein, Robert, Robert Scott, and Curtis Jones. "Measurement of 'Free-Riders' in Energy Conservation Programs." *Evaluation and Program Planning* 12, no. 2 (1989): 121–130. Useful discussion of free riders, those who are paid to conserve who would have done so even without subsidies.

Wetzler, James W. "Taxation of Energy Producers and Consumers." In *Free Market Energy: The Way to Benefit Consumers*, ed. S. Fred Singer. New York: Universe Books, 1984.

White, L. T., D. Archer, F. Aronson, L. Condelli, B. Curbow, B. McLeod, T. F. Pettigrew, and S. Yates. "Energy Conservation Research of California's Utilities—A Meta-Evaluation." *Evaluation Review* 8, no. 2 (1984): 167–186. Criticizes methodology of social science research in conservation; no studies prove much.

Winett, Richard A., and M. Nietzel. "Behavioral Ecology: Contingency Management of Residential Energy Use." *American Journal of Community Psychology* 3, no. 2 (1975): 123–133. Pamphlets and handbooks on conservation were ineffective.

Winett, Richard A., et al. "Effects of Monetary Rebates, Feedback and Information in Residential Energy Conservation." *Journal of Applied Psychology* 63, no. 1 (1978): 73–80. Those who increased energy use in a conservation experiment— ordinarily the subject of derision as "wasters"—had instituted savings measures before the experiment began.

Winkler, R. C. "Behavioral Economics and Water Conservation." In *Preserving the Environment: New Strategies for Behavior Change*, ed. E. Scott Geller, Richard A. Winett, and P. B. Everett. New York: Pergamon, 1982. Water conservation measures, such as feedback and rebates, proved ineffective in western Australia.

Wirl, Franz. "Analytics of Demand-Side Conservation Program." *Energy Systems and Policy* 13, no. 4 (1989): 285–300. Theoretical; proves Jevons' theorem about greater efficiency producing more energy use and shows futility of utility conservation programs.

Wirtschafter, Robert. "The Dramatic Growth in DSM: Too Much, Too Soon?" *Electricity Journal* 5 (Nov. 1992): 36–46. Expenditures on DSM are almost as large as spending on nuclear power during the boom 1960s.

"World Bank Charged with Ignoring Own Energy Policies." *Chemical & Engineering News* 72 (28 March 1994): 20. Bank rejects charges that it does not promote Third World conservation: "How many of [the two billion without access to electricity] can afford $25 lightbulbs?"

Yardley, Robert C. (Chairman of Massachusetts Dept. of Public Utilities). Letter to U.S. Environmental Protection Agency, 11 Feb. 1992. Monitored demand-side management programs for four Massachusetts utilities showed average savings of 52 percent of original engineering projections.

Yergin, Daniel. *Gasoline and the American People*. Cambridge, Mass.: Cambridge Research Associates, 1991. Retail gasoline prices in constant dollars were lower in 1990 than they were in 1972, 25 percent lower than in 1963, and 30 percent lower than in 1947.

Yergin, Daniel. "How to Design a New Energy Strategy." *Newsweek*, 11 Feb. 1991. Well-known energy writer mentions conservation as only one of five steps in a national program, but does not address the question of whether it exists at all. Useful data on the real gasoline price since 1950.

Zycher, Benjamin. "The Theoretical and Empirical Fantasies of Amory Lovins." Paper presented at the Western Economic Association International, Seattle, June/ July 1991. "We have Lovins making confident assertions about cost functions for things that are newly arrived and that have yet to be invented!"

Index

ABOUT THE AUTHOR

HERBERT INHABER is a principal scientist at a defense facility in South Carolina. A Fellow and member of the Board of Directors of the American Nuclear Society, he has published about 140 scientific papers in such journals as *Nature* and *Science* and five books, including *How Rich Is Too Rich?* (Praeger, 1992).